SOCIAL SERVICES IN SCOTLAND

SOCIAL SERVICES IN SCOTLAND

Edited by
JOHN ENGLISH

THE MERCAT PRESS
EDINBURGH

First edition published by Scottish Academic Press in 1979
This fourth edition published in 1998 by Mercat Press
53 South Bridge, Edinburgh EH1 1YS

ISBN: 1873644 779

Typeset in Times New Roman 10 point at Mercat Press

Printed in Great Britain by
The Cromwell Press, Trowbridge, Wiltshire

CONTENTS

Preface   vii
List of contributors   viii

1   Central and Local Government   1
     John English

2   Social Security   18
     John English

3   Health Services   40
     Michael Turner

4   Community Care and the Personal Social Services   72
     Rex Taylor

5   Children and their Families   91
     Malcolm Hill, Kathleen Murray, Kay Tisdall

6   Housing   118
     John English

7   Education   141
     Paul Littlewood

Bibliography   163
Index   172

PREFACE TO THE FOURTH EDITION

The late Professor Fred Martin and I had the idea for a book on the 'welfare state' in Scotland some twenty years ago, and we jointly edited the first two editions of *Social Services in Scotland.* It seemed to us that there was a need for a new book, in that four of the main 'social services'—the National Health Service, the personal social services, housing and education—have always been the responsibility of the Scottish Office and subject to separate Scottish legislation. Yet most textbooks either ignore Scotland or make only passing reference to its particular circumstances. As for social security, although cash benefits are administered on a uniform basis throughout Britain, a chapter on the topic was added because it seemed perverse to ignore such an important aspect of the welfare state.

It is now almost a decade since the previous edition of *Social Services in Scotland* appeared, and during this time there have been many important changes in both social conditions and service provision. This new edition has been completely rewritten, largely by new contributors. The first chapter is contextual, dealing with the Scottish Office, local government and public expenditure in Scotland, all of which are crucial to the social provision. Each of the chapters then deals with a particular aspect of the welfare state, covering both statutory and non-statutory services. But discussion of the personal social services has been split between two chapters: one focuses on care in the community for groups such as the elderly, and the other on services for children and families, including children's hearings.

I am indebted to the contributors who have made the book possible: with a project of this kind, both academic kudos and financial reward are modest. The demands of university life today mean that publication has taken longer than I expected but the material has been updated to include key decisions of the new Labour government during its first months in office.

I must also thank Mrs Margaret Bright who typed my own chapters and dealt with editorial changes to the manuscript as a whole. Not only was her work first rate but she tolerated my appetite for discovering endless corrections and improvements.

With devolution and the establishment of a Scottish parliament, much of whose time will be spent on social policy, there is unlikely to be a shortage of interesting developments in the coming years. But I hope that this edition of *Social Services in Scotland* will meet the needs of both students and teachers of social policy for a review of the Scottish welfare state today.

John English,
February 1998

CONTRIBUTORS

Central and Local Government	John English	*University of Paisley*
Social Security	John English	*University of Paisley*
Health Services	Michael Turner	*University of Paisley*
Community Care and the Personal Social Services	Rex Taylor	*University of Glasgow*
Children and their Families	Malcolm Hill	*University of Glasgow*
	Kathleen Murray	*University of Glasgow*
	Kay Tisdall	*University of Glasgow*
Housing	John English	*University of Paisley*
Education	Paul Littlewood	*University of Glasgow*

1
CENTRAL AND LOCAL GOVERNMENT

Devolution to Scotland and Wales is a flagship policy of the Labour government elected in May 1997. The new government's proposals for devolution and the establishment of a Scottish parliament (Cm 3658, 1997) were confirmed in a referendum and will lead to major changes in the way Scotland is governed and its relationship with the rest of the United Kingdom. But rather than speculate about the possible effects of devolution when a great deal of discussion of the detailed arrangements lies ahead—fascinating as that exercise might be—this chapter will deal with the current position. Nevertheless, it is worth pointing out that by far the most important proposed devolved powers relate to the 'welfare state'—health and personal social services, education and housing—where, over time, policy might increasingly diverge from that south of the border. Only social security, where Scotland is entirely integrated with the rest of the UK, will be an (enormously important) exception.

Scotland has long been a distinctive political and administrative community within the UK; while Scotland, England, Wales and Northern Ireland have a great deal in common and have existed under the jurisdiction of the same government, there are all kinds of differences in how things are done. These differences tend to be particularly significant in Scotland. There is a very long tradition of a separate Scottish legal system, national church and educational arrangements. During the present century central government administration has become increasingly distinctive as the Scottish Office has taken on wider functions, until it is now responsible for the bulk of economic and social policy north of the border. Scotland also has its own local government system. The level of public expenditure per head of population is substantially higher in Scotland than in other parts of the UK. Scottish legislation may or may not be different in substance—generally it is not massively different—but the existence of Scots law requires that there are usually separate acts of parliament for Scotland.

This chapter will therefore outline the development and functions of the Scottish Office, the main features of public spending in Scotland, and its system of local government. All these are important as the context within which social services operate because, as was pointed out above, with the exception of social security, they are separately administered in Scotland. Their main features may generally be similar on both sides of the border, but the differences are important enough to warrant separate study.

CENTRAL GOVERNMENT

Scottish administration between the Act of Union in 1707 and the mid-nineteenth century was a low-key affair, in the hands of a variety of ministers whose main activity seems to have been 'managing' the parliamentary support of Scottish MPs. Indeed, until the development of state involvement in poor relief, public health and education, there was little policy to be made and little to administer. Scottish affairs were nominally the responsibility of the Home Office though business seems generally to have been in the hands of the Lord Advocate. The Disruption of 1843, when the Church of Scotland split, was a crucial event in Scottish society, affecting both education and poor relief. The poor law had already been reformed south of the border in 1834, and the Poor Law Amendment (Scotland) Act, 1845 applied, spurred on by the Disruption and the breakdown in the previous voluntary system, the 'principles of 1834' to Scotland —though in a harsher form which nominally included a prohibition on any relief to the able-bodied. The Board of Supervision was created and under it non-elected parochial boards made up of local proprietors to administer the poor law in each parish. In 1867 the Board of Supervision was also given public health responsibilities. The Scotch Education Department, based in London, was set up in 1872 following the extension of elementary education throughout Scotland. By the late nineteenth century a number of semi-independent boards based in Edinburgh had been established to administer fisheries, lunatic asylums and prisons, as well as poor relief.

There had been calls for the appointment of a Scottish minister for some years when the Secretary for Scotland Act, 1885 was passed. The bill was introduced by a Liberal government and, when it fell, taken over by the Conservatives. At first the Scottish Office—headed by the Secretary for Scotland (a definitely lower status appointment with a lower salary than a secretaryship of state)—was a department with limited power and responsibility. The office was—and remained so well into the present century—a small organisation based at Dover House in Whitehall with at first virtually no presence in Edinburgh. The various boards and the Scottish Education Department continued with a substantial degree of independence (though the Scottish Secretary became ex-officio Vice President of the Committee of Council on Education in Scotland and effective head of that department). Furthermore, other departments tended to resist transfer of additional powers to the Scottish Office; for example the Home Office briefly succeeded in preventing the loss of responsibility for law and order in Scotland. The Scottish Secretary has, however, always enjoyed the honour of being Keeper of the Great Seal of Scotland (Gibson, 1985).

In 1892 the Local Government Board (LGB) for Scotland replaced the Board of Supervision, and elected parish councils superseded the parochial boards. The LGB was typical of the board system: located in Edinburgh with three active members—a chairman, an advocate and a medical man—it had an arms-length relationship with the Scottish Office at Dover House. Then in 1912 the Scottish Board of Agriculture was created. The administrative arrangements were, however, scarcely satisfactory because the Scottish Office was far from being an integrated department. Reform came in stages. The Scottish Secretary became a secretary of state in 1926, a matter of some prestige at a time when there were only some half dozen cabinet members with this title rather than, as today, practically every minister in charge of a department. The Scottish Office increased its presence in Edinburgh, and in 1928 the Boards of Health (which had replaced the LGB in 1919), Agriculture and Prisons became three departments comparable to the Scottish Education Department, though they remained legally separate bodies. The Scottish Office in its modern form dates from 1939, following the report of the Gilmour Committee (Cmd 5563, 1937) when the separate departments were abolished except as administrative divisions within a unitary organisation. At the same time most of its Edinburgh-based civil servants moved to newly-built St Andrew's House.

The Scottish Office is by no means the only government department with a presence or responsibilities in Scotland: two major examples are the Ministry of Defence and, of particular importance for social policy, the Department of Social Security (DSS). Other departments exercise certain functions in Scotland. The Home Office, for instance, is responsible for immigration and nationality throughout the UK. But the responsibilities of the Scottish Office have been extended considerably in the last 20 or 30 years, particularly in the fields of trade and industry. The Scottish Office now covers all or most of the responsibilities of seven Whitehall departments: Agriculture, Fisheries and Food, Education and Employment, Environment, Health, Home Affairs, Trade and Industry, and Transport.

Whereas all ministries have divisions of one sort or another, these are not much publicised or known to the general public. But because of the very wide range of its responsibilities (and perhaps because of its federal origins) the five departments into which it is divided tend to have a higher public profile than the Scottish Office itself. These departments are, however, merely a politically and administratively convenient way of dividing up the work, and they are reorganised from time to time, on the last occasion in 1995.

Since the Scottish Office felt it should polish up its public image a few years ago, the departments are now officially called, somewhat portentously, the Scottish Office Home Department and so on. The five departments are currently:

Agriculture, Environment and Fisheries Department: Includes responsibility for natural heritage, forestry, and water and sewerage.
Development Department: Mainly the equivalent of the Department of the Environment, Transport and the Regions it is responsible for housing, urban policy, local government and local government finance, town and country planning, new towns, and roads and transport.
Education and Industry Department: Scotland has had a separate education department since the nineteenth century; perhaps the recent amalgamation with industry reflects the creation of the Education and Employment Department in London. Responsibilities include schools, colleges, universities (since 1992), the arts, museums and libraries, and industrial and regional development.
Department of Health: Responsible for public health and the National Health Service.
Home Department: As well as police and fire, the courts and prisons, it is responsible for social work through the *Social Work Services Group.*

In recent years much of the executive work of central government—as distinct from policy making—has been transferred to 'next steps' agencies headed by chief executives and operating outside the main civil service structure. The Scottish Office is no exception, and agencies have been established, for example to run the prison service, public service pensions, the Scottish Record Office, fisheries protection and student awards. There are also a substantial number of non-departmental bodies ('quangos'); most are advisory but some are executive and responsible for considerable expenditure, including Highland and Islands Enterprise, Scottish Enterprise, Scottish Homes and the Scottish Higher Education Funding Council.

The relationship between the Scottish Office and London as far as policy-making is concerned can perhaps best be characterised as subtle. It has a degree of financial discretion within a generous overall expenditure ceiling through the operation of the Scottish block, discussed below, which is not enjoyed by other departments. Perhaps Edinburgh seems a long way from London, and Scotland is comparatively small, so the Cabinet may not always give too much attention to what happens north of the border. But that said, there is always a lively concern in the civil service about setting precedents, and a general assumption that policy in the different parts of the UK will move in parallel, unless there are specific reasons for divergence. On the whole Scotland follows England, though there are exceptions, and innovations are sometimes tried out north of the border: for example, the personal social services were reorganised in Scotland and local authority social work departments established in 1969, a couple of years before social services departments were set up; and it is well known that Scotland enjoyed the advantages of the community charge a year earlier than England and Wales. In the end, however, a great deal depends on the personality, political views and standing of the incumbent Secretary of State and his relationship with the Prime Minister. The majority of Scottish secretaries have been somewhat outside the mainstream of British politics and have not moved on to other posts; but interestingly the three who completed periods of office between 1979 and 1997—George Younger, Malcolm Rifkind and Ian Lang—were all promoted to higher things.

PUBLIC EXPENDITURE IN SCOTLAND

The social services which are discussed in this book are largely financed by the taxpayer so it is important to examine the level of public expenditure in Scotland and make some comparisons with other parts of the UK. The broad picture is that identifiable expenditure per head in Scotland is substantially higher than that in England and Wales, but it is necessary to look at the mechanisms whereby the level of spending is determined. The annual public expenditure round is a major element in British government and politics though it cannot be dealt with here in detail. Rather, the concern is with the effects on Scotland. Each year the Cabinet decides, in the light of the performance of the economy and the politically acceptable level of taxation, the total of public expenditure in the following financial year and its distribution between programmes. These decisions can be a matter of considerable controversy between ministers, each fighting for his or her share of the cake. In practice the argument is at the margin, about the increase (or sometimes decrease) for each programme in relation to the previous year's expenditure.

Changes at the margin are central to deciding public expenditure in Scotland, but for the most part the Secretary of State is not involved in the same sort of negotiations with the Treasury as other ministers. Instead, marginal changes to Scottish expenditure are derived 'automatically' through a formula, whereby Scotland receives a proportionate share (related to population) of comparable English (or English and Welsh) programmes. It should be emphasised that, as *de facto* in England, the previous year's expenditure is carried forward; the formula applies only to changes to Scottish expenditure, where it largely replaces *ad hoc* negotiation.

Public Expenditure Formulas

Public expenditure in Scotland was for many years determined, more or less, on the basis of the Goschen formula, introduced in 1888 by George Goschen, the Chancellor of the Exchequer. The Goschen formula gave Scotland 13.75 per cent of comparable expenditures in England and Wales, a proportion based on its contribution to the exchequer (Heald, 1992). The formula applied originally to education expenditure, but it came to be used more generally as a benchmark for public expenditure in Scotland until the late 1950s, by which time, with the declining share of the Scottish population in the overall total, it had become very favourable on an expenditure per head basis. The 'Goschen share' for Scotland was something the Scottish Office argued for in relation to specific programmes when it was thought politic to do so. Scottish secretaries were 'concerned to ensure that Scotland received its appropriate grant aid, normally assumed to be equivalent to the Goschen formula'. But this argument was not always used: 'With some grants already above the "Goschen line", but others below, it was, as one official wrote, "a two edged weapon" only to be "unsheathed" in extreme cases. It was possible that some Scottish needs would fall below the formula' (Levitt, 1992, p.68).

It was the prospect of devolution for Scotland and Wales in the 1970s which led the government to undertake a study of territorial spending needs. An interdepartmental study was carried out by the Treasury, the Scottish Office and other departments which, ironically, was published at the end of 1979 when devolution was no longer government policy. It dealt with expenditure programmes which were to have been devolved and included education (except universities), housing, and health and personal social services, but not social security. The study was intended to identify the effects of 'objective factors' outside the direct control of spending authorities, such as population density, age structure and mobility, which influenced relative expenditure needs (Treasury, 1979).

The *Needs Assessment Study* provided figures for identifiable expenditure per head (excluding social security) in each part of the UK from 1959-60; earlier statistics were not available. Identifiable Scottish expenditure per head relative to that in England (index 100) had been as follows:

1959-60	105
1962-63	118
1965-66	111
1968-69	134

1971-72	125
1974-75	118
1976-77	123
1977-78	128

It is interesting that the expenditure differential in Scotland's favour was very modest at the end of the 1950s: the Goschen benchmark, despite its use of anachronistic population relativities, does not appear to have ensured a particularly advantageous position for Scotland. Relative expenditure per head in Scotland then clearly increased quite substantially, though somewhat erratically, during the 1960s. Reasons for this include the vogue for regional policy at that time, which involved substantial expenditure in areas of high unemployment (which then included Scotland). The higher level of identifiable expenditure per head in Scotland has remained, with some year-to-year variations, down to the present time (see below); the most comparable figure in Table 1.1 for 1994-95 to the historical series—identifiable expenditure per head excluding social security compared with England—was index 135.

The estimates of relative need involved a good deal of judgement, and were indicative rather than precise. For 1976-77, it was estimated that Scotland needed to spend on relevant services (that is excluding social security) index 116 (England 100), in other words substantially less than the actual 123.

In 1978, the year before the *Needs Assessment Study* was published, a new formula, named after the chief secretary of the Treasury, Joel Barnett, was announced, based on relative populations in 1976. The formula was apparently applied from 1981-82 (Constitution Unit, 1996). The Barnett formula gave Scotland 11.11 per cent of changes to comparable England and Wales programmes (11.76 England programmes). Wales was dealt with similarly with different percentages.

One consequence of the existence of the formula is that Scottish expenditure levels are largely dependent on bargaining by other departmental ministers rather than by the Secretary of State. It appears, however, that the application of the formula is not entirely mechanistic and that negotiations do take place about special Scottish circumstances, though little is explicitly made public.

At about this time the Scottish block was formalised to include most expenditure within the responsibility of the Secretary of State. The block now includes over 95 per cent of this expenditure; the remainder is on agriculture, fisheries, food and forestry, and is negotiated on a bilateral basis. Expenditure within the Secretary of State's responsibility (or the Scottish block which is practically as large) constitutes over three-fifths of identifiable public expenditure in Scotland; most of the remainder is accounted for by social security. About a quarter of total public expenditure, on programmes such as defence which are essentially public goods, is not regarded as providing benefits which can be allocated to different parts of the UK, and is thus not identifiable in relation to the particular parts of the country.

The Barnett formula was revised in 1992 to reflect Scotland's falling share of the UK population revealed in the 1991 census. Scotland now receives 10.66 per cent of changes to England-only programmes (and 10.06 of the increasingly rare England and Wales programmes). But these new shares have been somewhat left behind by further decreases in Scotland's population share (which is, of course, advantageous in terms of expenditure per head).

In principle the Secretary of State has freedom to adopt a pattern of expenditure different from that south of the border; more can be spent on one service and less on another. In practice, however, this freedom is severely constrained. One constraint is political because the government find it hard (and probably would not wish) to justify radically different priorities in Scotland from those in the rest of Britain. Second, although intra-government and civil service relations are private, it seems unlikely that the Treasury fails to exercise its beneficent control over the details of Scottish expenditure, notwithstanding the existence of the block.

Operation of the formula: The working of the formula and the determination of Scottish public expenditure are, in the final analysis, undoubtedly complex. However, in outline the system is fairly straightforward and, given its significance, it is perhaps worth giving some (hypothetical) examples of its operation. For the purposes of exposition, Scotland will be compared simply with England (and on the basis of purely illustrative figures).

Suppose the following: Scotland has 10 per cent of England's population; the formula gives Scotland 10 per cent of expenditure changes in England; and total expenditure is Scotland index 125 and England 1000 (that is index 125 and 100 *per head* respectively). Each round in the operation of the formula can be conceptualised as involving two financial years; at the next operation of the formula the second year of the previous round becomes year one.

Expenditure in year one is: England   1000
                                     Scotland   125

Assume expenditure in year two in England (on relevant programmes) is increased by 5 per cent so that: England becomes   1050 (1000 plus 50)
                                     Scotland becomes   130 (125 plus 10 per cent *of 50*)

Thus Scotland gets a 4 per cent increase in expenditure, compared with 5 per cent in England. This is because Scotland's expenditure in year one is not 10 per cent (the formula percentage) of England's but 12.5 per cent. Consequently 10 per cent of England's increase is equal to only 4 per cent of Scotland's year one expenditure.

The effect of the formula (assuming public expenditure is not reduced in cash terms, when Scotland would lose less than England and the disparity would be increased) is slowly to eliminate Scotland's higher expenditure per head, so eroding the differential. The speed with which this happens depends on the size of *cash* increases in England, regardless of whether these are real increases or adjustments for inflation.

Suppose that expenditure in cash terms doubled in England. The effect on Scotland would be to increase expenditure from index 125 to 225 (125 plus 10 per cent of the 1000 English increase), that is an 80 per cent rather than a 100 per cent increase. Compared with English expenditure, Scotland's expenditure per head would fall from index 125 to 112.5. In other words, a doubling of cash expenditure in England would halve the differential in Scotland's favour. This effect might, on the basis of past experience, to some extent be counteracted by Scotland's relative population diminishing unless the formula is regularly updated. How soon this might happen depends on the extent of inflation and real expenditure increases; a very modest three per cent average annual increase—made up of, say, two per cent inflation and one per cent real increase —would double cash expenditure in 24 years, while a five per cent average increase would take 15 years.

Public expenditure is changed (in practice almost always increased) in cash terms for two reasons: first, to take account of inflation and/or, second, to increase (or reduce) expenditure in real terms. As for the effect on Scotland, the primary consideration, as was pointed out above, is the size of cash increases, and only secondarily how far these are related to inflation or real expenditure changes. While cash increases will always tend to move Scottish expenditure closer to the UK average, those related to inflation are unequivocally bad for Scotland; if, for example, real expenditure is flat but there are cash increases to take account of inflation, Scottish expenditure will fall in real terms. (That, in fact, is fairly close to what is happening at the moment.) Real increases in English expenditure, on the other hand, are only bad for Scotland in relative (or sour grapes) terms: real Scottish expenditure will increase in absolute terms but more slowly than that in England so the differential will, as before, be diminished. Thus Scotland should welcome low inflation with, if possible, rising real expenditure; the worst of all worlds is high inflation but flat (or, even worse, diminishing) real expenditure.

Scottish Public Expenditure Levels

In 1995-96 the Scottish block was nearly £14bn, rather more than five per cent of total government expenditure (excluding debt interest). Identifiable expenditure in Scotland was more than one and a half times as large as the block, mainly because of the inclusion of social security. By no means all of the block is spent directly by the Scottish Office or bodies such as the National Health Service, Scottish Homes or the Scottish Higher Education Funding Council; over two-fifths goes to local authorities in Revenue Support Grant, other grants, and capital allocations (Cm 3214, 1996).

Statistics on identifiable public expenditure per head in Scotland for 1994-95, compared with the UK and England, are in Table 1.1. The index of Scottish expenditure levels should be reasonably robust but may not be precisely accurate (in particular the comparison with England uses the author's calculations rather than those of the Treasury). The published index figures sometimes vary quite widely between years in a way which is not always easy to relate to real changes.

Expenditure per head on programmes within the Scottish block is more than a quarter greater than the UK average, and over a third more than the (lower) English level. If expenditure within the block had been at the same level per head as the UK average in 1994-95, the total would have been some £3.7bn less (the Scottish 'excess'); if social security is included (which approximates total identifiable expenditure) the excess would have been about £4.6 bn. The excess would have been greater relative to English expenditure per head: perhaps £4.8bn and £6.4bn respectively. To some extent this Scottish excess is undoubtedly warranted by particular Scottish circumstances; for example, a large part of Scotland has very low population densities (though not many people live in these areas) which result in higher costs for providing services of a comparable standard; and people living in Scotland suffer from poorer

TABLE 1.1: *Identifiable Public Expenditure Per Head in Scotland, 1994-95*

	UK = 100	ENGLAND = 100	SCOTTISH BLOCK %	TOTAL IDENTIFIABLE EXPENDITURE %
Health & PSS	122	126	35	22
Education	126	131	28	17
Law, order, etc	105	111	9	5
Other environmental services	132	142	8	5
Transport	105	104	7	4
Trade, industry, energy & employment	168	203	6	4
Housing	171	197	6	3
National heritage	132	132	1	1
SCOTTISH BLOCK	127	135	100	61
Agriculture, fisheries, food & forestry	192	251	-	2
Social security	108	111	-	37
TOTAL	121	128	-	100

NOTE: 'Welfare State' programmes are italicised.
Source: HM Treasury, *Public Expenditure: Statistical Analyses 1996-97,* Cm 3201, 1996

health status which puts a greater burden on the health service. As discussed above, the 'appropriate' level of expenditure is impossible to calculate with any precision though the actual levels do seem implausibly high in terms of greater Scottish 'needs'; and the excess is around twice as high as the Treasury's estimate in the late 1970s (Treasury, 1979). In reality, of course, the level of Scottish expenditure has as much if not more to do with politics than objective 'needs'.

Some individual services can be briefly examined. The high expenditure on housing is at least partly a reflection of the larger social rented sector in Scotland; its counterpart is lower tax expenditure on mortgage interest tax relief. As far as health is concerned, the NHS is probably better resourced in Scotland even taking into account the evidence of greater illness (see Chapter 3). In 1993-94 some 13 per cent more hospital in-patients were treated per head of population than in England; there were about a third more NHS staff and average GP list size was nearly one-fifth smaller. As for education, in 1994 Scotland had some 16 per cent fewer primary and 11 per cent secondary pupils per teacher (Central Statistical Office, 1995). Scotland also spends relatively more on higher education, partly because a higher proportion of young people undertake degree courses, partly because of the prevalence of four-year courses, and partly because there is a net importation of students from south of the border. The Scottish Office took over funding of universities in 1992; current Universities Funding Council expenditure was included in the block, but, whereas only the formula percentage of annual increases in English and Welsh higher education spending is received each year, Scottish universities spend a substantially greater proportion of the UK total. Consequently, either expenditure will have to be transferred within the block from other services to higher education, or the sector will have to be squeezed in one way or another.

Social security is an exception among social services or indeed identifiable expenditure in general, in that policy and administration are a matter for the DSS, and expenditure is nothing to do with the Secretary of State for Scotland or the Scottish block. Interestingly, social security expenditure per head in Scotland is much closer to that in England or the UK than any of the other social services; in fact, even index 108 in 1994-95 compared with the UK (and 111 compared with England) is higher than in recent years when, on occasion, it has been below 100. All this obviously raises the question of how far, if consistent policy were applied throughout the UK, Scottish conditions would result in higher spending levels in other services. As social security expenditure is demand-led rather than cash limited, variations in need should tend to be reflected in expenditure levels.

It is somewhat unsatisfactory to look solely at conventional public expenditure and to ignore tax expenditures, that is reliefs and allowances (apart from those which are intrinsic to the structure of the system, such as income tax personal allowances). Unfortunately, information about many tax expenditures is rather sketchy both in terms of their total value and their incidence in different parts of the UK. One tax expenditure about which quite a lot is known is mortgage income tax relief; in the mid-1990s Scotland had for a number of years been receiving about seven per cent of UK expenditure, slightly less than Scotland's share of mortgages, or nearly 80 per cent of average expenditure per head (Scottish Office, 1995a). The cost of this relief varies according to prevailing interest rates, though currently Scotland is 'losing' less than £100m annually, notwithstanding the growth in owner occupation. This lower tax expenditure on mortgage interest relief, as pointed out above, is to some extent the counterpart of higher conventional housing expenditure in Scotland with its larger social rented sector.

A contentious topic is the extent, if any, to which Scotland's share of public expenditure (including non-identifiable expenditure) exceeds the Scottish contribution to tax revenues. Estimates are sensitive to the assumptions which underlie them and these vary widely; and there is no doubt that the methodology adopted can be influenced by politically motivated assumptions about whether Scotland benefits financially from the Union. The approach taken here is fairly simple but, it can be argued, essentially robust. First, Scotland's contribution to UK tax revenue (excluding North Sea oil taxation) is close to its population share at some 8.9 per cent and 8.8 per cent respectively in 1993-94 (Scottish Office, 1995a). North Sea oil revenues are now modest, amounting to some one per cent or less of government receipts, so even if a substantial proportion were allocated to Scotland the effect on its share of UK taxation would be small. (North Sea oil revenues were much larger in the 1980s, and it could be argued with some plausibility that—on the basis that most of the oil 'belonged' to Scotland—England was being subsidised; but it is difficult to see that this argument has any relevance to the present and future.) Second, it is assumed that non-identifiable expenditure including interest on the national debt should be allocated on a population basis, on the grounds that everyone benefits (or not) equally from defence, foreign relations, the royal family and so on. Consequently, the fiscal deficit in Scottish tax receipts compared with expenditure can be broadly equated with the 'excess' of identifiable expenditure relative to the UK average, something between £4bn and £5bn. This substantial additional expenditure, essentially a transfer from south of the border, goes mainly to provide a more generously financed welfare state in Scotland.

LOCAL GOVERNMENT

Three of the social services discussed in this book—education, (social) housing and the personal social services—are mainly the responsibility of local government. The system of local government in Scotland was reorganised in 1996 but before outlining the new structure the historical background should be mentioned. Local government, apart from the ancient burghs, was really a nineteenth century creation, a response to the growing responsibilities which the state was assuming in poor relief, public health and education. The period of almost a century down to 1929 was marked by a plethora of specialist local bodies responsible for particular services: parochial boards and then parish councils for the poor law, separate education authorities and so on, as well as county councils and town councils with more general functions. Local government was different from today in another way; it raised almost all its own revenues from the rates, a property tax under its own control, and thus enjoyed the freedom and self confidence that stem from financial independence. There was a major reorganisation of local government in 1929 which established or reconstituted 33 county councils, 24 town councils of large burghs, 171 town councils of small burghs, and 199 district councils in counties (so-called landward areas). The system of government grants also was systematised and extended in 1929 to allow rates on industry to be reduced to assist economic recovery, but in the process increasing the financial dependence of councils on the exchequer.

This structure of local government lasted with some amendment until 1975 when it was radically reformed and replaced by the system of regional and district councils which remained until 1996. The 1975-96 system was based on the 1969 report of the Royal Commission on Local Government in Scotland chaired by Lord Wheatley (Cmnd 4510, 1969). The report stated that reform should seek to ensure that local government could have a responsible and positive role, provide services in the most satisfactory manner, and bring electors into the decision-making process as much as possible.

The 1975 system, which was broadly based on Wheatley's recommendations (though the number of councils was rather greater than proposed), consisted of three all-purpose

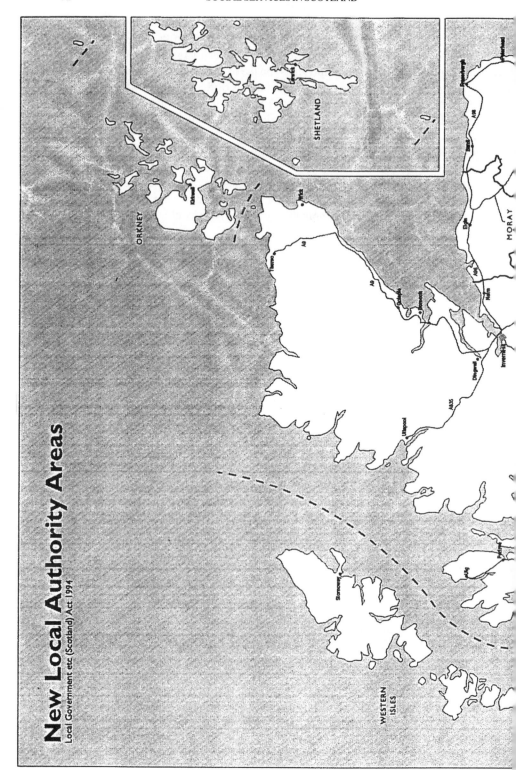

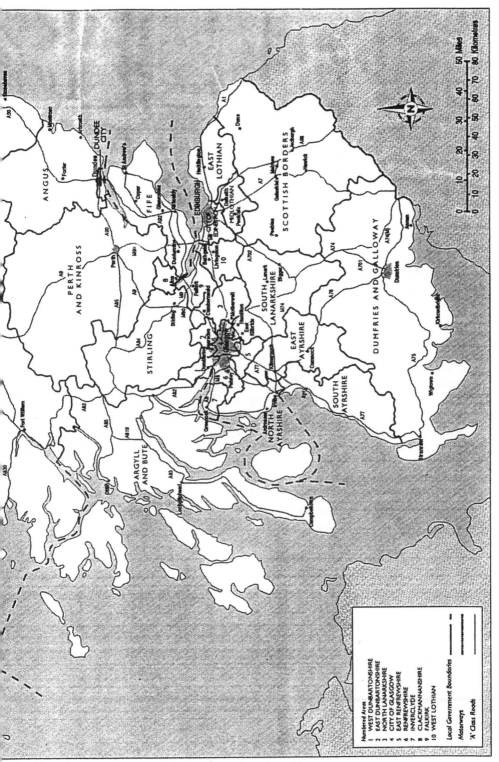

FIGURE 1.1: *New Scottish Local Authority Areas*

islands councils (which continue in existence), and elsewhere a two-tier structure of nine regional councils and 53 district councils. The population of the authorities varied widely: that of regions from Strathclyde, with nearly half the Scottish population, to Borders with some 100,000, and of districts from Glasgow with three quarters of a million to Badenoch and Strathspey with little more than 10,000. The regions were the predominant local authorities responsible for the main services including social work, education, police and fire. Housing, which was the most important district function, went to the lower tier after a good deal of argument; but the division of responsibility for social housing and the personal social services under regional social work departments was on the whole unfortunate (see Chapter 6). Additionally, over 1,000 community councils were established as debating forums to represent the demands and grievances of local areas. The Convention of Scottish Local Authorities (COSLA) was set up by the new councils collectively to represent their interests, particularly in relations with central government.

The two-tier system of local government was subject to a good deal of criticism by advocates of unitary authorities: the government tended to feel that the latter would be more economical and would get rid of the Labour-controlled monolith of Strathclyde; while the opposition parties were vulnerable to jibes about a 'third tier' of government in view of their policy of establishing a Scottish parliament and were somewhat reluctant to defend the *status quo*. The government issued consultation papers in 1991 and 1992 proposing a structure of single-tier authorities. It was asserted that the existing system was based on thinking of the 1960s which envisaged a large role for the public sector in economic planning and the delivery of services. But there was 'now little support for that approach to economic development, and a general recognition that services are better delivered by competing private businesses'. Local authorities had 'a less comprehensive planning role than the Wheatley Commission envisaged'. There was therefore less need 'for the very large authorities of the sort Wheatley recommended' (Scottish Office, 1992). Furthermore, people were confused—which is certainly indisputable—about the responsibilities of regions and districts, and this confusion was inimical to the proper accountability of councils. It was difficult to identify with large authorities, and there was overlap, duplication and potential conflict between the tiers. The main objection made to change, according to the government, was that the cost and upheaval of reform was not justified as the existing structure was working satisfactorily. The government believed, however, that transitional costs would be exceeded by longer-term savings.

In Scotland, as in Wales, the government did not appoint an independent local government commission but introduced legislation following a consultation exercise. (Interestingly, in England, despite the government's preference for unitary authorities, the local government commission's review of different areas has for the most part resulted in the preservation of counties and districts. However, the exercise has verged on the shambolic and no doubt ministers wished they could have followed the example of Scotland and Wales by carving up the local government map in the privacy of Whitehall.) In the 1992 consultation paper the government put forward four illustrative options with from 15 to 51 unitary authorities (including the three existing islands councils). The extreme options were rather in the nature of straw men, being very closely based on the existing regions (though breaking up Strathclyde) and districts. There was a basic trade-off between the potential cost saving of a small number of larger authorities and, to the government, the political attractiveness of small ones. In the event, the Local Government (Scotland) Act, 1994 provided for 29 new unitary authorities which, together with the islands councils, resulted in a total of 32 local authorities. Though the Conservatives would, of course, deny it, some of the decisions about boundaries may have been influenced by political considerations; in particular East Renfrewshire to the south of Glasgow, with its convoluted boundaries, was the subject of adverse criticism that it was an artificial entity designed in an (at least initially) unsuccessful attempt to ensure that at least one council would be under Conservative control.

The new local authorities vary widely in size, both in terms of population and area. Twelve of the new local authorities cover the same areas as former district councils (three with altered names); four the areas of the Borders, Dumfries and Galloway, Fife and Highland regional councils; thirteen are new or altered areas (including Dundee and Glasgow where part of the former district was removed); and there are the three islands councils which continued in existence (Table 1.2 and Figure 1.1). They range in population from Glasgow with well over 600,000 to Clackmannanshire with less than 50,000 (leaving aside the even smaller islands councils). Some cover large rural areas, including the enormous Highland council, while others, among them a number of the biggest in population terms, are compact urban areas.

The eight Scottish police forces continued in existence but are run by new police authorities with representatives of councils in the areas served; similar arrangements were made for the fire service. Water and sewerage services, which used to be the responsibility of regional councils, might well have been privatised, but after strong opposition the government retreated and the three new water authorities, covering the East, North and West of Scotland, remained in the public sector.

Local Government Finance

The main areas of current expenditure by local authorities are education (39 per cent of the total in 1995-96), social work (16 per cent) and police (9 per cent). It should be noted that although providing rented housing is an important local authority function, its finances are segregated in Housing Revenue Accounts and are separate from the arrangements discussed here; furthermore, it is no longer permissable to subsidise council housing from general revenues (see Chapter 6). Apart from the cost of housing benefit, where councils essentially act as agents for the DSS, almost all local authority expenditure except that financed locally comes from the Scottish block. Local authorities are responsible for spending between 40 and 50 per cent of the block, and their expenditure per head is some 40 per cent higher than in England.

Over 80 per cent of local authority current expenditure is financed by central government through Aggregate External Finance (AEF) in three forms: specific grants, Revenue Support Grant (RSG), and non-domestic rates. Specific grants are paid in aid of expenditure on certain services, the most significant being for the police service (about three-quarters of the total), and in total amount to less than ten per cent of AEF.

TABLE 1.2: *Population and Land Area of the New Scottish Local Authorities*

	Population (1993)	Land Area (000s hectares)
Aberdeen City[1]	218,220	19
Aberdeenshire[4]	223,630	632
Angus[4]	111,020	218
Argyll & Bute[4]	90,550	693
Ayrshire, East[4]	123,820	125
Ayrshire, North[2]	139,020	88
Ayrshire South[2]	113,960	120
Clackmannanshire[2]	48,660	16
Dumfries & Galloway[3]	147,900	644
Dunbartonshire, East[4]	110,220	17
Dunbartonshire, West[4]	97,790	16
Dundee City[4]	153,710	7
Edinburgh, City of[1]	441,620	26
Falkirk[1]	142,610	30
Fife[3]	351,200	132
Glasgow, City of[4]	623,850	18
Highland[3]	206,900	2,578
Inverclyde[1]	89,990	16
Lanarkshire, North[4]	326,750	47
Lanarkshire, South[4]	307,100	177
Lothian, East[1]	85,640	68
Lothian, West[1]	146,730	43
Midlothian[1]	79,910	36
Moray[1]	86,250	224
Orkney[5]	19,760	99
Perth & Kinross[4]	130,470	531
Renfrewshire[4]	176,970	26
Renfrewshire, East[4]	86,780	17
Scottish Borders[3]	105,300	473
Shetland[5]	22,830	144
Stirling[1]	81,630	220
Western Isles[5]	29,410	313

Notes: 1. Former district council area (9)
2. Former district council area with altered name (3)
3. Former regional council area (4)
4. New or altered area (13)
5. Continuing islands council (3)

Source: Scottish Office, *The New Councils*, 1995b.

The remainder of AEF is made up of RSG (about 70 per cent) and non-domestic rates (about 20 per cent) which are not tied to any particular service so that councils have some freedom to set their own priorities.

The purpose of RSG is that each local authority should be able to provide the same standard of service and charge the same council tax for houses in the various valuation bands. About one-third of RSG is distributed between areas according to their need to incur expenditure on a client group assessment (number of children, old people, etc). The remaining two-thirds is used to compensate for differences in the average council tax yield per dwelling (that is to subsidise areas with a high proportion of houses in lower valuation bands).

Non-domestic (business) rates used to be set by councils, but when domestic rates were abolished with the introduction of the community charge the former became the responsibility of central government which distributes the revenue to local authorities as, in effect, a grant. They are now set at a standard rate in the pound of rateable value so that businesses are no longer burdened by the high rates which used to be charged by profligate local authorities. The removal of discretion over the level of non-domestic rates was a major step in reducing the financial autonomy of local government.

So far as sources of revenue under their control are concerned, local authorities receive some income from fees and charges but apart from this they rely on the council tax introduced in 1993 to replace the community charge or poll tax. The council tax is a return to a property tax. The government makes assumptions about appropriate levels of expenditure and therefore council tax. Provided RSG operates properly, as explained above, at assumed expenditure levels the council tax would be the same in all areas. There tend to be complaints from COSLA and individual local authorities about the reasonableness of government expenditure assumptions and RSG levels, but a particular difficulty which arose with local government reorganisation, it was alleged, was a failure to take sufficient account of the ending of intra-regional subsidies to large urban areas. The government was, of course, reluctant to accept this, but it was claimed by some councils, for example Glasgow, that their services were put under additional pressure. In fact, most local authorities spend above the level assumed for RSG purposes but below a higher limit at which the council tax would be capped by the government. (Local authorities usually do not even try to exceed this limit because to do so would only be a political gesture and they would be forced to reduce the council tax.) Quite apart from any threat of capping, the high level of central government grant means that there is an intense gearing effect. For example, if at the level of expenditure assumed by the government the council tax would constitute ten per cent of a local authority's revenue but it decides to spend five per cent above this level, the council tax would be 50 per cent higher.

Capital expenditure: In principle capital expenditure (on buildings, etc) is financed by borrowing, though some is met by current revenue. Borrowing obviously has implications for future current expenditure to meet loan charges. Central government keeps close control over capital expenditure through capital allocations, though to some extent capital receipts are permitted to raise the limit on them. Capital allocations form part of the Scottish block because they count as public expenditure; however they are not grants from central government but consents for councils to borrow.

2
SOCIAL SECURITY

The objective of this book is to examine Scottish social services, most of which are subject to separate legislation, display significant differences from provision in the rest of the UK and will be the responsibility of a Scottish parliament. Cash benefits are an exception, and are provided on a uniform basis in England, Scotland and Wales; the Department of Social Security (DSS) is responsible for policy, and the Benefits Agency for day-to-day administration. Nevertheless, it is appropriate to include a chapter on social security because of its importance, both to recipients and in terms of public expenditure. Not to do so would be to give a very partial view of the 'welfare state' in Scotland. This chapter provides an outline of the benefits system, but it is concerned with broad issues of social security policy rather than with the details of welfare rights.

DEVELOPMENT OF SOCIAL SECURITY IN BRITAIN

At the end of the nineteenth century the only source of cash income from public funds available to those in need was outdoor relief from the locally administered and financed poor law. The harsh terms on which poor relief was given meant that it was the last resort of a destitute minority of the population. The history of social security during the first half of the present century is to a large extent an account of how provision was made outside the poor law (and on a national rather than a local basis) on terms which were acceptable to the population as a whole (Gilbert, 1966; 1974).

In the early 1900s there was a new awareness of the extent of poverty with the research of Charles Booth in London and Seebohm Rowntree in York (Booth, 1903; Rowntree, 1901). They demonstrated that poverty was a serious problem and that its chief causes were old age and sickness. At the same time there was widespread dissatisfaction with the poor law and a feeling that it should be reformed. Although some believed that its administration ought to be tightened up and that the principle of less eligibility should be enforced, the more general view was that the poor law should be liberalised and made less deterrent. A Royal Commission on the Poor Laws and Relief of Distress (that is unemployment) was set up in 1905 and reported in 1909 (Cd 4499, 1909). But in 1908 the recently elected Liberal government introduced the old age pensions, the first social security scheme in Britain apart from the poor law. It was felt to be undesirable that large numbers of old people should be obliged to resort to poor relief and there had been a growing demand for pensions. Two features of the new scheme should be emphasised: first, pensions were financed from general taxation (rather than from local rates or special insurance contributions); and, second, they were paid subject to a means test. Nevertheless, pensions were quite unlike the poor law; a standardised national means test was used, and most people aged 70 with an income below a specified level had a right to a pension. Once the scheme was fully established, some two-thirds of individuals over 70 were receiving pensions.

The introduction of health and unemployment insurance in 1911, by David Lloyd George and Winston Churchill, respectively the Chancellor of the Exchequer and President of the Board of Trade, was the most important measure in the social security field until after the Second World War. It marked the adoption in Britain of contributory social insurance—or national insurance—as a method of financing social security. Contributory insurance is the basis of many benefits today. The creation of entirely new contributory schemes was politically attractive for a number of reasons. First, insurance contributions by employers and employees were a convenient way of raising revenue which did not seem to be just another tax: old age pensions had turned out to be more expensive than expected and the Treasury was opposed to new schemes financed primarily out of general taxation. Second, poor law reform was unattractive because of the enormous task of reconstructing local government administration and finance which it involved. Third, many advocates of poor law reform had a highly paternalistic approach and believed that relief should be 'conditional': that anyone receiving assistance from the state should be required to behave in such a way that dependency would be ended as soon as possible. Contributory benefits, on the other hand, could be presented as a quasi-contractual return on contributions rather than a gift from the state demanding character reform. And the absence of a means test further emphasised the distinction between contributory national insurance and the poor law. This approach of defining rights to benefit and of avoiding the personal investigation of claimants is still central to the national insurance system.

National health insurance was the more significant of the two schemes. It covered all manual workers and lower-paid white collar workers—the bulk of the labour force. National health insurance had two aspects: a cash sickness benefit and medical benefit. The latter was basically the free services of a general practitioner and free drugs (and became part of the National Health Service in 1948). Sickness benefit was payable for up to six months, when it was replaced by a lower disablement benefit. There was also a lump-sum maternity benefit.

Unemployment insurance, the first state-run scheme of its kind in the world, was small-scale and experimental, applying only to certain trades, such as building and iron-founding. The scheme was administered through the recently established labour exchanges where the unemployed had to register in order to claim benefit. This was payable for a strictly limited period of one week's benefit for every five contributions, with not more than 15 weeks' benefit in any 12 months. The scheme was primarily intended to tide over the normally employed workman for short periods. It did little for those in casual employment who would soon run out of benefit even if they had paid enough contributions to qualify in the first place.

During less than a decade before the First World War, therefore, the beginnings of a system of social security benefits were established in Britain by Liberal governments. But the years between the wars, dominated by economic crises and mass unemployment, saw only relatively modest improvements. In 1920 unemployment insurance was extended to practically the same categories of workers as were covered by health insurance. But the post-war boom soon collapsed, unemployment greatly increased and the insurance scheme entered a decade of chaos. It was politically unacceptable to force large numbers of the long-term unemployed onto poor relief, so unemployment insurance was adapted to cater for them. The rules were relaxed until an unemployed person could draw benefit practically without limit, and as a consequence outgoings exceeded income from contributions with the result that the exchequer had to make up the difference out of general taxation. The insurance basis of the scheme had been practically destroyed (Gilbert, 1974).

In the political crisis of 1931, when economies in public expenditure were demanded to balance the budget, the National Government both cut benefits (their real value had increased owing to falling prices) and limited entitlement to unemployment benefit to six months. The long-term unemployed who ran out of insurance benefit could now obtain allowances only after a means test; initially local authorities administered these transitional payments. But the divorce between providing and spending money was unsatisfactory, and in 1934 a new body, the Unemployment Assistance Board (UAB), was created to administer the allowances. This was an important innovation because for the first time responsibility for 'social assistance' was given to a national body. The UAB, which set up a network of area offices, in 1948 became the National Assistance Board responsible for all social assistance.

These developments affecting the unemployed were significant for another reason because, though means testing had always been central to the poor law, only relatively small numbers of people had experienced it (except that for old age pensions which was very different). The means test for the unemployed was on a 'household' basis, the needs of everyone living in the same house being aggregated. An unemployed son could therefore be ineligible for assistance and obliged to rely on his parents. Sometimes unemployed children moved into lodgings to get some income of their own. The experience of the unemployed in the 1930s was an important factor in the widespread antipathy towards means testing at the time of the Beveridge report.

The other innovations during the inter-war period affected pensions. There were a number of criticisms of the existing scheme. First, the pension age of 70 was seen as too high; many found it difficult to carry on working until then. Second, the means test was disliked. Third, there was no provision for widows. The government decided to extend the principle of contributory insurance to pensions in 1925. For those who had been insured the pension age was reduced to 65 and the means test abolished, as well as widows' and orphans' pensions being introduced. (The lower age of 60 for women, which is now being phased out, dates from 1940.) Thus by the Second World War an extensive range of cash benefits had developed in Britain, mainly on the basis of contributory insurance. But they had limitations; for example, there were many separate schemes none covering precisely the same categories of people, they were administered by different organisations and the level of some benefits was very low. As well as gaps in provision for the non-employed, the problem of inadequate wages in relation to family requirements was ignored completely.

The Beveridge Report

While the war was in progress the government started to consider reconstruction when peace came, and in 1941 an inter-departmental committee of civil servants under the chairmanship of Sir William Beveridge was appointed to undertake a 'survey of the existing national schemes of social insurance and allied services'. Beveridge, who had long been concerned with social security, wanted far more radical reforms than had originally been envisaged and about which civil servants could not properly express views in public. They therefore became advisers and the report, published in 1942, was signed by Beveridge alone (Cmd 6404, 1942). Though many changes have subsequently been made, social security benefits in Britain still owe much to the recommendations of the Beveridge Report and it is useful to examine what he was seeking to achieve.

The theme which dominates the Beveridge Report is the objective of guaranteeing to every citizen an income at subsistence level or, in other words, sufficient resources to keep people out of poverty (or what he called 'want'). In proposing rates of benefit Beveridge relied on pre-war poverty studies such as those of Rowntree, who acted as an adviser. Beveridge believed that the role of the state in social security should be limited to providing a subsistence income. He recognised that many people would wish to have a higher income when they were not working but believed that this should be obtained through voluntary insurance.

Beveridge identified two causes of poverty: the interruption or loss of earning power (for example during sickness, unemployment or old age), and the failure of wages to relate to the needs of families of different sizes. He believed that the abolition of poverty required a 'double redistribution of income' from those currently at work to those not at work, chiefly through social insurance; and from individuals and small families to larger ones through family (or, as he called them, children's) allowances.

The main part of the report was concerned with interruption or loss of earning power. Beveridge wholeheartedly approved of social insurance; he believed that people preferred benefits in return for contribution and without a means test. (There is no technical reason why non-contributory benefits should be means-tested but in practice they usually are; family allowances, now child benefit, have been the major exception.) Social insurance should continue to be the main method of providing incomes for those not at work and it would be necessary to improve the existing schemes in three directions: they should be extended to cover persons (chiefly white collar workers) and risks then excluded, and benefit rates should be raised to a subsistence level.

Social insurance was, however, to be only one of three methods of providing social security; the others were to be voluntary insurance and national assistance. The role of voluntary insurance in providing an income in excess of the subsistence level has already been mentioned but, as Beveridge's specific ideas about it have not had a great impact, this aspect of his proposals may be left aside. Social insurance on its own would not be capable of providing everyone with an income even at the subsistence level, and to supplement it (or to act as a 'safety net') there should be a non-contributory national assistance scheme of means-tested allowances for those in need.

National assistance would cover all categories of need including those still met by cash payments from the poor law.

Assistance was envisaged as having only a very limited permanent role in meeting the few needs not covered by insurance benefits. (Beveridge proposed that increased retirement pensions should be phased in over 20 years so that in the interim assistance would cater for large numbers of old people. But higher pensions were paid immediately after the war.) There were in essence three kinds of need for which assistance would be required. First, there would be those who had not fulfilled the contribution conditions for insurance benefit, for example because they had not worked for a sufficient period. (The unemployed who run out of insurance benefit are in a rather similar position, but this limitation was a divergence from the Beveridge Report which did not propose a time limit on eligibility.) Second, there would be those in circumstances (or 'contingencies') which were thought not sufficiently widespread to warrant an insurance benefit; in practice lone parents (apart from widows) have been the largest group in this position, but Beveridge did not foresee the rapid growth in their numbers. Third, there would be those who, although entitled to an insurance benefit, had exceptionally large needs. Insurance benefits were to be set at a level sufficient to provide a subsistence income for those with normal needs, but they would be inadequate in cases such as a high rent or illness requiring a special diet. Only in this third category of need would assistance be paid in addition to insurance benefits.

Beveridge did not regard inadequate wages in relation to family needs as falling strictly within his terms of reference, and instead he dealt with family allowances as one of three 'assumptions' which were essential to the success of his plan for social security (the others were a national health service and the maintenance of full employment). As wages are unrelated to family needs, a combination of low income and dependent children can be a cause of poverty. But Beveridge was not only concerned with family allowances as a method of preventing poverty. He was also concerned about the possible overlap between the level of wages and benefits (especially during unemployment) from the point of view of work incentives. (This phenomenon is now known as the unemployment trap and is discussed below.) Without family allowances, paid whether the head of the household was working or not, either benefits for larger families would have to be set below the subsistence level (by paying very meagre amounts for children) or in some cases they would be higher than the wage which a claimant could earn.

Beveridge proposed family allowances, on a non-means-tested basis paid to the mother, and financed by the exchequer, of eight shillings a week which was his estimate of the subsistence cost of keeping a child. Family allowances were to be paid in respect of second and subsequent children so that separate child additions in the case of other benefits would not be required for them. Exclusion of the first child was ostensibly justified on two grounds. First, Beveridge believed that 'very few men's wages are insufficient to cover at least two adults and one child'. Second, he said that it was desirable that the cost of maintaining children should be shared between the family and the state. In reality Beveridge was also constrained by the level of expenditure to which the Treasury was willing to agree. Exclusion of the first child approximately halved the cost of any given level of allowance, as about half of all dependent children are first or only children. On the assumption that wages were adequate for a one-child family, a subsistence level allowance would prevent additional children pushing a family into poverty, but the alternative of a smaller one payable in respect of every child could not do this.

The bulk of the recommendations of the Beveridge report were accepted by the wartime Coalition government and implemented in uncontroversial acts of parliament. Family allowances were introduced before the end of the war, and the rest by the post-war Labour government. Family allowances were first paid in 1946 while the other measures came into force in 1948. Nevertheless, there were divergences from the recommendations of the Beveridge report, mainly affecting the rates of benefit, which were crucial.

In the case of national insurance, the Coalition government took the view that the subsistence rates of benefit proposed by Beveridge would be too expensive, and it decided that they should instead merely provide a 'reasonable insurance against want' (Cmd 6550, 1944). If the rates of national assistance had been similarly reduced, the relationship between insurance and assistance proposed by Beveridge would have been maintained, albeit at a lower level of payment, and the former would still have been deemed sufficient in all 'normal' cases. Those receiving insurance benefits would only have required to have them supplemented by assistance where 'exceptional' needs existed. But national assistance rates were actually set at a higher level, approximating to the real value of Beveridge's subsistence scale (Deacon, 1982); consequently a substantial minority of those entitled to national insurance benefits, particularly those without a separate source of income such as an occupational pension, were entitled to have them supplemented by assistance.

What happened in practice can be clarified by focusing on the treatment of housing costs, or what Beveridge referred to as 'rent'. He recommended that a notional amount should be included in insurance benefit rates which would generally be enough to meet rent, so that only those with exceptionally high housing costs would require assistance for this reason. In practice, however, insurance benefit rates were only slightly higher than national assistance rates, but the latter paid housing costs in addition. The notional rent element in national insurance disappeared, and housing costs were, until the introduction of housing benefit in 1982, an important cause of entitlement to assistance amongst insurance beneficiaries.

The much greater reliance on assistance than Beveridge intended—stemming partly from the limitation of entitlement to unemployment benefit and the growth in the numbers of single parents as well as from the distortion of relative payment levels outlined above—had important consequences. Apart from an excessive reliance on what was in Beveridge's eyes a less desirable form of social security, the problems have centred on the incomplete take-up of means-tested benefits. The problem of low take-up must, however, be balanced against the provision of higher benefits for a given expenditure through the concentration of resources on those with demonstrated financial need. Unless expenditure on social security could have been substantially increased, slightly more generous insurance benefits would have meant markedly lower rates of assistance. It is not clear that on balance this would have been to the advantage of the poorest households; after all only a minority of eligible people fail to claim means-tested benefits.

Another divergence from Beveridge's recommendations was in the level at which family allowances were set. On grounds of cost the Coalition government set allowances at only five shillings a week so that when they began to be paid after the war they fell far below the subsistence needs of a child. Not only were allowances initially inadequate to guarantee that family size would not be a cause of poverty but the reluctance of successive governments to uprate them to take account of inflation meant that they became increasingly ineffective.

The Beveridge report represented a major step forward in social security provisions and some of its proposals were radical, such as the extension of insurance benefits to the whole population and the attempt to limit the role of means testing. But in others, like the emphasis on subsistence level benefits financed by regressive flat-rate contributions, it was conservative. The way in which the recommendations were implemented, however, has meant that the new benefits have not been completely successful in achieving Beveridge's primary aim of abolishing poverty.

The Fowler Reviews

A substantial number of changes, albeit often modest in scope, were made over the years to the Beveridge system after 1948. Among the more significant developments were the replacement of national assistance by supplementary benefit in 1966 in order to give the social assistance safety net a better image to encourage take-up; family income supplement was introduced in 1971 to provide a means-tested (and therefore low-cost) alternative to increased family allowances for low wage households with children; the state earnings related pension scheme (SERPS) started in 1978; and in the late 1970s child benefit was phased in to replace family allowances and child income tax allowances. By the mid-1980s, however, the government was becoming increasingly aware of what it saw as shortcomings in the social security system and, in the words of a green paper, felt that three 'main objectives' should be pursued: first, 'meeting genuine need' by giving greater priority to families with children; second, consistency with the needs of the economy by restraining expenditure growth and improving work incentives; and, third, making benefits easier to administer (Cmnd 9517, 1985). Four civil service reviews had been set up by Norman Fowler, the then Secretary of State for Social Services, which resulted in the green paper, then a white paper (Cmnd 9691, 1985) and legislation in 1986. The important changes to the benefits system were implemented in 1988.

The Fowler reviews, which dealt with retirement, children and young people, supplementary benefit and housing benefit, were essentially concerned with making means-tested benefits work better. The exception was the scaling down of the SERPS and the introduction of personal pensions as a third alternative to it and occupational pensions. Means-tested benefits had become increasingly important and supplementary benefit was particularly problematic. Its predecessor, national assistance, had originally been intended as a small-scale safety net but in the event it had a very substantial number of claimants for the reasons explained above. In principle, national assistance and supplementary benefit provided an income precisely adjusted to meet the needs of each household. Hence the safety net was complicated and expensive to administer, and not well designed for a mass role. Then there was concern about the incentives problems of the poverty and unemployment traps (discussed below). Finally, there was a good deal of evidence that while many of the elderly had a reasonable, and improving, standard of living, families with children, particularly the unemployed and lone parents, were doing less well. Consequently the government sought to streamline assistance, improve work incentives and, to some extent, shift resources from the elderly to families with children. But the exercise was conducted on a 'nil-cost' basis, and any additional expenditure had to be balanced by savings elsewhere in the social security programme.

Income Support: Supplementary benefit was replaced by a combination of income support and the social fund. The basic weekly supplementary scale rates were generally straightforward to administer, and these became, with some modifications, income support. Extra weekly amounts to meet special needs, such a heating or diet allowance, were abolished and replaced by 'premiums' to cover easily identifiable categories such as families with children and the elderly. (In fact, the only significant income support claimants not entitled to any premium were the unemployed without children.) In effect different claimant groups receive different weekly rates depending on the government's view of their likely needs (and perhaps deserts). There is an element of what at the time was often referred to as 'rough justice' with gainers and losers; the latter were particularly claimants who had received substantial amounts for special needs (although supplementary benefit in payment was not reduced in cash terms).

Social Fund: Lump-sum grants under supplementary benefit were replaced by the social fund which is formally separate from income support. The significance of the distinction is that the social fund is discretionary and cash limited; dissatisfied applicants cannot appeal to an independent tribunal but may only have their cases reviewed by a procedure within the DSS. The social fund has a fixed annual budget which cannot be exceeded (rather than expenditure being demand-led and determined by claimant entitlements).

The social fund has two roles: to provide interest-free loans, normally only to people already receiving income support, and to pay community care grants to enable individuals to live in their own homes rather than in institutions. The justification for loans rather than the grants they replaced (apart from saving money) is that the purposes for which they are made—to buy clothing or bedding for example—are in principle covered by income support. The implication is that someone asking for a loan has not budgeted properly. Loans are normally recovered from future income support payments.

Family Credit: Family income supplement was replaced by a basically similar but more generous benefit, which was consequently available to more households. The intention was to improve the financial position of low earners with children and thus improve work incentives. As is explained below, this may have alleviated the unemployment trap but at the cost of drawing more people into the poverty trap. However, a move to a net income means test (also explained below) meant that practically no-one would be actually worse off after a pay increase.

Housing Benefit: The means test was simplified and also put on a net income basis. Housing benefit for households with incomes significantly above the income support level was drastically cut back. This particularly affected the elderly, especially through reductions in the rates rebate element which hit many owner occupiers. While the cutbacks in SERPS will result in large expenditure savings in the longer term, the reductions in housing benefit eligibility for the slightly better off provided immediate savings which financed the somewhat higher benefits for families with children.

Developments to 1997

There have been further changes to benefits since the Fowler reviews were implemented in 1988. The DSS started carrying out internal reviews of benefits on a sector by sector basis, putting expenditure under close scrutiny. The objectives were stated to be better targeting of those in need, encouraging more self-provision, and providing more work incentives (Cm 2813, 1995). These reviews are a reason why, as discussed below, the increase in expenditure on social security is expected to slow in coming years.

Incapacity benefit replaced sickness benefit and invalidity benefit in 1995. Expenditure on the long-term sick had been increasing rapidly and basically the aim was to tighten up on the availability of benefit. Sickness was in most cases certified by patients' own GPs, and they were seen as fairly ineffective gatekeepers. Incapacity benefit introduced a new, 'more objective', all-work test applied to most claimants after 28 weeks. This test is operated by doctors directly employed by the Benefits Agency. Although the expectation was that the new test would reduce the number of claimants receiving incapacity benefit (though possibly resulting in some registering as unemployed), thus significantly reducing expenditure, it does not in fact seem to have been particularly effective in this respect.

Job seeker's allowance replaced unemployment benefit and income support for the unemployed in 1996. It may not be unfair to suggest that the new benefit was to some extent a presentational renaming, but there were substantive changes. Availability for work and job search requirements were further tightened, but the key development was that eligibility for contributory, non-means tested, benefit was reduced from a year to six months (and no longer includes increases for dependants). The unemployed then move on to income-related job seeker's allowance, on a similar basis to income support which, in their case, it replaced. Again the new benefit is expected to reduce expenditure.

Two further changes were made, affecting assistance with housing costs. Since 1995 new income support claimants do not have their mortgage interest met for nine months; house buyers are expected to take out insurance. Eligibility for housing benefit was tightened up in 1996: private sector rents are now only taken fully into account up to the local average for the type of property; and single people under 25 only receive benefit on rents for non-self-contained accommodation.

The Labour Government

Major changes to the benefits system are likely to take some time to emerge, though before the end of 1997 there was controversy about Labour's decision to implement cuts to benefits for single parents announced by the previous government. 'Welfare' soon emerged as an important, and controversial, aspect of the new government's policies: their aim is to get as many as possible of the unemployed, sick and single parents back to work, thus both improving their standard of living and reducing expenditure. 'Welfare to work' is a flagship policy, and a number of policy reviews have been set up.

THE BENEFITS SYSTEM

Before moving on to discuss policy issues in social security, it is useful to outline the current benefits system. The main social security benefits are listed in Figure 2.1, which divides them into six categories according to whether they are contributory or means-tested or neither; and into income maintenance benefits, which may provide a household's main or only income, and those designed to meet an additional need of some kind. It should be noted that, with the exception of SERPS, none varies according to previous earnings. In the spirit of the Beveridge plan, Britain, unlike many other countries, has a basically flat-rate benefits system. The categorisation of benefits according to how they are financed—from national insurance contributions or general taxation—and whether they are means-tested, is fundamental to understanding social security.

Contributory (National Insurance) Benefits: The academic term for these benefits is 'social insurance'. They are financed through national insurance contributions paid by employees and employers, and eligibility depends (apart from being elderly, sick, unemployed, etc.) on having paid these contributions. But they are not means-tested and other income is not taken into account. Beveridge intended national insurance to be the backbone of the benefits system, and they still account for about half of total expenditure on benefits though their importance used to be even greater.

Means-tested (Income-related) Benefits: The academic term for these benefits is 'social assistance'. In contrast to contributory benefits, this category is financed from general taxation so there are no contribution conditions for eligibility. Beveridge was not very keen on means-tested benefits—he thought the contributory principle was a better way of organising social security—but, as explained above, he recognised they would be needed for people whose needs were not met by national insurance. Consequently, he proposed national assistance as a means-tested safety net. In the event, three particular sets of circumstances have been important in causing dependence on assistance. First, until the 1970s the bulk of recipients of national assistance (supplementary benefit from 1966) were old people having their retirement pensions topped up, mainly because housing costs were included in assistance but not in national insurance benefits. Second and third, however, are lone parenthood and unemployment which have become much more significant since the 1970s. Lone parents (apart from widowed mothers who are eligible for national insurance benefits) caring for children full time are the only significant group to whom the state is willing to provide a social security income but where there is no contributory benefit. Consequently lone parents who are not in paid employment are generally dependent on assistance, now in the form of income support. Unemployment benefit was limited to 12 months (and now contributory Job Seeker's Allowance is limited to six months) so that the long-term unemployed were also dependent on income support (now on non-contributory

FIGURE 2.1: *Main Social Security Benefits, 1997*

	Income maintenance	Supplementary income
Contributory (National Insurance)	Job Seeker's Allowance (contributory)[1] Incapacity Benefit[2] Retirement Pension (basic) Widow's Pension Widowed Mother's Allowance	State Earnings Related Pension Scheme (SERPS)[3]
Means-tested (or income related) Benefits	Income Support Job Seeker's Allowance (non-contributory)[1]	Social Fund[4] Family Credit Housing Benefit Council Tax Benefit Disability Working Allowance
Non-contributory (or contingency) Benefits	Severe Disablement Allowance Invalid Care Allowance Retirement Pension (non-contributory) Guardian's Allowance	Child Benefit Attendance Allowance Disability Living Allowance

NOTES: 1. Contributory Job Seeker's Allowance for six months; thereafter non-contributory JSA.
2. Generally statutory sick pay, paid by employer, for first six months.
3. Employees must contribute to SERPS or an occupational pension or a personal pension.
4. Lump-sum loans or grants; linked to income support.

JSA). Failure to pay contributions, generally because someone has never worked owing to disablement of some kind, has always been a comparatively small cause of dependence on assistance.

Means-tested benefits have become more important and now account for about one-third of benefit expenditure, nearly twice the proportion in 1979. This growth is partly because of the introduction of new benefits, such as family credit for low-income families in work, and partly because of the growth of some claimant groups, especially lone parents and the unemployed.

Non-contributory (Contingency) Benefits: These are a sort of the hybrid of the first two categories: they are not means-tested but they are financed from general taxation so that there are no contribution conditions. With the exception of family allowances which were proposed by Beveridge (now incorporated in child benefit), non-contributory benefits were mainly introduced in the 1970s and most are provided for the disabled. These were thought desirable partly because some of the disabled did not qualify for insurance benefits because they had never paid contributions. Those which have an income maintenance role are paid at a rate well below that of other benefits and most recipients also claim income support, so their practical significance is limited. Including child benefit, non-contributory benefits account for about one-sixth of total expenditure.

SOCIAL SECURITY POLICY: OBJECTIVES AND CONSTRAINTS

Social security policy, like all aspects of social policy, pursues a number of objectives but has to work within a number of constraints. Policy has to try to achieve a reasonable balance between these objectives and constraints because, in the final analysis, they are incompatible. In other words, it is unlikely that any particular objective can be fully achieved, but neither can any be ignored. As well as administrative feasibility (where, for example, supplementary benefit came near to falling down) there are perhaps three crucial factors which provide the context for policy:

Cost of benefits: the level of public expenditure has to be politically acceptable.

Adequacy of benefits: the coverage and level of benefits should be satisfactory.

Maintenance of incentives: the benefits system should not discourage work and saving.

In essence, any two of these objectives/constraints could be achieved fairly easily. If a lot more were spent on benefits, they could be both generous and non means-tested—means testing is the main cause of damaged incentives. If benefits were at a very low level, they could have an acceptable cost and be non-means tested. If incentives were ignored, generous means-tested benefits would not be excessively expensive. In fact policy is always a compromise between these considerations, and each will now be considered.

Cost of Benefits

The social security programme is not only by far the largest public expenditure programme but (except for the social fund) it is 'demand led' and not subject to cash limits. Because people have a legal right to benefits if they fall into defined circumstances, the exchequer has to find the money if expenditure exceeds forecasts, for example because of increased take-up or higher unemployment.

Expenditure on social security grew eightfold in real terms between 1949-50 (the first year of the post-Beveridge system) and 1995-96; from less than five per cent to 13 per cent of GDP; and from 14 per cent to one-third of total public expenditure. The real growth in expenditure was nearly five per cent a year, over twice as fast as GDP. There is a variety of reasons for increased expenditure since 1948: a more comprehensive system with new benefits, higher benefits, and social and demographic changes (Department of Social Security, 1993).

Table 2.1 compares the proportion of benefit expenditure on broad client groups in 1978-79 and 1995-96; during this period expenditure rose by over 80 per cent in real terms or four per cent annually (despite the fact that since 1980 benefit rates have in principle not been uprated except to take account of inflation). The elderly are still

TABLE 2.1: *Benefit Expenditure by Client Groups, 1978-79 and 1995-96*

	1978-79 %	1995-96 %
Elderly	56	44
Long term sick and disabled	11	24
Short term sick	5	1
Families[1]	16	19
(of which lone parents)	(6)	(11)
Unemployed	8	10
Widows and others	4	2

Note: 1. Includes child benefit; one parent benefit; family income supplement/
         family credit; maternity benefits; means-tested benefits to lone parents;
         housing benefit for people in work.

Sources: Department of Social Security, *The Growth of Social Security,* 1993;
         *Social Security Departmental Report: The Government's Expenditure
         Plans 1996-97 to 1998-99,* Cm 3212, 1996.

the most important client group in expenditure terms though their dominance has diminished to some extent, to well below half the total. Expenditure on the elderly increased by about half in real terms over the 17-year period. The long-term sick and disabled have become much more important, a trend which in part reflects economic changes whereby middle-aged men with indifferent health lost jobs which in other circumstances they would have often kept to retirement age. Expenditure on this group increased by about 300 per cent over the same period. The sharp reduction in spending on the short-term sick is linked to the introduction of statutory sick pay paid through employers. Expenditure on lone parents increased almost as rapidly as on the long-term sick. Two points might be made about the unemployed: their number goes up and down according to the state of the economy; and although unemployment is a serious problem it is fallacious to suggest that it is the major reason for the increasing cost of social security.

Growth in expenditure to the end of the century, however, is projected to be not much more than one per cent annually, partly because of changes to the system (such as the introduction of incapacity benefit). The social security programme is likely to fall as a proportion of GDP.

To return to the constraints on policy making, social security is clearly a very large programme where there are still pressures for further growth, even if these have been reduced. Improvements to all social services are likely to have public expenditure implications which will be unwelcome to any government; but these implications tend to be particularly significant in the case of social security. Consequently, although increasing expenditure might solve a lot of problems in social security policy, this is unlikely to be practical politics. Indeed, the Labour government is giving at least as much emphasis to holding down public expenditure as did their predecessors, in order to fulfil their pledge not to increase income tax and VAT. And particular emphasis is being put on trying to reduce 'welfare' expenditure so that, in the political rhetoric, more can be spent on hospitals and schools.

Adequacy of Benefits

Moving on to the second objective of social security policy, the principal concern is the level of benefits, though their coverage is also important. It would obviously not be satisfactory if benefits, though generous for those eligible to receive them, did not cover contingencies widely recognised as justifying the payment of social security. However, though benefits in Britain have their limitations, their coverage is comparatively broad, particularly with the introduction of new benefits since 1948 such as family income supplement (now family credit) for low wage families with children.

As was mentioned earlier, the Beveridge report sought to ensure that the benefits system would provide a subsistence income to all, so as far as possible, to prevent poverty. When the new system was introduced in 1948, the normal benefit rate (based somewhat loosely on Beveridge's recommendations) for a single retirement pensioner, for example, was equivalent to about 20 per cent of average male manual earnings. Initially benefits were uprated irregularly—no doubt because it took some time for policy makers to come to terms with the then new phenomenon of sustained inflation—but since the 1970s upratings have been annual. Criteria for uprating benefits after 1948 were not at first explicit, but it is clear that policy was to keep them broadly in line with average earnings. In 1973 a distinction was made between 'long-term' benefits (retirement pensions, invalidity pensions, and widows' benefits as well as long-term supplementary benefit rates) and 'short-term' benefits (sickness benefit, unemployment benefit and ordinary supplementary benefit rates). Until 1980 long-term benefits were uprated in line with average earnings or inflation, whichever was higher, whereas short-term benefits were uprated in line with inflation. As earnings usually rise faster than inflation, an increasingly wide gap opened between long and short-term benefits. It was difficult to justify a substantial and growing difference in terms of the ostensible rationale of the greater needs of long-term claimants (except for the unemployed who never got the higher rate).

Between 1948 and the early 1980s short-term benefits approximately doubled in real value while long-term benefits increased about two and a half times. Long-term benefits increased modestly relative to average earnings, but to a greater extent relative to net earnings (because of increases in income tax and national insurance contributions paid by the employed). The Conservative government elected in 1979 decided that, from the 1980 uprating, the link between long-term benefits and average earnings would be abandoned, and since then all benefits have been adjusted for inflation. Their purchasing power is therefore static, and households dependent on benefits have been pegged at the same standard of living. Average earnings increased by approximately two-fifths in real terms between 1980 and 1996, so that the single retirement pension fell from about 21 per cent to 15 per cent of average earnings. Until 1980 most of those dependent on benefits broadly participated in generally increasing standards of living, but since 1980 they have been left behind (Bradshaw and Lynes, 1995). It should be pointed out, however, that income inequality has increased and lower earnings have generally risen by less than the average. Indeed, the lowest have scarcely increased in real terms. Consequently, while some households moving on to benefits have experienced an increasingly sharp fall in income relative to their previous earnings, the gap has *not* tended to widen in the case of the lower paid. Put another way, the pre-1980 uprating regime would have seen a significant increase in benefit income relative to earning capacity in the case, for example, of most of the long-term sick whose benefits used to be linked to average earnings. This would have had implications for work incentives (the unemployment trap) which are discussed below.

Beveridge's notion of appropriate benefit levels was, as has been suggested, directly related to his objective of preventing poverty. In other words, the amount of benefit appropriate to a household of any particular composition was by implication its 'poverty line'. Indeed, though no government has ever accepted the equivalence, social assistance (national assistance, supplementary benefit or income support) scales have often been referred to as the 'official' poverty line. And in a very important sense benefit rates—in the tradition of Beveridge and his concern to guarantee a subsistence income to all in order to eradicate poverty—are implicitly a poverty line. This approach is sometimes criticised on account of its circularity; if, to help the poor, benefits are increased, more people will be defined as poor. But this objection is surely misconceived: if the government decides that the minimum standard of living should be increased and consequently raises benefit levels, by the same token it makes the implied poverty line more generous. That some people have incomes which fall below the poverty line—because of shortcomings in the benefits system such as inadequate coverage or low take-up—is a separate issue.

Furthermore, benefit levels, even if they are not an ideal way of defining poverty, are arguably the least unsatisfactory approach available. Social research, though it can provide persuasive evidence about living standards at different income levels which may influence political thinking and policy making, cannot itself directly produce a poverty line: a definition of poverty is of little practical consequence unless it obtains widespread support, for example by being endorsed by a major political party. A very powerful consideration will always be earnings: benefit rates—and implicitly poverty lines—are unlikely to be set at a higher level than wages, except perhaps those of a small minority of the lowest paid. Ideas of what constitutes a socially acceptable minimum standard of living below which society strives to prevent people falling—essentially what is meant by poverty—will differ according to time and place. In the final analysis defining a poverty line is a political decision. As for the current levels of benefits, probably few people would take the view that the standard of living of households solely dependent on them is excessively generous though there is more argument about whether they are too low and ought to be increased. But despite the reluctance of some commentators to accept the basically relative nature of poverty, it is difficult to think of a poverty line that has remained unchanged in real terms over a long period in the context of rising general standards of living.

The cost of benefits was discussed in the previous section, and this is clearly affected by uprating policy. It was the Labour Party's intention as late as 1992 to restore the earnings link in the case of long-term benefits such as retirement pensions, but this policy is no longer on the political agenda. The structure of the benefits system has changed since 1980—some benefits have been replaced by new ones—so that it is not possible to say precisely how much more would now be spent annually had the earnings link been retained. But it is difficult to believe that retention of the earnings link would not by now imply additional annual expenditure of at least £20bn. Argument about the earnings link has tended to centre on retirement pensions, which account for over £10bn of the saving, though in practice it might be difficult to ignore at least other long-term benefits. As far as the basic pension is concerned, given that the majority of the elderly have significant additional income from occupational pensions and savings, and have enjoyed above average increases in living standards, it is perhaps difficult to argue that higher rates should be a priority for public expenditure. The answer may well be a divergence between contributory benefits and social assistance, with income support rates being increased in real terms. Alternatively, some kind of 'guaranteed pension', means-tested but separate from income support, may be politically more attractive for presentational reasons. By focusing extra resources on low income households, such policies would be comparatively cheap, though at the cost of drawing more people into dependence on means-tested benefits, which, as discussed below, are not without problems of their own.

Maintenance of Incentives

While 'moral hazard'—the tendency to maximise one's own well-being at the cost of society's—may affect most tax-financed services to some extent, it is much less significant in, say, the NHS than in the case of cash benefits, particularly those available to individuals of working age. A realistic approach to social security policy must recognize that the availability of benefits inevitably tends to affect behaviour, sometimes in a socially undesirable way: it may involve perverse incentives. Some incentives, of course, are desirable from the point of view of society (for example, to refrain from work when genuinely ill in order to assist recovery) but others are undesirable (for example, to prefer unemployment to work). While all benefits potentially alter behaviour, it is often argued that in certain circumstances means-tested benefits can be particularly significant from the point of view of incentives. Some of the perverse incentive effects of benefits (not only means-tested ones) have come to be labelled as various 'traps'.

Poverty Trap: This is the best known 'trap' but it is not always properly understood and the term is sometimes used merely as a vague adverse criticism of the benefits system. The poverty trap has a specific meaning and refers to those, mainly families with children, who are working for relatively low wages and are entitled to means-tested benefits (family credit and housing benefit). If they increase their earnings there is little change in net income (unless the pay increase is very substantial). Income tax and national insurance contributions take about one-third of most people's extra income, but those claiming means-tested benefits see these sharply reduced as well. Before 1988 when the Fowler reforms were implemented a family might be worse off after a pay increase though this was unusual; now, with net income means tests for family credit and housing benefit, it is very rare to be worse off though the net gain can be small. The calculation below illustrates a typical example of how the poverty trap can affect a family with children.

Pay increase	£1.00
minus income tax (20%)[1] and NICs[2] (10%)	30p
Residue	70p
minus Family Credit taper[3] (70%)	49p
Residue	21p
minus Housing Benefit[4] and Council Tax tapers (80%)	17p
Net income increase	4p

Notes: 1. Lower rate on incomes up to approximately £7,000.
2. National insurance contributions.
3. Loss of family credit delayed for up to six months until current award ends.
4. Tenant and therefore eligible for housing benefit.

Over a wide range of earnings (up to more than £200 a week but depending on number of children and rent level) the net income of a family increases only very slowly. The DSS has estimated that approximately 100,000 families face marginal withdrawal rates of 90 per cent or more, and over 400,000 of 80 per cent or more (Cm 3213, 1996).

The term is perhaps a slight misnomer in that most families caught in the poverty trap are not 'poor' in the sense of having an income below the income support level. The poverty trap became a problem in the early 1970s owing to a combination of factors: the income tax threshold had fallen so that almost everyone in employment paid tax, national insurance contributions were put on an earnings-related basis, and new means-tested benefits available to those in work were introduced. The poverty trap is the inevitable result of in-work means-tested benefits (especially when combined with low tax thresholds and earnings-related national insurance contributions). It is undesirable because it reduces incentives to undertake training, move to a better paid job or to work longer hours, and therefore tends to damage the economy.

In principle the poverty trap could be alleviated in a variety of ways. First, means-tested benefits for those in work could simply be abandoned; the poverty trap would then be eliminated but low earners would have to manage on possibly very inadequate incomes, the position before the 1970s. Second, an attempt could be made to increase earnings through a minimum wage policy. A minimum wage would benefit some people caught in the poverty trap (provided they did not lose their jobs) but the majority of those affected would be young people and married women who are not in the poverty trap. But a minimum wage, except perhaps at a very low level which would not have much point anyway, would certainly increase unemployment; and no remotely feasible minimum wage could meet the needs of families with a number of children or high rents, so benefits would still be required for some low earners. Third, the burden of income tax and national insurance contributions on the lower paid could be reduced, so leading to higher take-home pay, but this would be expensive as everyone in employment would benefit. Fourth, child benefit could be very substantially increased which would reduce the need for family credit and housing benefit. In essence this was Beveridge's approach in his proposal for family allowances. It is unlikely, however, that increased child benefit will be an acceptable option, particularly when there is recurrent political debate about whether this benefit should even be retained in its present form. In reality, it is difficult to see that much will be done about the poverty trap because of the public expenditure implications of alternatives to means-tested benefits paid to those in work. In fact, their use has been tending to increase. Furthermore, as is explained below, there is a trade off between increasing incentives to take work in the first pace—dealing with the unemployment trap—at an acceptable cost and eliminating the poverty trap. In-work means-tested benefits cause the poverty trap but alleviate the unemployment trap.

Unemployment trap: This problem arises when benefit income during unemployment (and to an extent during sickness in that unfitness for work is often not absolute and there is an element of choice on the part of the claimant) exceeds or is near to in-work income. Whereas the poverty trap is concerned with net income increases for someone already at work who earns more, the unemployment trap is concerned with a comparison of in-work and out of work income (the replacement ratio). The problem tends to be confused with the poverty trap, and the two do have some features in common. Nevertheless, the unemployment trap is a distinct problem and, while some policy measures would alleviate both it and the poverty trap, others would deal with one and make the other worse. This point was made about in-work means-tested benefits at the end of the previous section. It must be emphasised that, unlike the poverty trap, the unemployment trap is *not* caused by means-tested benefit available to those in work; in fact family credit and housing benefit reduce it.

Income when unemployed is normally job seeker's allowance and housing benefit (plus any undeclared informal earnings); in-work income equals gross earnings *minus* income tax and national insurance contributions *plus* benefits (means-tested and non-means-tested) *minus* work expenses. These components of income in and out of work suggest how in principle the replacement ratio, and therefore the unemployment trap, could be reduced. In theory, out-of-work income could be reduced by making the benefits available to the unemployed lower; but, as was suggested above, benefits are scarcely generous and few people would argue that this is an acceptable approach to alleviating the unemployment trap. Consequently attention is focused on the other side of the equation, in-work income, where a number of possibilities exist, some of them essentially the same as solutions to the poverty trap discussed in the previous section. First, a minimum wage would increase earnings and reduce the replacement ratio for some households, but it would have the drawbacks mentioned in the context of the poverty trap. Second, income tax and national insurance contributions paid by low earners could be reduced, so increasing take-home pay, but would be expensive. Third, child benefit could be substantially increased but, again, would be expensive. (Higher child benefit would increase net income in work without increasing out-of-work income because it is offset against child additions in other benefits including job seeker's allowance.) All these measures would simultaneously reduce both the poverty and unemployment traps. But this is not true of in-work means-tested benefits which operate in opposite directions as far as the poverty and unemployment traps are concerned. They alleviate the unemployment trap by increasing in-work income relative to out-of-work income but at the same time worsen the poverty trap; indeed, they are the main cause of that problem. Increasing eligibility for family credit, and housing benefit for those in work, would have these effects.

From the point of view of practical policy, however, this fifth approach to dealing with the unemployment trap is very attractive because it is comparatively cheap. To increase the incomes of low earners with children through higher family credit would involve only a fraction of the cost of making a similar increase through higher child benefit. But the drawback, of course, is that dealing with the unemployment trap will draw more households into the poverty trap. In fact this dilemma is always present in government thinking about social security, for example in the Fowler reviews, and in practice the aim is to achieve a reasonable compromise between the two problems. In-work means-tested benefits are used to improve work incentives—and to provide a reasonable standard of living for low earners—while endeavouring to avoid making the poverty trap too severe (though some families can currently lose over 90 per cent of a pay increase).

Another concern about means-tested in-work benefits, if their use is widespread, is that they are likely to depress wages. This might be called the Speenhamland effect after the pre-1834 system of relief in aid of wages which the Poor Law Amendment Act sought to eradicate. When the bulk of a wage increase is offset by reduced benefits there is obviously an incentive for employers and employees to collude at taxpayers' expense. At present the number of households receiving family credit, though increasing, may be small enough to mean that the effect is slight, but piloting of a new earnings top-up scheme, which extends a family credit type benefit to single people and couples without children, started in eight areas in 1996. If a benefit on these lines were to be made generally available, it is difficult to see that this would not tend to depress the level of lower earnings.

The DSS calculates replacement ratios using data from the family expenditure survey, and it is estimated that in 1995-96 only 15,000 working households faced replacement ratios exceeding 100 per cent, 35,000 exceeding 90 per cent, 165,000 exceeding 80 per cent and 510,000 (or some four per cent of relevant households) exceeding 70 per cent (Cm 3213, 1996). It is unlikely that any particular replacement ratio is crucial but most people would expect to gain a substantial margin of additional income when working, particularly when work expenses and loss of opportunity for informal earnings are taken into account. The DSS estimates do not take account of expenses such as the cost of travelling to work, and these obviously increase replacement ratios. There are, however, two types of households which are liable to be severely affected by the unemployment trap, and where in some cases taking a modestly paid job may not be a realistic financial proposition. First, lone parents often have to incur substantial child care costs if they go out to work; partly as a result of this, dependence on income support is widespread where there are young children. The cost of child care is now met to a limited extent by an additional allowance within family credit though this has by no means solved the problem. Second, owner occupiers who are unemployed (or sick) have their mortgage interest met by job seeker's allowance (or income support) after nine months, but when working for modest wages receive nothing comparable to housing benefit; tenants on the other hand do not have to meet any rent until their in-work income exceeds the income support level.

There is now increasing interest in the DSS in moving beyond the unemployment trap as a solely financial equation, and in attempting to ease the practical problems of transition from benefit to work. Employment (plus in-work benefits) may provide a higher income than job seeker's allowance but this is not the only consideration for the unemployed. There is likely to be a delay before family credit is assessed and paid, and in the meantime income will fall sharply; and while job seeker's allowance provides a predictable and secure (if modest) income, a new job may not turn out to be permanent and an individual then has to reapply for benefit. The DSS has therefore introduced a number of measures to smooth the transition into work. An attempt is being made to ensure that family credit and housing benefit claims are dealt with quickly to avoid a drop in income when moving into work. Furthermore, although entry wages commanded by a formerly unemployed individual are often comparatively modest, if the family income can be made up to a level where he or she is willing to take a job, subsequently increased earnings frequently mean that social security support is then no longer needed.

Savings Trap: A third trap, which potentially mainly affects the elderly, is a disincentive to save (or make higher pension contributions) if the additional income when retired results in reduced means-tested benefits. The savings trap is not a major issue in social security at the moment because only about one in seven pensioners receive income support. But if contributory pensions remain fixed in value, as seems likely, and a future government were to increase income support in real terms, allowing poorer households to share in increasing general prosperity, numbers eligible for assistance would increase and the savings trap might become more significant. In one respect, however, a version of the savings trap is already an issue. Residential and community care is only available free on a means-tested basis, and people have to run down most of their savings and possibly sell owner-occupied houses before they qualify.

Low Take-up of Benefits

The previous discussion has been primarily (though not entirely) concerned with means-tested benefits, and this is an appropriate place to mention another problem with means-testing, though it is not a matter of incentives. Take-up of non-means-tested benefits is generally very high but a significant minority of people who are entitled to means-tested benefits do not claim them. Most income-related benefits have an estimated take-up of around 80 per cent of those eligible though the figure is probably about 70 per cent in the case of family credit where there has always been a particular problem. But take-up is related to eligibility and is highest where the largest amounts are involved and where the benefit may provide someone's only substantial income. This is no doubt a factor in the lower take-up of family credit where, by definition, it is a supplement to employment income. On the basis of the proportion of the possible total expenditure on means-tested benefits, take-up is higher than in terms of the number of eligible individuals.

A degree of low take-up seems to be an inherent problem of means-tested benefits, though perhaps in a slightly different sense than with the poverty trap. That problem is an absolutely unavoidable result of in-work means-tested benefits; it is a matter of arithmetic (though the effects on work effort are the result of behavioural responses). Low take-up, on the other hand, is an essentially behavioural matter. Thus, although in principle take-up could no doubt be increased to some extent, it is difficult to see how the problem could ever be entirely eliminated.

In broad terms, low take-up can be seen as having two causes. First, people may not claim because they do not realise they are eligible for a benefit; in other words, means-tested benefits have an extra layer of complication. Better advertising of benefits might do something to improve knowledge about them. Second, there is what can be called the 'cost' of claiming means-tested benefits; not, for the most part, actual out of pocket expenses, but cost in terms of a distaste for making a claim—sometimes referred to as the 'stigma' of claiming—and the time and effort involved. Many people have more or less negative feelings about applying for these benefits which, though they are a 'right', necessarily involve an investigation of their financial affairs. They may also have to spend time completing lengthy application forms. If they have little other income they are likely to claim anyway; but if they are eligible for only a modest payment on top of wages or a national insurance benefit some may not bother. This reluctance to claim—which in so far as it reflects a determination to be self-reliant is perhaps not altogether undesirable—would be very difficult to overcome.

THE FUTURE OF SOCIAL SECURITY

The main features of social security in Britain have been outlined, and the objectives of policy and the constraints within which it is developed—cost, adequacy of benefits and minimisation of perverse incentives—discussed. The cost of benefits is an unavoidable and ever-present political issue, though some commentators take the view that rapidly increasing expenditure is no longer a major threat. Before 1997 the Conservative government was pursuing incremental change, benefit by benefit, in an attempt to improve targeting and contain the growth of expenditure. Measures included the introduction of incapacity benefit and jobseekers' allowance. And as the economy grows, provided that the real value of benefits is not increased, the social security programme may well fall as a proportion of GDP. The real concern should arguably be that benefits—and therefore the standard of living of recipients without other income— will seem less and less adequate as most employment and *rentier* incomes do continue to increase in real terms. As mentioned above, the Labour government elected in 1997 is reviewing various aspects of social security policy, particularly 'welfare to work' and pensions, and significant proposals for change are likely to emerge.

As far as pensions are concerned, Labour seems finally to have abandoned any attempt to restore the link between the level of the basic state retirement pension and real increases in average earnings. Consequently, its value will slowly fall to a nugatory level relative to earnings, which are likely to rise on average by perhaps two per cent a year. Labour seems to have no policy on the basic pension except to allow it to fade away. The main focus is now on second-tier (earnings-related) pensions—occupational, SERPS or personal—and an attempt to develop a more satisfactory set of arrangements. Following cutbacks in the Fowler reviews and more recently, SERPS is no more than a shadow of the original scheme. Labour's main interest, however, is in reforming personal pensions, which since their introduction in 1988 have been beset by mis-selling (mainly to individuals who would have been better off remaining in occupational schemes) and high charges. 'Stakeholder' pensions—basically a tightly-regulated version of personal pensions with low charges—are promised. The pay-as-you-go principle—that current contributors pay current benefits—on which SERPS and national insurance generally operate has become an unfashionable basis for pensions. The alternative is funding—where contributions are invested to pay the future pensions of today's contributors—but moving to funded provision, already the basis of personal and most occupational schemes, comes up against what might be called the 'pay twice' problem. The current generation of workers would both have to contribute towards their own pensions and finance unfunded pensions currently in payment. But because of the importance of occupational and personal pensions in Britain, the state's unfunded pension liabilities are modest compared with most other European countries. One significant change to the benefits system which has already been brought forward is the replacement of family credit by a working families tax credit which will be paid throught the employer, normally to the man in a couple. The objective seems to be to reduce the stigma of 'welfare' and thus improve take up, and to bring home more directly to men the financial advantages of low-paid work compared to unemployment. Single mothers will not be greatly affected but women in couples will generally lose income, and the proposal is controversial. In a sense this is a return to the original proposal for family credit, which was to have been paid through employers until the government was forced to abandon the idea, because of widespread opposition from women's groups.

The future development of social security policy in Britain is, of course, uncertain but it seems likely that the attempt to target expenditure where 'need' is greatest will be pursued, as will the enhancement of the role of the private sector, particularly in the case of pensions. In the 1960s and 1970s some commentators on social security as it had evolved since 1948 were critical of the growing importance of means-tested benefits and urged a return to the principles of the Beveridge plan—higher contributory benefits and child benefit to diminish the role of means-testing. Perhaps 'back to Beveridge', with its implications for substantially increased public expenditure, was never practical politics, but it is certainly not so today

It is now almost half a century since the Beveridge plan was implemented in 1948; by the 1960s attention was being drawn to shortcomings but the assumption tended to be that only comparatively minor improvements were needed to a basically sound system. But in the last 20 years, and particularly in the last decade, it has become accepted that at least some of Beveridge's ideas are no longer appropriate to a society which has seen major economic and social change: it is certain that social security policy and the benefits system will continue to evolve.

3
HEALTH SERVICES

This chapter is concerned with the provision of health care in Scotland, focusing principally on the organisation and performance of the National Health Service. It examines the creation of the NHS in 1948, its reorganisation in 1974, and the wholesale changes to the service brought about by the white paper, *Working for Patients* (Cm 555, 1989). Finally, a number of issues and problems are examined, including the NHS 'internal market', GP fundholding, the Patient's Charter, and the policies of the new Labour government and its white paper, *Designed to Care* (Cm 3811, 1997). (Other issues of relevance to the NHS, in relation to its interface with community care, are discussed in Chapter 4).

HISTORICAL OVERVIEW

Despite the common assumption that the NHS is national in the sense of covering the whole of the UK on a uniform basis, there is considerable organisational variation in the service as it has operated in England, Scotland, Wales and Northern Ireland. In the case of Scotland, from its inception in 1948 the NHS has operated in the context of distinctively Scottish systems of law, education and local government (see Chapter 1). Thus separate legislation, in the form of the National Health Service (Scotland) Act, 1947, was required to set up the service in Scotland. Moreover, while the Scottish legislation enacted the same principles and basic structures as those established for England and Wales by the National Health Service Act, 1946—comprehensive medical care, available to all free at the point of need and financed essentially out of general taxation—these were introduced within a distinctive health care setting.

Historically, medical education in Scotland (based initially on the universities of Glasgow and Edinburgh) had developed a separate tradition from that in England. From this emerged a Scottish medical establishment based on the Royal College of Physicians (Edinburgh), the Royal College of Surgeons (Edinburgh) and the Royal College of Physicians and Surgeons (Glasgow). With the expansion of medical schools (located in Edinburgh, Glasgow, Dundee and Aberdeen), their associated teaching hospitals and other voluntary hospitals in the cities and larger towns in the eighteenth century, medical provision in Scotland began to grow in size and scope. In consequence, by the end of the nineteenth century, most Scottish towns had their own hospitals, while more doctors were being produced than were required to deal with Scotland's medical needs so that a significant number had to move south of the border and elsewhere (Hamilton, 1981).

Prior to the advent of the NHS in 1948, medical treatment in Scotland for those unable directly to pay for their own care was funded in a variety of ways. As well as voluntary hospitals, financed by charitable donations, rudimentary provision under the poor law was extended by the early twentieth century in a few areas (including Edinburgh and Glasgow) to include separate hospitals which provided care of a reasonable standard. Care was also available for working people through friendly societies and trade unions, which engaged doctors on a contract basis to treat their members. Then in 1911 Lloyd George's National Insurance Act provided free GP care for manual workers (but not their families), financed by employers, employees and the state.

As well as poor law and voluntary hospitals, Scotland also had an exchequer-funded forerunner of the NHS in the Highlands and Islands Medical Service set up in 1919. The service provided salaried nursing staff to deal with the special medical needs of remote and sparsely populated areas. Nonetheless, health care in Scotland before 1948, though extensive, was not comprehensive in scope nor freely available to the whole population.

Structurally, the NHS in Scotland was founded on the same tripartite principle as in England and Wales, covering (1) hospital and specialist services; (2) family practitioner services; and (3) community and auxiliary health services. Hospital services were placed under the control of five regional hospital boards: Northern (Inverness); North-Eastern (Aberdeen); Eastern (Dundee); South-Eastern (Edinburgh); and Western (Glasgow). These boards were responsible for 65 boards of management which directly operated the hospital service. Family practitioner services, including GPs as well as dental, ophthalmic and pharmaceutical services, were regulated by 25 executive councils. Finally, 55 local health authorities (departments of city or large burgh councils or, in landward areas, county councils) were charged with the provision of community services, including health visitors, district nurses, and maternity and child welfare services. The Scottish Secretary and the Scottish Office in Edinburgh—rather than the Ministry of Health in London—were responsible for the operation of the service in Scotland.

The medical profession in Scotland accepted the state's assumption of increased responsibilities for health care in 1948 more readily than some of their colleagues south of the border. For patients, the health service represented an assurance of treatment which was not based on contributions or eligibility tests. For both doctors and patients, the new system still permitted private medical practice: those with the means to do so could continue to purchase private treatment; equally, doctors could continue to engage in private practice alongside their NHS responsibilities.

It became apparent by the 1960s, however, that there were problems with the tripartite structure of the service—in particular, there was insufficient linkage in terms of planning and communication between hospitals, GPs and local authority services. In consequence, as part of a consultative process with a broad range of interested parties, the Scottish Secretary published a green paper in 1968, *Administrative Reorganisation of the Scottish Health Services* (Scottish Home and Health Department, 1968). This led to a white paper in 1971, *Reorganisation of the Scottish Health Services* (Cmnd 4734), which set out firm proposals for the service. The National Health Service (Scotland) Act, 1972 which implemented the proposals came into force in 1974.

THE REORGANISED NHS: 1974-89

The 1974 reorganisation of the NHS in Scotland established five new types of administrative structure. First, and most important, the regional hospital boards and hospital boards of management, local health authorities and executive councils were replaced by 15 health boards which were given responsibility for all aspects of the service. Second, a Scottish Health Services Planning Council was established to identify health care needs and to develop plans to meet these. Third, the Common Services Agency was created with responsibility for a variety of services which required provision on a Scotland-wide basis. Fourth, mechanisms were established to represent the views of producers and consumers of health care with the creation of a system of professional advisory committees and local health councils. Finally, the new post of Health Service Commissioner was introduced to deal with patient complaints involving non-clinical matters.

Health Boards

The arrangements adopted for Scotland in 1974 were different from those south of the border: England and Wales retained a regional tier of administration whereas Scotland was organised as, in effect, a single region. But on both sides of the border an attempt was made to align health service and local authority boundaries. Thus the boundaries of the 15 Scottish health boards (Figure 1) were broadly in line with those of the nine regional and three islands councils also established in 1974 (see Chapter 1). The main exception was Strathclyde Region, which included four health boards (Argyll and Clyde, Ayrshire and Arran, Greater Glasgow, and Lanarkshire).

The 15 health boards were given resources which varied extremely widely, reflecting considerable differences in the size and health needs of the populations served. Thus, within three years of the reorganisation, the Greater Glasgow Health Board was operating with a current expenditure total of nearly £17m, 46 hospitals (containing over 14,000 beds), and over 550 consultants to deal with a population of over one million. At the other end of the scale, Orkney Health Board had a current expenditure less than £2m, two hospitals (with 124 beds), and one and a half consultants to meet the needs of its 18,000 population. The variation in resources between boards led, however, to considerable interdependence, with smaller boards looking to larger ones (for example, Greater Glasgow) for the provision of specialist services. Accordingly, allowance had to be made in the allocation of resources to each board for cross-boundary flows of patients as well as the composition of its resident population.

The health boards were responsible for the planning and provision of health services within their areas, with a broad measure of autonomy over the use of resources.

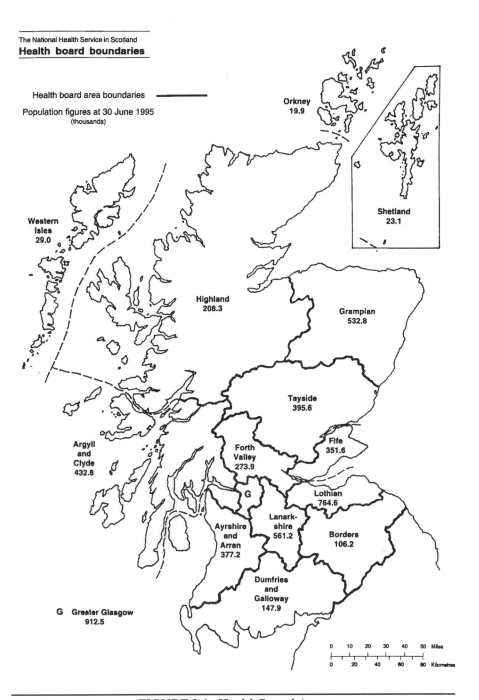

The National Health Service in Scotland
Health board boundaries

Health board area boundaries ━━━━━━

Population figures at 30 June 1995
(thousands)

Orkney
19.9

Shetland
23.1

Western
Isles
29.0

Highland
208.3

Grampian
532.8

Tayside
395.6

Argyll
and
Clyde
432.8

Forth
Valley
273.9

Fife
351.6

G

Lothian
764.6

Lanark-
shire
561.2

Ayrshire
and
Arran
377.2

Borders
106.2

Dumfries
and
Galloway
147.9

G   Greater Glasgow
912.5

| 0 | 10 | 20 | 30 | 40 | 50 Miles |

| 0 | 20 | 40 | 60 | 80 Kilometres |

FIGURE 3.1: *Health Board Areas*

But, to ensure a unified system of care throughout Scotland, the boards were made directly responsible to the Secretary of State who appointed their members. Day-to-day management of the boards was delegated to a team of chief officers (the Chief Administrative Medical Officer, Chief Area Nursing Officer, Board Treasurer and Board Secretary). Initially, most of the 15 boards were subdivided for administrative purposes into districts; but, following a consultative document (Scottish Home and Health Department, 1979), the district structure was progressively abolished.

Under the new policy of 'localism', health boards devolved management to the unit level, with each unit being based on one or more hospitals and made responsible for its own administration and finance, nursing, ancillary services and community medicine. In part, this move was related to the Griffiths Report on NHS management which recommended the appointment of general managers who would be responsible for organisational efficiency (Griffiths, 1983). The new focus on the unit level greatly facilitated the introduction of general management into the service. A variety of problems, including poor industrial relations, planning and management difficulties stemming from conflicting area and district administrative tiers, and the constantly rising cost of health care provision, had already been identified in the *Report of the Royal Commission on the National Health Service* (Cmnd 7615, 1979). The royal commission had been set up by the Labour government in 1976 to consider 'the best use and management of financial and manpower resources of the NHS'. Amongst the report's 117 recommendations were administrative simplification, better use of resources, improvements in medical procedures (by establishing a system of medical audit, and improved preventative care by extending screening programmes).

The Scottish Health Services Planning Council

The Planning Council was set up in 1974 to co-ordinate the views of the major participants in decisions on planning and resource allocation matters. Its remit was expanded in 1978 to include advising the Scottish Secretary on health service matters and reviewing development of the NHS in Scotland. It comprised a member (normally the board chairman) from all 15 health boards, six representatives of the Scottish Home and Health Department and a representative from each Scottish university with a medical school. The council's chairman was appointed by the Secretary of State.

The council's most distinctive contribution came in 1977 when its working group on health resources developed a new mechanism for equalising the allocation of resources between health boards: *Scottish Health Authorities Revenue Equalisation* (Scottish Home and Health Department, 1977). In essence, SHARE is the Scottish counterpart of the better-known Resource Allocation Working Party (RAWP) of 1975 in England. The Planning Council was abolished in 1991 following the introduction of the NHS 'internal market' (see below).

The Common Services Agency

The Common Services Agency was set up in 1974 to meet health service needs that required to be handled on a Scotland-wide basis. Its functions therefore included responsibility for the provision of ambulance and blood transfusion services, legal advice, planning and implementation of major capital projects, health education, and training services. Like the Planning Council, the CSA was operated under a management board comprising representatives from all 15 health boards as well as the Scottish Home and Health Department.

Professional Advisory Committees

In the 1974 reorganisation provision was made for advice on the planning and implementation of health services from the various professions working in the NHS. Thus professional advisory committees were established to advise on the provision of the particular professional service with which they were involved: medical, dental, nursing and midwifery, pharmacy, scientific, and professions allied to medicine.The Planning Council was required to consult with the advisory committees while, in addition, these were linked to the Scottish Health Service Advisory Council which advised the Scottish Secretary. Advisory committees were also established at health board level. However, the abolition of both the Planning Council in 1991 and the Advisory Council in 1993 resulted in some diminution of the influence of the national professional committees.

Local Health Councils

The 1974 reorganisation also created local health councils (LHCs)—similar to community health councils in England and Wales—to represent the interests of the public in local health services. LHC membership (varying from 15 to 20) is drawn from a variety of interested bodies including local authorities, trade unions and voluntary bodies. The number of LHCs has varied considerably, from 48 (some health boards having several) to the current total of 18 (most boards now having only one).

On the face of it the LHCs appeared to offer NHS consumers a useful mechanism for reviewing the performance of the service and making recommendations for improvements to the health boards. The boards were required to consult LHCs on major changes in local services (for example, hospital closures and major redeployments of resources). However, in practice they have proved to be less than wholly successful. Not only did they fail to develop any meaningful community identity, but they have also had a low profile from the standpoint of the patients. Moreover, they have lacked the expertise and grasp of health service issues possessed by the professional advisory committees. In consequence they have not made much impression on either health boards or the public whose interests they were set up to represent (Bochel and McLaren, 1979).

The Health Service Commissioner

Established in 1974, the office of Health Service Commissioner (the health 'ombudsman') investigates complaints from patients or their representatives about maladministration or failure to provide appropriate services. Crucially, to protect the medical profession's jealously guarded clinical autonomy, the commissioner was specifically prohibited from dealing with complaints stemming directly from questions of clinical judgement.

The commissioner has not been entirely successful as a vehicle for complaints. In part this relates to the fact that complaints must be made in written form within 12 months of the grievance coming to the patient's attention, and then only after the relevant authority—usually a health board—has failed to resolve matters. Furthermore, with no separate Scottish commissioner, few patients in Scotland have been aware of the service available to them. Matters were not helped by the unwillingness of a number of health boards to publish their own complaints ratings.

THE REFORMED NHS AND THE 'INTERNAL MARKET'

Reform as a Response to Crisis

The most radical reorganisation in the history of the NHS since 1948 followed the publication in 1989 of a white paper, *Working for Patients* (Cm 555). From their election in 1979, the Conservatives under Margaret Thatcher's leadership pursued a 'New Right' agenda of promoting free market economics, and rolling back the scope of the state's activities. Within the NHS, their general policy of attacking bureaucracy and inefficiency in the public sector focused particularly on 'excessive' layers of administration. Accordingly, health board districts (and a tier of administration in England) had been abolished. In 1989, however, the spur for wholesale reform of the NHS came from more than ideological imperatives. It was also prompted by a sense of growing crisis from the mid-1980s, as various factors combined to highlight a service facing growing demands for treatment which were increasingly outstripping its ability to deal with them.

On the demand side, the NHS faced—as it has continued to face—major expenditure implications stemming from advances in medical technology. It is not that such advances increase the cost of what health care can already achieve—on the whole they tend to decrease it—but they result in new and more effective treatments. Conditions can be better treated or treated for the first time, and there is naturally a demand that the new procedures should be available from the NHS. The Department of Health estimated in the early 1980s that the hospital and community health service budget in England would require an annual real increase of 0.5 per cent simply to ensure adequate provision for new technology (Ham, Costain and Benzeval, 1988).

A second major demand on NHS services was—and continues to be—the steady rise in the population aged over 65, which constitutes the largest single category of NHS patients. Thus, in Scotland, while the population as a whole fell by 81,000 between 1970 and 1994, the numbers of those aged 65-74 rose by 36,000, those aged 75-84 by 63,000, and those aged 85 and over by 39,000. This trend has created considerable cost burdens for the NHS owing to the much higher health expenditures *per capita* required by the elderly. Indeed, calculations by the Scottish Home and Health Department indicate that while NHS expenditure on those aged over 65 accounted for 30 per cent of NHS expenditure in 1979, it rose to 39 per cent by 1992, and was

Table 3.1: *NHS Expenditure in Scotland by Age Group, 1995-96*

	Expenditure Per Head £
Births	3,603
0-4	595
5-14	400
15-44	483
45-64	751
65-74	1,468
75-84	2,920
85 and above	4,954

Source: Scottish Office, *Serving Scotland's Needs: The Government's Expenditure Plans 1997-98 to 1999-2000,* Cm 3614, 1997.

projected to rise even further to 46 per cent by 2018 and to almost 60 per cent by 2040 (Scottish Office, 1994). Some measure of the contrasting expenditure levels incurred by different age groups is indicated in Table 3.1.

On the supply side, constraints on available resources limited the capacity of the NHS to meet the increasing demands imposed upon it. The Conservative government required public expenditure restraint (as well as greater efficiency) throughout the public sector, and this clearly included the NHS. While health spending never fell in real terms during the 1980s, a tighter regime was imposed, resulting in the average annual real increase in expenditure on hospital and community health services in England dropping to 1.6 per cent. Given the widely used estimate that NHS spending required an annual increase of at least two per cent in real terms to meet rising demands—in addition to the effects of rising costs—an expenditure shortfall was clearly indicated. But the government contended that any spending shortfall could be bridged by 'cost improvement programmes' producing annual efficiency savings amounting to 0.5 per cent of the budget. Nevertheless, the Social Services Select Committee estimated the cumulative spending shortfall on hospital and community health services between 1981-82 and 1987-88 as £1.9 bn (Timmins, 1988; Harrison, 1989).

In addition to the debate about a shortfall in NHS funding, the sense of crisis in 1987 was sharpened by the increasing number of cancelled operations and bed closures. But this problem seems to have been less serious in Scotland than south of the border, which is perhaps not surprising given the substantially higher level of funding (see below). There was the thorny problem of pay within the NHS which had become a major issue for virtually all levels of staff: the government endeavoured throughout the 1980s to restrain the pay recommendations from the independent pay review bodies for the clinical and nursing professions.

A further, and perhaps deeper seated, supply side problem concerned the use to which available resources were put in the NHS. In 1985 the American economist Alain

Enthoven produced a highly critical study of weaknesses in the service, which focused particularly on the perverse incentives operating on cash-limited health authorities, clinicians and managers which militated against efficiency (Enthoven, 1985). He found that hospitals which treated more patients simply used up their funding more rapidly, leading to unused capacity (in the form of bed closures and idle staff) towards the end of the financial year since additional patients attracted no extra funds. Equally perverse was the reverse situation where poor service resulted in a reduced demand for treatment but carried no automatic decrease in budgets. Enthoven also highlighted problems and perverse incentives stemming from the compensation arrangements for cross-boundary flows (where patients from one health authority were treated by another).

In December 1987, the government sought to pacify its critics with the announcement of additional funding of some £100m to deal with bed and ward closures; Scottish health boards received £7.6m. However, it remained clear that the difficulties in the service were not simply concerned with funding issues; remedial action was required to deal with very real problems of how funding was to be better employed in the delivery of health care. In an effort to be seen to be doing something about the NHS 'crisis', Mrs Thatcher, during a live BBC *Panorama* interview in January 1988, announced that she was setting up a ministerial review—chaired by herself—to examine the future of the NHS, covering all aspects of the service. However, while the review's small group of senior ministers subsequently considered alternative methods of funding the NHS (including the introduction of compulsory health insurance), these were discarded in favour of maintaining the *status quo* of financing the service out of general taxation.

In its deliberations over alternatives for reshaping service delivery to make it more cost effective, the review group considered and discarded the American system of health maintenance organisations on the grounds that they could not be successfully adapted for British needs in large working class areas. What emerged were proposals based on Enthoven's ideas of an 'internal market' within the NHS which separated the purchasers of health care from those who provided it. This would bring into play market dynamics, with purchasers of care able to shop around for the 'best buys', while providers would be forced by competition into offering care at the lowest possible price. An aspect of this internal market was that money would follow the patient— hospitals would be paid for actual work done—so that hospitals which provided treatment more efficiently and competitively would attract more patients and thereby gain additional funding, thus reversing perverse incentives highlighted by Enthoven.

The results of the ministerial review exercise and its reform package were published in the white paper, *Working for Patients*, and fuller details of the proposals were subsequently set out in a series of working papers. Stressing that it sought to build on the foundations of the existing NHS, the white paper indicated that the service would continue to be funded mainly from general taxation and reaffirmed the principles of free universal health care available on the basis of medical need and not on the ability to pay. However, its reform proposals set out a transformation of the organisation and delivery of treatment. Although it included some dozen proposals, the key aspect of the white paper was the creation of a purchaser/provider division to separate the purchasing of medical services from their provision and management. Thus two types of purchasers were established: health boards (district health authorities in England), and general practices which qualified for, and wished to have, their own budgets as GP fundholders. Services would be provided on the basis of purchasing contracts made with hospitals and other provider units (such as community and ambulance services), including NHS trusts, hospitals and units initially managed directly by health boards, and hospitals in the private sector.

The Reformed Purchasing Arrangements

The proposals in *Working for Patients* were enacted in the National Health Service and Community Care Act, 1990 (unusually there was no separate Scottish legislation); its provisions relating to the NHS came into force in April 1991, although those affecting community care did not do so until 1993 (see Chapter 4).

Under the 1990 act, health boards continued to be charged with assessing the health needs of their local populations, but their major activity was now to be the purchasing of care—provided by others—to deal with these needs. While the boards retained responsibility for the management, and provision of treatment within, hospitals and units that remained under their control as directly managed units (DMUs), it was clearly intended that their role as providers of services would disappear as more and more hospitals and other units became self-governing trusts. The transition to NHS trusts was relatively rapid: by April 1995 all units on the mainland of Scotland were operating under trust status.

Changes were also made to the method of allocating resources to enable health boards to meet their populations' health care needs. Provision for cross-boundary patient flows under SHARE became unnecessary after 1991 (though this feature is to be re-introduced as part of the Labour government's proposed abolition of the internal market). The revised system employed a formula based on a board's resident population, weighted to reflect the health and age distribution of that population (including the number of elderly people) and the relative costs of providing services. A short transition period for adjustment was necessary for 'over-financed' boards which had been financed to provide services for patients from outwith their areas.

As indicated above, health boards remained responsible for ensuring that their resident populations could obtain access to a comprehensive range of services; they also retained their strategic planning role. To ensure adequate health care provision, the 1989 white paper identified two broad categories of services: 'core' services and 'other' services.

Core services: These were defined as those to which patients required guaranteed local access. It was left to each board to consider in the light of its own circumstances which core services should be provided in its area: thus 'locally' for some people would continue to mean provision at a hospital in a neighbouring board area. In broad terms, the white paper set out five broad categories of services that were considered to be 'core':

- Accident and emergency (A and E) departments.
- Immediate admissions to hospital from an A and E department, including a significant proportion of general surgery.
- Other immediate admissions, such as most general medicine and many hospital geriatric and psychiatric services.
- Out-patient and other support services needed in support of the categories above.
- Public health, community-based services and other hospital services requiring provision on a local basis.

Other Services: These were identified as services where there would be a greater element of choice about where a patient could be treated and where there would be an element of competition in supply. Services to be regarded as 'other' comprised the following:

- Elective acute care surgical treatments for which there are long waiting lists (for example, hip replacements, cataract removals and hernia repairs) and for which it could advantage patients to have them provided at a hospital other than their local one.
- Services not provided within every health board area, such as ear, nose and throat (ENT), ophthalmology and oral surgery.
- Other services for which patients may wish to choose the location (for example, some long-stay care for elderly people).

GP Fundholding: In line with the Thatcher government's policy of devolving decision-taking as closely as possible to the level of the patient, the role of purchasing agent was extended to the new category of GP fundholders. As outlined by *Working for Patients*, the eligibility criteria for fundholding status were threefold:

- The registered list of the practice should exceed 11,000 patients. Smaller practices could group together for the purpose of meeting this criterion.
- The practice should be able to demonstrate its ability to manage budgets, as evidenced by adequate administrative support, and information technology and information systems.
- All members of the practice should agree to the fundholding application.

The original list size of 11,000 patients for fundholding practices was quickly cut to 9,000; subsequent reductions brought this down to 3,000 by 1996. This gradual introduction of fundholding reflected the need to proceed with caution at the outset, since there were no pilot studies to help shape the process.

Fundholding practices would operate with budgets allocated by their health board on the basis of their number of patients, weighted for age and other factors. Practice budgets enabled GP fundholders to purchase a range of hospital services directly for their patients:

- A defined group of surgical, in-patient and day case treatments covering most elective procedures (for example, hip replacements and cataract removals). Emergency admissions and medical admissions were excluded.
- Out-patient services.
- Diagnostic investigation services.

Besides the purchase of hospital services, practice budgets also covered approved costs of practice staff and accommodation, as well as the costs of prescribed drugs and appliances. Fundholding practices could overspend by a maximum of five per cent of their budget in any one year, but had to make a corresponding reduction the following year. Any practice overspending in excess of this limit, or persistently underspending, would trigger a health board audit of practice procedures. In addition, any overspending in excess of five per cent for two successive years could lead to the loss of fundholding status (subject to appeal to the Secretary of State). However, the fundholding system did permit practices to employ small budget surpluses for improvement of their premises.

Purchasing Contracts

The purchasing of patient services by health boards and GP fundholders was to be effected by three kinds of contracts with providers.

- *Block Contracts:* Health boards or GP fundholders would pay the hospital or service unit a fixed annual fee for patient access to a defined range of services, with the individual contracts setting out the broad volume and the standards of treatment to be provided. Block contracts were viewed at the outset as particularly suitable for provision of core services.
- *Cost and Volume Contracts:* These were designed for the provision of elective treatments for which there is choice about where and when these should take place. Essentially, the provider would be paid a fixed sum for a baseline level of treatments, with additional sums for cases treated above that level, at a price for each additional case established in advance.
- *Cost Per Case Contracts:* These were set up for additional referrals not covered by the previous two types of contract. The provider would be paid on a case-by-case basis, either where a health board or GP fundholder had no regular contract with the provider, or where additional treatments were being purchased over and above the terms of the contract. (In the absence of a regular contract with a provider non-fundholders have to obtain health board

approval for an Extra Contractual Referral.)

The object of the purchaser/provider split was to introduce an 'internal market' within which the dynamics of competition would work to develop a more efficient and cost-effective health service. However, at the outset, health boards were directed to establish contracts with providers which reflected their current patterns of service, rather than moving to alternatives to get the 'best buy'. Thus, under this 'steady state' approach, the internal market was developed on the basis of managed rather than open competition (Ham, 1991; Klein, 1995).

A further problem for development of the internal market was the relatively slow growth in the number of GP fundholding practices. This was particularly the case in Scotland where only 11 per cent of practices (21 per cent of individual GPs) had gained fundholding status by October 1995. However, by April 1996 this had risen considerably, with 34 per cent of practices operating as fundholders, covering 42 per cent of patients. In England and Wales, the growth of fundholding proceeded much faster, with fundholding practices covering 40 per cent of patients by April 1995, rising to 52 per cent of patients by April 1996. In consequence, the NHS found itself dealing with two sets of patients: those whose fundholding GPs could purchase elective treatment for them directly from health care providers, and those in non-fundholding practices whose GPs had to commission their treatment indirectly through the health board as the purchaser of care. This situation produced allegations of a 'two-tier' system of treatment which will be discussed later.

The New 'Providers': NHS Trusts

The policy of enabling NHS hospitals and other provider units to become self-governing NHS trusts was part of the Conservative government's approach of devolving decision-taking power to local operational level. Thus self-governing trust status would 'make hospitals more responsive to the needs of their patients, to secure local commitment and to achieve greater value for money' (Scottish Home and Health Department, 1989a). However, the introduction of NHS trusts was also part of a wider strategy to make clinicians and other medical professionals less powerful and more accountable to management, particularly in the use of hospital resources. Closely linked to this was the desire to curtail further the power of national trade unions by granting to trusts responsibility for setting pay and conditions of service for all levels of staff locally.

Each NHS trust was to be run by a board of directors, with a non-executive chairman appointed by the Scottish Secretary (in England by the Secretary of State for Health), and an equal numbers of executive and non-executive directors. The non-executive directors were to be appointed by the Secretary of State in consultation with the trust chairman (in the case of teaching hospitals one of these members being drawn from the relevant medical school). Non-executive directors were to be appointed for their personal contributions to trust management affairs and not as interest group representatives. The executive directors were to comprise the general manager of the hospital or other unit, the medical director (who may have clinical responsibilities), the senior nurse manager, and the finance director.

To operate as self-governing providers of health services within the NHS, the hospital trusts were provided with an extensive range of powers and freedoms under the 1990 legislation:

- To acquire, own and dispose of assets to ensure the most effective use of them.

- To borrow, subject to an annual financial limit.

- To retain operating surpluses and build up reserves.

- To set management structures without direction from health boards or the Scottish Home and Health Department.

- Freedom to employ the staff considered necessary, to determine their pay and conditions of service, and to conduct industrial relations.

Hospital trusts were to be funded predominantly by revenues from the sale of their services to health boards and GP fundholders, but income could also be derived from private patients. Besides meeting their normal operating costs (including staff salaries, medical equipment and capital spending), trusts had three basic financial requirements imposed on them: first, to earn at least six per cent return on their assets; second, to maintain a break-even performance year upon year; and, finally, to stay within their annual external financing limits (imposed by the Treasury to curb trust borrowing which counts as public expenditure) . The need to price contracts with purchasers required NHS trusts to invest substantially in the provision of financial and management information systems.

One of the main objectives of creating self-governing trust hospitals was to end the disincentives to efficiency identified by Enthoven. Thus trust hospitals, as masters of their own affairs, could be rewarded by increased revenues stemming from improved efficiency and greater cost effectiveness. However, this thinking was premised on the running of a genuinely competitive internal market. Instead, from the outset a managed 'steady state' system was operated under which health authorities had to retain their historical providers in making contracts for core services, rather than switching to competitors. Nonetheless, some element of competition did exist in contracts for elective treatment. Thus, Bartlett and Le Grand (1994) were able to conclude in their early study of trust performance that 'at least as far as trusts are concerned, the conditions for the quasi-market to promote greater efficiency, choice and responsiveness do appear to be broadly in place, or, at least, moving in the right direction.'

A further objective of the reformed system was to bring about greater clinician accountability for the use of resources. As one of the working papers accompanying *Working for Patients* emphasised: 'Consultants are increasingly responsible for the direct or indirect commitment of substantial levels of resource' (Scottish Home and

Health Department, 1989b). The government had previously tried to address this with the appointment of the more 'business focused' general managers in the wake of the Griffiths Report in 1983. However, the new managers had been unable to make much of an impact in hospitals and units where powerful clinician interests prevailed in decisions about the use of resources (Strong and Robinson, 1990; Harrison, Hunter, Marnoch and Pollitt, 1992). Accordingly, the 1989 reforms sought to create an environment within which management could establish clinician responsibility and accountability for use of resources.

Within trusts, the general manager was given responsibility for ensuring that a detailed job description was agreed with every consultant, subject to annual review. Besides dealing with the main duties of the post, each job description was to set out details of budgetary and other management responsibilities as well as arrangements for participation in medical audit. Changes were also made in the appointment of consultants, with selection criteria altered to take into account a candidate's willingness and ability to meet requirements for the management of resources, and the inclusion in the selection process of a senior manager to assist in making this assessment.

Beyond the more formal and explicit mechanisms outlined above, the dynamics involved in operating self-governing trusts provided further possibilities for developing clinician accountability. The success of each trust was dependent on its ability to generate revenues and contain costs, and this clearly required all participants to stay within budgetary parameters set by the trust business plan. Accordingly, the new working environment of trust hospitals became one in which both clinicians and managers had a vested interest in working more collaboratively. Indeed, Bartlett and Le Grand (1994) discussed hospital trusts in terms of 'labour-managed co-operatives'.

HEALTH CARE NEEDS AND RESOURCES IN SCOTLAND

Historically, Scotland has received a substantially higher NHS budget on a *per capita* basis than England and Wales. At the same time, however, it can be shown that Scottish health needs—as measured by the mortality data—are also greater. This section considers these related phenomena.

Scotland's Health Needs

When comparisons are made on an inter-generational basis, it is clear that the health of people in Scotland has improved considerably since the beginning of the present century, as underscored by the fact that life expectancy for both Scottish men and women has risen by approximately 25 years. However, a much darker picture is presented when the comparisons are made with other western industrialised countries, with the mortality and morbidity data showing Scotland's health record to be a relatively bad one. Scottish males born in 1990 could expect to live on average to 71 years of age, a lower level of expectation than males in 14 other industrialised countries, including England and Wales. The Chief Medical Officer for Scotland noted that

> Scotland's health [is] conspicuously worse than that of most other industrial

Table 3.2: *Hospital Patient Data and Standardised Mortality Ratios by Health Board, 1994-95*

	Population	Hospital Inpatient Discharges	New Outpatients Attending Consultant Clinics	Day Cases	Standardised Mortality Ratios
Scotland	5,132,400	824,346	2,576,573	326,765	100
Argyll & Clyde	433,000	57,401	211,522	23,546	104
Ayrshire & Arran	377,000	53,853	172,929	22,042	100
Borders	105,700	14,203	37,530	3,876	90
Dumfries & Galloway	147,000	23,423	63,099	11,566	87
Fife	352,100	37,362	139,970	23,670	94
Forth Valley	273,400	34,068	122,934	18,182	96
Grampian	532,500	81,838	242,134	18,969	92
Greater Glasgow	916,600	201,066	634,844	79,780	113
Highland	207,500	32,248	89,992	9,366	97
Lanarkshire	561,961	70,035	240,100	27,568	108
Lothian	758,600	138,444	356,825	60,740	96
Orkney	19,810	1,691	4,916	518	94
Shetland	22,880	2,192	9,837	1,067	92
Tayside	395,000	70,581	239,497	25,212	95
Western Isles	29,310	3,938	10,444	663	100

Sources: Information and Statistics Division, NHS in Scotland, *Scottish Health Statistics 1995*; and *Annual Report of the Registrar General for Scotland 1995.*

countries [in] mortality from coronary heart disease and from cancer, dental health, and the smoking and drinking habits which contribute to a wide spectrum of disorders, including coronary heart disease and cancers of several kinds (Scottish Office, 1994a).

However, as Table 3.2 indicates, within Scotland itself there is a wide variation in mortality rates between the populations of the 15 health board areas. Thus three boards stand out as having standardised mortality ratios (SMRs) above an index level of 100—Argyll and Clyde, Greater Glasgow, and Lanarkshire—all of which contain communities with even higher SMRs (for example, Inverclyde 116, Glasgow City 121 and Monklands 121). As the table also indicates, these three boards have much higher numbers of both in-patient and out-patient cases (though the numbers in Greater Glasgow also reflect cases from elsewhere). Finally, all three boards have populations with a high incidence of social deprivation, which has been shown to be closely linked to significantly higher levels of morbidity and premature death (Carstairs and Morris, 1991).

Table 3.3: *Excess Mortality Under 65 in Scotland Compared with England*[1]

	Males %	Females %	Both %
1984	+25	+28	+26
1989	+28	+29	+28
1994	+34	+31	+32

Note: 1. Based on standardised mortality ratios.
Source: Scottish Office, *Health in Scotland 1995.*

Besides social deprivation, a further major causal factor in Scotland's bad health record is poor lifestyle. Thus the incidence of cigarette smoking in Scotland (both male and female) is much higher than most other industrialised nations including England and Wales, while the Scottish diet (extremely high in saturated or animal fats and low in dietary fibre) is widely acknowledged as one of the most unhealthy in the western world.

Recognising that action was needed to deal with this depressingly bad health record, a set of priorities and related targets was set out by the government in a 1991 policy statement on health education in Scotland (which paralleled a similar exercise in England). However, the Scottish targets were tightly focused on areas in which the Scottish health record was conspicuously bad, including premature death from coronary heart disease (CHD) and cancer, as well as ill health stemming from smoking and high alcohol consumption.

In his report, *Health in Scotland 1995* (Scottish Office, 1996), the Chief Medical Officer for Scotland confirmed that Scotland was likely to meet or even exceed the targets for reduction in mortality before the age of 65 in cancer (a 15 per cent reduction over the period 1986-2000) and CHD (a 40 per cent reduction). In other areas, there was less good news to report. On the smoking reduction targets, whilst that for the over 25s remained achievable, surveys had shown no reduction in the smoking rates of secondary schoolchildren since 1986. Equally depressing were survey results showing no change in the numbers of men drinking excessively and a probable increase in the proportion of women doing so. Finally, whilst there had been gains in reducing Scottish mortality rates under the age of 65, the Chief Medical Officer indicated that there was a growing 'health gap' between Scotland and England. As Table 3.3 indicates, this health gap (measured in terms of the percentage of excess mortality under age 65 in Scotland compared with England) has widened over the period 1984-94. While unclear about the reason for the increasing gap, the report commented that 'the explanation is more likely to be found in the social and economic differences between the two countries than in the efficacy of medical treatment or of health promotion campaigns'.

Scottish Health Expenditure and Resources

Scotland has enjoyed a consistently higher level of spending on health services than England and Wales. In 1994-95, spending on health and personal social services (HPSS) accounted for 35 per cent of the block grant from the Treasury and for 22 per cent of all identifiable public expenditure in Scotland (see Chapter 1).

Comparing Scottish average *per capita* HPSS spending levels over the five years ending in 1994-95 with that in with other parts of the UK (with the UK indexed at 100), Scotland's spending stood at 122, with England at 97, Wales at 108 and Northern Ireland at 112. Owing to the inadequacy of historical statistics it is unclear when the much higher Scottish *per capita* HPSS expenditure arose but it was identified by the *Needs Assessment Study* (Treasury, 1979). Given Scotland's bad health record, it can reasonably be contended that the advantageous spending relativities should be preserved at least to some extent: the actual ones are, however, substantially greater than those suggested by the *Needs Assessment Study*. But the much higher *per capita* level of HPSS expenditure has not been reflected in any significant health gains in Scotland relative to the health record of England.

As can be seen from Table 3.4, within Scotland there is a wide variation in the health care resources allocated to each of the 15 health boards. Essentially, these reflect the relative needs of the various boards' populations indicated by SMR levels. However, in some cases the hospital and staffing resources deployed by the larger boards (notably Greater Glasgow) also reflect arrangements made for the specialised care needs of other areas.

Finally, the level of NHS resources is augmented slightly by expenditure generated from private purchasing of health care, either by health insurance companies or directly by private individuals. In the UK as a whole there has been a substantial growth in private health insurance: the number of people with health insurance cover rose from 2.3 million (4.1 per cent of the population) in 1975 to an estimated eight million (13.6 per cent of the population) in 1996. However, in Scotland there is a much lower coverage, a level of only four per cent of the population in 1993 compared with 12 per cent in England (Orton and Fry, 1995).

Similarly, the number of private sector acute hospitals has increased appreciably; the UK total rose from 150 hospitals with 6,671 beds in 1979, to 224 hospitals with 11,391 beds in 1993. However, here again Scotland presented a different picture, reflecting the low coverage of private health insurance: Scotland had only 11 acute private hospitals with 680 beds, four of which with 459 beds were in the Greater Glasgow area. Furthermore, the latter included 260 beds at the controversial Health Care International (HCI) Medical Centre in Clydebank which was established to cater for patients drawn exclusively from overseas. (HCI received some £28m in development assistance and an additional £10m for site preparation from the Scottish Office.) However, after its opening in 1994, it became clear that the hospital was unable to attract more than token numbers of overseas patients, and it went bankrupt after five months. Then, under new ownership, the hospital began admitting British patients, including NHS patients treated under purchasing contracts from a number of Scottish health boards and health authorities in England.

Table 3.4: *Health Care Resources by Health Board, 1994-95*

	Population	Total Revenue Expenditure £	Expenditure per Head £	Staff[1]	Available Staffed Beds
Scotland	5,132,400	4,070,367	762	137,714	42,351
Argyll & Clyde	433,000	329,977	762	10,625	3,592
Ayrshire & Arran	377,000	267,618	710	8,360	2,575
Borders	105,700	85,388	811	2,632	812
Dumfries & Galloway	147,000	118,454	801	4,244	1,226
Fife	352,100	243,223	693	7,036	2,455
Forth Valley	273,400	195,689	717	7,191	2,504
Grampian	532,500	372,259	705	12,893	4,414
Greater Glasgow	916,600	772,838	844	26,068	8,548
Highland	207,500	164,139	793	5,616	1,674
Lanarkshire	561,961	366,961	654	10,583	3,855
Lothian	758,600	574,463	762	20,210	6,287
Orkney	19,810	17,685	895	496	150
Shetland	22,880	20,294	889	448	137
Tayside	395,000	327,681	829	12,322	3,857
Western Isles	29,310	33,609	1143	885	265

Note: 1. Whole time equivalents.
Source: Information and Statistics Division, NHS in Scotland, *Scottish Health Statistics 1995.*

ISSUES IN THE REFORMED NHS

As discussed earlier in this chapter, the reform of the NHS in 1991 involved a radical restructuring of the service, the most significant aspect of which was the purchaser/provider split. While the reforms initially attracted strong hostility from opposition parties, professional associations and trade unions within the NHS, and were distinctly unpopular with the general public, they have now become embedded within the fabric of the service. Indeed, few of the critics have continued their wholesale rejection of the reforms. Nonetheless, a variety of unresolved issues continue to affect the reformed service.

The NHS Internal Market

Perhaps the biggest surprise about the NHS reform road mapped out by the Conservatives in 1989 is that, having set out for the market, they failed to arrive. It seems extraordinary to have invested so heavily in trumpeting both the necessity for, and the advantages of, the dynamics of market competition in order to bring about greater efficiency and cost-effectiveness, and then to have switched to a system of 'managed competition' which worked to negate the free operation of the market.

However, the historical structure and location of NHS hospital provision made it difficult to introduce a genuinely competitive market. The prevailing pattern prior to the reforms was the result of public sector planning specifically designed to avoid duplication of services and to gain economies of scale. This was the case not just in Scotland (where the wide variation in health board populations necessitated the planning of specialist provision on a national basis), but also throughout England where regional specialities had been promoted. In addition, both patients and GPs often favoured locally provided services which they were accustomed to use. As a result, as Ranade has pointed out, the NHS presented problems of 'spatial monopoly' to reformers seeking to operate an internal market within it (Ranade, 1994).

There were, of course, other difficulties facing the introduction of competition between service providers. The NHS had operated until 1991 with little detailed costing of treatments and services; the system of contracting services required for the functioning of the purchaser/provider split thus had to surmount a considerable information deficit. Consequently, the reforms were accompanied by an almost frenetic rush to introduce new information technology, management and accounting systems, and contract preparation and invoicing procedures. More broadly, it was necessary to come to terms with the new world of business plans, capital charging and borrowing limits. Given the massive level of adaptation required (and the absence of the pilot projects advocated by Enthoven), there was little real alternative to the 'steady state' approach.

A further justification for the steady state approach to contracting was the government's need to avoid the strict logic of market competition, that the strong flourish and the weak perish if they remain uncompetitive. Since it was politically unacceptable that uncompetitive hospitals should fail under the pressures of market competition, it was necessary for purchasers to continue to use their existing providers rather than pursue 'better buys' elsewhere. Thus the internal market was a 'managed market'.

Finally, mention should be made of a feature of the NHS internal market that came in for strong criticism from free market advocates: the fact that the consumers of the service, the patients, were excluded from direct participation. Thus David Green of the Institute of Economic Affairs, who was an advocate of health care reform on the basis of lessons from the private health care system of the United States (Green, 1988), discussed the market model set out in *Working for Patients* in highly dismissive terms:

It can be called a 'defence-industry procurement' model of competition, in which relatively few suppliers submit tenders to provide goods or services stipulated by a Government agency. This produces results which are very different from a 'consumer sovereignty' model of competition in which the paying customers can choose from among a range of suppliers, thus signalling their approval or disapproval of the service offered (Green, Neuberger, Young and Burstall, 1990).

Management Issues

Expansion of Management and Administration: A major cost associated with implementing the reform was, as mentioned above, the heavy investment required in personnel management and information technology to create a financial and managerial infrastructure. Thus, in Scotland between 1989 and 1995, the number of administrative personnel (measured in whole-time equivalents, and including senior management personnel) rose from 15,223 to 22,339, an increase of 47 per cent (compared with a 13.5 per cent increase in England). In a health service which had prided itself on historically low administrative costs, the sharply increased costs of management and administration were cause for concern. However, it should be borne in mind that the previous low level of spending was also linked to a lack of capacity to cost specific treatments and care. In consequence, while low administrative costs may have suggested an efficient system, they may also have masked inefficiency; only when costs are fully known can informed judgements be made about efficiency and effectiveness.

Local Pay Bargaining and Conditions of Service: Despite the cohorts of general managers brought into the service following the Griffiths Report of 1983, responsibility for pay and conditions was not substantially devolved to local personnel management prior to the *Working for Patients* reforms. Indeed, a 1991 survey, undertaken by the National Association of Health Service Personnel Officers, Scotland (NAHSPO), provided the following assessment of personnel management in the pre-reformed NHS:

> Traditionally personnel management in the Service has had both operational and strategic dimensions. The main thrust of its contribution, however, has been operational—providing support services and 'fire fighting' problems and issues as they arise... The true strategic functions of human resources planning, organisational development and facilitating performance have been relatively under-developed... The capability to effectively create, integrate and implement a comprehensive human resource management agenda has not been developed (NAHSPO, 1991).

NAHSPO also identified a number of key areas in which personnel management skills appeared underdeveloped, including the employee relations, manpower utilisation, and local pay determination and negotiation. Also standing in the way of local pay determination were the independent pay review bodies for professional staff, and the Whitley Councils covering ancillary workers, which set national pay levels. The Whitley Council system had operated in the NHS from the outset, providing a negotiating forum for management and unions. The influence of the Whitley system had, however, been eroded by the introduction of competitive tendering for ancillary services in 1983, which removed from private contractors the requirement to meet national rates of pay and conditions of service. Furthermore, the pay awards recommended by the independent pay review bodies were increasingly underfunded by government from the mid 1980s, with NHS management instructed to finance the shortfall from cost savings.

Nonetheless, national pay mechanisms were viewed, both by government and by some inside the NHS, as a barrier to allowing local labour markets to set pay and service conditions, and thus to address staff recruitment difficulties or permit savings on pay. One aspect of the *Working for Patients* reforms was that NHS trusts would assume responsibility for bargaining over pay and conditions with their own staff. The development of trusts provided a spur for decentralisation of three personnel functions: staffing levels and the local skill mix, policy covering employee relations, and local pay determination (Secombe and Buchan, 1994). But the government delayed the implementation of these reforms, and the reason for the delay in grasping the nettle of local pay and conditions was straightforward: NHS management was swamped by the task of dealing with major changes required for operating the purchaser/provider split and therefore had no capacity to deal with much else. The assumption of responsibility for pay and personnel issues by local management presented an extremely testing challenge, particularly in a labour-intensive service with over a million staff employed by several hundred separate units. But the result was that, when action was finally taken, the Conservative government was faced with a growing labour relations problem in the NHS which might prove electorally damaging with the latest possible general election date approaching.

The government proceeded to implement local pay bargaining in 1995, with trade unions and professional associations acquiescing with reluctance. Not all trusts conceded the maximum local element awarded by the pay review bodies—this was, after all, the point of the exercise—but the nurses' representatives took the view that they should have done so, despite the principle of local bargaining having been conceded by the union side. Also in 1995, the Royal College of Nursing changed its rules to permit its members to take industrial action. The arguments about local pay bargaining have rumbled on: it is a logical concomitant of NHS trusts being responsible for managing their own affairs but, on the other hand, distasteful to many employees and their representatives who prefer the more monolithic, pre-internal market, service. In 1997, however, the Labour government's white paper, *Designed to Care,* implied that the role of local bargaining over pay and conditions of service will in future be severely restricted.

GP Fundholding and Allegations of a 'Two-Tier' Service

As noted earlier, GP fundholding brought with it allegations of a 'two-tier' system of patient care, within which patients of fundholding practices received preferential treatment from trust hospitals. Despite guidelines that equity between patients should be maintained in all purchaser/provider contracts, a steady stream of newspaper articles from 1993 highlighted instances of differential treatment. In essence, the claims about a two-tier system stemmed from the greater freedom accorded GP fundholders in directly purchasing patient services from providers using their practice budgets. Thus fundholding practices could contract with hospitals offering the shortest waiting times or most competitive rates. In contrast, non-fundholding practices remained dependent on their local health board buying patient services on their behalf.

The Conservative government made clear at the outset that GP fundholders and their patients would obtain benefits from the new system, including faster treatment. However, while non-fundholding practices lacked contractual independence, they were not necessarily totally impotent; they could still put pressure on the health board to switch its purchasing contracts to hospitals providing better or faster services. The government's position was that fundholder freedom of contract did not create a 'two-tier' service for patients but actually increased the incentives for providers to make themselves more competitive to all purchasers, health boards and GP fundholders alike. The difficulty with such a defence is that it was dependent on the assumption that the competition in question was between competing *providers* and not competition between different *purchasers* for services from a given provider. However, this assumption was by no means wholly credible: it appeared to fly in the face of numerous reported instances of providers giving preference to the patients of fundholding practices.

An example of the pressures on providers to differentiate between purchasers was provided by a report in the *Herald* newspaper in January 1996, disclosing that Glasgow Royal Infirmary had been canvassing the views of its senior clinicians on the possible adoption of a two-tier referral system. Under this system, preference would be given not only to GP fundholders but also to health boards outside Glasgow whose contracts could increase the trust's revenues. The letter to consultants from the hospital's Medical Advisory Committee justified such a course of action as follows: 'Despite what might be a natural inclination for us to reject the notion of differential access, there is a real threat if the aspirations of individual purchasers are not met then important sources of revenue for the trust will be lost' (MacDermid, 1996). A spokesman for the trust's chief executive, however, stressed the continuation of equity for all patients, claiming that the letter had merely been intended to canvass views.

Notwithstanding reported cases of preferential treatment, however, the evidence for the operation of a two-tier *system* was somewhat mixed. Reviewing the findings from various research studies, Whitehead (1994) found that on the negative side there was some cause for concern because:

> there is evidence that situations have developed in which the will to succeed financially, or even just survive, has overridden the concern to ensure that everyone has access to the same high standard of service. In the new contract culture, deals have been struck which deliberately give preference to some patients above others, on financial rather than clinical grounds.

More positively, however, Whitehead could also state that:

> there are reports of people striving very hard to adapt to the new structures and ways of working to make sure the new arrangements are still based on equity principles. Co-operation between some Family Health Service Authorities, DHAs and fundholders…has resulted in contracts being set that do not contain clauses giving preferential treatment to one set of patients over another. There are examples where consultants have resisted pressure to choose patients on financial grounds.

A parallel review by Glennerster, Matsaganis, Owens and Hancock (1994) argued that for fundholding to be successful there would inevitably be some degree of inequality of patient treatment. They concluded that the greater the gains from fundholding, the more inequality is likely to result. However, they were opposed to scrapping the fundholding scheme: instead, they advocated a policy of extending 'the benefits of bottom-up funding and negotiating to those who are not fundholders.' Thus two-tier service would vanish once fundholding is made universal.

Given the spread of GP fundholding after a rather slow start (especially in Scotland)—to the position in 1996 when more than more than 40 per cent of NHS patients in Scotland and more than half in England were covered by fundholding practices—expansion of coverage to 100 per cent of patients appeared to offer one solution to the equity problem. But the change of government in 1997 resulted in further expansion of fundholding being frozen and then its abolition being announced (see below).

The Patient's Charter

The Citizen's Charter, introduced in 1991 by the Conservative government, was viewed as a means of prompting public sector management to make their organisations more responsive to the needs of consumers. A number of charters were subsequently brought in for specific services, including the Patient's Charter for the NHS. In the context of the reformed NHS, the Patient's Charter could be viewed as something of a 'fig leaf' to cover the stark reality that, while *Working for Patients* talked about 'extending patient choice' and making the service 'more responsive to the needs of patients', patients were excluded from the contracting process at the heart of the changes. Moreover, nothing had been done even to involve local health councils, which were supposed to represent patients' interests, in any meaningful consultative role about the establishment and operation of hospital trusts or GP fundholding.

Essentially, the Patient's Charter was presented as means of improving the quality of service by establishing a range of patient rights and service standards which would be supplemented by local charters developed by health boards, specifying standards in greater detail. Of the ten national charter 'rights', seven are basically a reiteration of those already possessed by patients, including the right of access to treatment on the basis of need regardless of the ability to pay, the right to be registered with a GP, the right to prior informed consent to treatment, and the right of access to medical records. The three newly-established 'rights' are a right to detailed information about local health services (including prevailing quality standards and maximum waiting times for treatment), a right to medical treatment within two years of being put on a waiting list, and a right to a prompt and full investigation of complaints about the service.

The charter's 'rights' are, however, not capable of legal enforcement; rather, they are a set of expectations that patients ought be able to count on being delivered by purchasers and providers of their health care. Even the standards set out in the charter were less significant than they appeared: for example, the NHS in Scotland had already established a maximum waiting time for treatment of 18 months, six months less than the 24 month maximum announced for England and Wales. Moreover, as

Table 3.5: *Waiting Times and Length of Waiting Lists, Scotland*

	1991 %	1993 %	1995 %
Under 3 months	52.8	54.0	60.7
3-6 months	18.8	20.7	22.2
6-12 months	15.6	16.1	14.8
Over 1 year	12.7	9.2	2.3
Of which over 2 years	4.5	2.8	0.1
Numbers on waiting lists	60,693	59,225	50,133

Source: Information and Statistics Division, NHS in Scotland, *Scottish Health Statistics 1995.*

Baggott (1992) has pointed out, some of the pre-existing rights reiterated by the charter were not always effective. Thus the right to be registered with a GP continued to be denied to some homeless people. On the other hand, ministers on both sides of the border pushed hard to get health boards and authorities fully involved in the drive to implement charter targets. In Scotland this had the effect of achieving greater openness, with health boards—some of which had previously refused to do so—now required to publish their waiting times. Moreover, the publication of waiting times was accompanied by more focused efforts to reduce them.

The data for Scottish in-patients in Table 3.5 show that, over the period 1991-95, significant reductions were achieved, both in terms of total numbers on waiting lists and of the percentage of patients waiting more than one year. However, the picture concerning day case waiting times was somewhat different: while there had been a fall in those waiting more than a year for treatment, from 18 per cent of cases in 1991 to less than two per cent by 1995, the overall number of day cases on the waiting list rose from 19,173 to 29,570. Some caution is necessary concerning both the fall in in-patient, and the rise in day case waiting lists. These should be viewed in the context of a rapid rise in the use of day case surgery in the 1990s, which accounted for just over half of all elective treatment by 1995. Nevertheless, it can be seen that overall the goal of bringing down the length of waiting times was being realised.

As discussed above, the charter process set in train greater openness in the health service by requirements imposed on health boards—later extended to NHS trusts—to make available more information about patient services. This was expanded considerably in Scotland with publication in 1994 of so-called 'league tables' setting out comparisons of clinical outcomes for patients in 30 Scottish hospital trusts. Based on 17 performance indicators, which included seven for acute hospitals requiring data on treatment outcomes, the Scottish clinical outcome tables differed markedly from the earlier hospital trust league tables south of the border: the English tables did not deal with outcomes, but were restricted to comparisons of waiting times in out-patient and accident departments, in-patient waiting times for some common specialities and the percentage treated as day cases. The Scottish statistics revealed considerable variation between hospitals; but in an attempt to pre-empt their interpretation as league tables of 'best' and 'worst' performers, the NHS Chief Executive and the Chief Medical Officer for Scotland emphasised that the indicators were being published with the aim of stimulating discussion of reasons for the disparities and action which might be taken, such as the use of clinical audit.

When a second set of Scottish clinical outcomes data was published in 1996, there was a new focus on patient survival rates in various clinical categories rather than on mortality rates. While initially somewhat crude—and controversial—the publication of the outcomes tables may be viewed as significant in two ways. First, it was a manifestation of attempts to promote greater openness in the health service; second, it expanded the information base available to the purchasers of health care in the internal market and their patients.

Privatisation

While Margaret Thatcher may have pledged at the 1987 Conservative conference that 'the NHS is safe in our hands', critics of the NHS reforms continued to view them with grave suspicion. Given the privatisation of nationalised industries, it came as no surprise that efforts were made to bring market forces into the public services sector. In the case of the NHS, the introduction in 1983 of competitive tendering for ancillary services (for example, laundry, catering and cleaning services) was viewed with suspicion by the trade unions, and some health authorities and clinicians, as heralding a privatisation agenda for the health service. However, this view was somewhat undercut by the results, with in-house providers winning 60 to 80 per cent of contracts awarded in each round of the tendering process (Baggott, 1992).

Accusations of a privatisation agenda appeared to be given new life in 1988 with Mrs Thatcher's announcement of the ministerial review to consider the future of the NHS which resulted in *Working for Patients*. While the review rejected proposals to fund health care through private insurance schemes, it did come up with the idea of the internal market and a purchaser/provider split. Yet, despite claims from Labour's then health spokesman, Robin Cook, that the advent of NHS trusts meant that hospitals 'opted out of the NHS', the reforms essentially involved employing some of the dynamics of a market system within the framework of a reconstructed but publicly operated health service. Thus NHS trusts remained within the public sector and were accountable to ministers who held ultimate control over their assets.

That said, two aspects of the reformed NHS clearly did offer potential points of entry for the private sector. The first concerned the ability of purchasers to place contracts for patient services with private sector providers, though in practice the purchasing of private treatment by health boards and GP fundholders has so far been fairly marginal. The second was that by 1996 NHS trust hospitals had become the UK's largest providers of services for private patients, surpassing BUPA hospitals and BMI Healthcare. Indeed, with nearly 17 per cent of the private health care market in

1996, pay beds in trust hospitals represented such a threat to private sector hospitals that the largest medical insurers were developing 'preferred provider' arrangements to ensure the latter's survival (Timmins, 1996). While trust revenues benefited considerably from the additional funding generated by private patients, critics contended that trust hospital pay beds also promoted private practice by NHS consultants to the detriment of NHS patients.

Meanwhile, NHS trust hospitals became the focus of speculation concerning their potential for fuller development if they were privatised. Such a notion was promoted in the *Sunday Times* by R. Lilley, a former NHS trust chairman:

> Hospital trusts with appropriate assets could become public limited companies (plcs). Released from the vagaries of government funding cycles and electoral fortunes, they could plan their long-term futures and benefit from the competition and boardroom discipline that always leverage quality and customer choice to the top of the agenda.
>
> Tight performance contracts between [NHS] health purchasers and hospital plcs would ensure a quality of treatment that is impossible to achieve in the confused consensus of today's arrangements.

To critics countering that this would mean the end of the cherished NHS principles of free and universal health care, Lilley offered a robust response:

> From the patient's point of view nothing would change. Services would remain free at the point of need, paid for by taxation. Currently, health care is 'purchased' on our behalf, by health purchasing commissions and GP fundholders, who are already free to buy treatment from the private sector. A mixed market, with all the benefits of competition leading to better quality and lower costs, is yet to emerge. By developing the private sector a true market will develop (Lilley, 1995).

While the Conservative government showed no interest in moving to privatise trust hospitals, it nevertheless did introduce a new element into the privatisation debate by extending coverage of its private finance initiative (PFI) to the NHS in 1993. (The PFI is designed to utilise private capital, for example to build and equip a hospital which is then rented by the NHS, probably at greater cost in the long term than if it had been publicly financed: the private sector requires to make a commercial return on its investment.) In 1994 hospital trusts were required to examine the possibilities for involving the private sector before capital projects would be approved. Thus a variety of collaborative ventures with the private sector was set in motion, including the provision of services for a new community hospital in Stonehaven by Grampian Healthcare Trust, and the building of a general hospital near Wishaw by the Law Hospital NHS Trust.

However, Ham (1994) has argued that the question of hospital ownership is a 'diversion' and that the real issue is one of providing quality care for patients. In his view, what matters more is the preservation of the founding principles of the NHS by maintaining its public funding and universal coverage. Thus he concluded that:

> the NHS that is emerging from the reforms may be likened to a national health insurance organisation, with provision being the responsibility of a range of public and private agencies. If this is what ministers have in mind, debate should focus on how at a local level this insurance or purchasing function should be discharged... It is this, far more than the privatisation or not of trust hospitals, that affects whether patients will still have access to appropriate and necessary services.

LABOUR AND THE FUTURE OF THE NHS

The Labour party initially adopted a strongly hostile position towards the main proposals in *Working for Patients*, which they portrayed as undermining the whole basis of the NHS as a national, public service by introducing alien values of competition into health care. Thus a policy document in 1990, *A Fresh Start for Health*, made it clear that the Conservative reforms would be swept aside, a commitment which was carried into the 1992 general election. However, two years later the party issued a consultation paper, *Health 2000*, which reflected an acceptance that a return to the pre-reform NHS was no longer possible and that compromises with the basic purchaser/provider framework would be required.

Labour's revised approach to health care was subsequently set out in the policy document, *Renewing the NHS: Labour's Agenda for a Healthier Britain* (Labour Party, 1995). While it reiterated the party's opposition to a health market, it declared the party did not 'seek change for its own sake'. The goal for Labour was to recreate the NHS as 'a single organisation, working locally and nationally, with shared objectives, [whose] staff will work once more for a truly national, integrated service'. The party now accepted that 'the planning and delivery of care are distinct responsibilities [which] should be kept separate'. However, 'comprehensive health care agreements' with hospitals, which would retain managerial responsibility for day to day decisions about the delivery of care, would replace 'costly and bureaucratic annual contracts'. To avoid recreating the perverse incentives against efficiency identified by Enthoven in 1985, financial incentives might allow hospitals to retain a proportion of efficiency savings. Finally, the 1995 document reiterated the party's commitment to abolish GP fundholding, but proposed to replace it with a system of 'GP commissioning' under which practices would 'team up' with the local health authority to commission services for their patients: 'Health authority commissioning decisions [would] be required genuinely to reflect the preferences of local GPs'. The problem with Labour's proposals is that they would at least reduce the real control fundholders currently exercise over patient care by having their own budgets.

Labour in Office

The election of a Labour government in May 1997 held out the prospect of changes to the NHS internal market, as well as continuing debate over the adequacy of funding levels. Before and during the election campaign, it was widely reported that the financial condition of the NHS had become critical, as evidenced by rising waiting lists, the cancellation of non-urgent operations and the denial of costly drug treatments. Financial pressures had been increased by a severe squeeze on NHS expenditure: while in real terms growth in Scotland had averaged 2.5 per cent over the previous decade (Cm 3551, 1997), the health budget was increased by only 1.4 per cent for 1997-98 (Cm 3614, 1997). These increases should, however, be seen in the context of the perhaps three per cent annual real growth necessary to meet the rising demands and costs affecting the service. Because of Labour's pre-election commitment to stay within the public expenditure plans of the previous government, it seemed unlikely that there would be a major easing of the very tight NHS spending limits for at least two years: it was clear that the service faced the prospect of continuing difficulties.

The new government sought to gloss over NHS budget difficulties by implementing its pledges to 'cut bureaucracy' to secure savings which could be used for increased patient care, and to utilise the private finance initiative (PFI) for some new hospital projects. The Scottish health minister made an immediate commitment to provide £10m for additional patient care spending from cuts in NHS bureaucracy. In June 1997 approval of six PFI funded projects was announced, including a new Edinburgh Royal Infirmary and two new Lanarkshire hospitals at Law and Hairmyres. In all some £400m in hospital building spending was contemplated for 1997-98, the largest ever programme in Scotland.

Labour's first budget in July 1997 added £1.2m to NHS expenditure in 1998-99 from the contingency reserve; Scotland's share was £107m. Then in October, following continued disquiet about the financial position of the service, the government 'found' some £300m from other departmental budgets—a proportion of which was to go to community care in an attempt to free hospital beds blocked by the elderly—of which Scotland received £17m, to be spent during the coming winter.

There was an indication of the Labour government's resolve to take action on modifying the NHS internal market within three weeks of its election with an immediate freeze on the expansion of GP fundholding. The ending of 'two-tier' hospital waiting lists came in July when Secretary of State for Health announced that, from April 1998, NHS trusts would be required to operate common waiting lists for all non-urgent patients. However, this change was less significant north of the border since it addressed a problem mainly experienced in England where fundholding was more developed. In a further move against the internal market, all health boards and trusts were instructed to develop plans for cutting administrative costs.

The NHS White Papers

The Labour government unveiled its plans for 'abolishing' the internal market and ending GP fundholding—though not the purchaser/provider split—in white papers published in December 1997: *Designed to Care* (Cm 3811) from the Scottish Office and *The New NHS: Modern, Dependable* (Cm 3807) covering England. Although both reflected similar themes of co-operation in place of competition, and long-term arrangements between purchasers and providers rather than short-term contracts, there were significant differences in the proposals. It can be argued that the new arrangements in Scotland implied a more radical shift away from *Working for Patients*, in that, with the end of fundholding, GPs will have no responsibility for commissioning hospital care. But south of the border fundholding had become too widespread for it to be politically feasible simply to remove GPs from the commissioning process. Consequently, it was proposed—very much along the lines put forward by Labour in opposition—that groups of GPs should take over the commissioning of most hospital care; the bulk of NHS expenditure would then pass through their hands.

The new NHS structure in Scotland, which will come into operation in April 1999, is outlined in Figure 3.2. The 15 health boards will remain very much as before and they will be responsible for 'strategy and planning', while 'operational management' will be the responsibility of Primary Care Trusts (PCTs) and Acute Hospital Trusts (AHTs). While there was 'no intention of turning the clock back to a time when the NHS was run by a crude command and control system', the distinction between purchasers and providers of care would remain. Health boards will prepare rolling five-year Health Improvement Programmes (HIPs) covering issues such as health promotion, needs assessment and resource allocation. Development of HIPs should be 'a genuinely co-operative process in which local Trusts, GPs and others participate actively.' HIPs may propose changes to services, but their effects must be planned for in advance, another move away from the original notion of an internal market (Cm 3811, 1997).

It seems to be envisaged that there will be a number of PCTs in each health board area, and they will be made up, at least in part, of GPs and other primary care professionals. As well as their main responsibility for general practice, PCTs will operate some hospital services, in particular for people with learning difficulties, the mentally ill and the frail elderly. In rural areas PCTs may be responsible for acute care in community hospitals. GP practices will be expected to group themselves into Local Health Care Co-operatives (LHCCs), covering 'natural communities' of 25,000 to 150,000. LHCCs may hold budgets for primary and community health services (but, unlike their counterparts south of the border, not acute hospital care).

Most hospitals will be run by Acute Hospital Trusts (AHTs) and, except in Glasgow and Lothian, there will be only one in each health board area. Thus most boards will have a one-to-one relationship with a single AHT. Trusts will be funded on the basis of Trust Implementation Plans (TIPs) which 'will set out the range and quality of services that each Trust is to provide and the funds to be allocated to do so.' Funding for the forthcoming year will be agreed when the health board approves the TIP. There will be a return to some sort of provision for cross-boundary patient flows in the SHARE formula. Health boards will be given power of approval over capital spending and senior medical appointments to prevent trusts pursuing 'alternative strategies' to those of the HIP. Thus, although the delivery of care will remain the responsibility of trusts which will continue to be separate legal entities, and health care strategy will be formalised in HIPs and TIPs, in many ways there will be a return to the position before

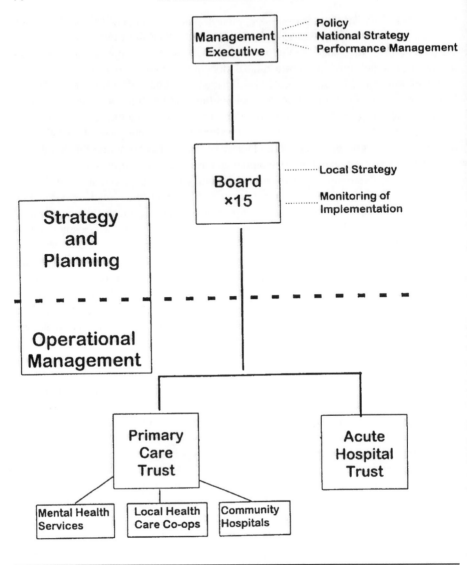

FIGURE 3.2: *The New NHS Structure in Scotland*

Working for Patients. But perhaps the point is also that, especially in Scotland, the internal market has never operated in the way originally envisaged.

The key difference in the proposals for England is that, following the end of fundholding, most hospital care will be commissioned by GPs through Primary Care Groups (PCGs). This will be done through Long Term Service Agreements rather than annual contracts. The NHS Executive will produce model agreements. As was suggested above, this arrangement is, in effect, a recognition of the considerably greater importance of fundholding south of the border; in Scotland it is possible straightforwardly to abolish fundholding and leave GPs with a purely advisory role as far as acute hospital care is concerned. Although fundholding will be ended on both sides of the border, in England, *all* GPs are potentially to be given a role, through PCGs, in commissioning care. The point has already been made that not all fundholders may find this an adequate substitute for loss of their practice budgets. PCGs will have at least a similar status to LHCCs in Scotland, advising health authorities on commissioning, but they are expected generally to assume responsibility for managing the health care budget in their area. Commissioning, through Long Term Service Agreements, will be undertaken in the context of the health authority's HIP.

CONCLUSION

Enormous changes have taken place in the NHS since the introduction of the *Working for Patients* reforms in 1991. These changes were initially opposed by virtually all the professional bodies representing clinicians and nursing staff, but after a few years the new structures were more often than not being defended by these former critics in the face of proposals for further reorganisation from Labour. In part this change reflected the successful consolidation of the purchaser/provider split and the widening coverage of GP fundholding. The Labour government is only partially reversing the Conservative reforms, particularly south of the border.

On the continuing issue of the adequacy of NHS funding, it seems unlikely that the service can hope for more than a continuation of modest real growth in resources from future chancellors of the exchequer of either major party. Informal rationing of NHS care has, of course, always taken place, but the question is increasingly being asked—though rarely in public by leading politicians—whether the service will be able, even in principle, to provide universal access, very largely free at the point of use, to a full range of medical care. A government may one day address the difficult issues of what the NHS can realistically provide and/or new sources of finance apart from taxation, but the likelihood for the immediate future is probably more muddling through.

The NHS has existed for almost 50 years and the likelihood is that it will continue into the foreseeable future, in more or less its present form, as an institution enjoying enormous public support. The reforms which followed *Working for Patients* have undoubtedly involved both gains and losses, but realistic debate is about the balance between the two and not whether the changes were wholly good or wholly bad. The same will, no doubt, be said about those now proposed by the Labour government. The NHS will have to continue to adapt and it will undoubtedly do so: the central issue will be how the service can square the circle of, on one hand, the ever increasing capabilities of medical science and consequent rising expectations, and, on the other, the seeming unwillingness of the political system to provide more than a modest real increase in funding from taxation. Scotland is, of course, considerably better placed, with its substantially higher expenditure per head than England and Wales; but tensions between demand for care and available finance are still likely to be felt on both sides of the border.

4
COMMUNITY CARE AND THE PERSONAL SOCIAL SERVICES

The personal social services, which provide care and support for groups such as the elderly, mentally ill and people with learning difficulties, have become increasingly important in the last 20 or 30 years. Indeed, although qualified social workers, residential and day-care staff and home helps, to mention some of the staff involved, have existed for many years, it was not until the 1960s that the term personal social services gained currency. Their identity was reinforced by the creation of social work departments in Scotland and, slightly later, social services departments in England and Wales (see Chapter 5). At the same time there has been a major, and continuing, change of emphasis, from institutional provision—such as mental hospitals—to care in the community. This chapter examines the comparatively recent emergence of community care as an important aspect of the welfare state, summarises the major legislation, assesses its impact, and describes the changing pattern of care. The main emphasis of this chapter is on adults in need of care, and Chapter 5 deals with the personal social services as they relate to children and their families.

The Scottish Office recently issued a multi-volume *Guidance Package* for social work departments covering children and families, criminal justice and community care (Social Work Services Group and Social Work Services Inspectorate, 1996). About half of the *Package* is devoted to community care, which reflects its increasing dominance in social work departments' activities. Indeed, in most Scottish social work departments around 70 per cent of the total budget is spent on supporting community care services for the frail elderly, the mentally ill and people with learning difficulties.

PRE-GRIFFITHS: THE SCOTTISH DIMENSION

In Scotland, as in the rest of the UK, services for the elderly, mentally ill and people with learning difficulties have had a long history of neglect. In the 1950s and 1960s critics often referred to them as Cinderella groups or services to emphasise their comparative neglect, usually in relation to the acute hospital sector. A number of reasons have been advanced for this situation (Means and Smith, 1994), the most important of which has probably been the historic policy of institutionalisation. Discomfort, stigma and neglect *within* institutions also contributed to the negative image of those *outside* their walls. As a consequence, there was little public pressure to improve benefits and services so as to allow people to remain in the community with comfort.

TABLE 4.1: *Mentally Ill and Mentally Handicapped Hospital Patients, Scotland and England, 1986*

	Scotland	England
Mentally ill	14,500	60,300
Rate per 100,000 population	282	128
Mentally handicapped	5,401	34,200
Rate per 100,000 population	105	72

Source: Titterton, *Caring for People in Scotland,* 1990.

To the extent that the policy and practice of institutionalisation did have this effect, it is likely that it was greater in Scotland than elsewhere in the UK. In Scotland the balance of care between its institutional and community forms has long been biased towards the former. Health expenditure per head has traditionally been higher than in England (see Chapter 3) and, within health expenditure, that on hospitals proportionately greater, but that on community services proportionately less. Exact comparisons are difficult, but Titterton (1990) has shown that, as late as the mid-1980s, Scotland had over twice the number of psychiatric in-patients in relation to population and over one and a half times the number of mentally handicapped patients (Table 4.1).

Comparisons in the balance of care for the frail elderly are also biased in the direction of greater institutional provision north of the border. By the late 1970s Scotland had 15 geriatric beds per 1,000 population aged 60 and over, one and a half times the English provision.

Coinciding with these differences in the balance of care, there have also been historic differences in the welfare mix, that is between statutory, voluntary and private provision. Scotland has shown more enthusiasm than England for collectivist solutions and, accordingly, the role of the public sector has generally been stronger north of the border. Where alternative providers have been sought, voluntary organisations have generally been favoured over the private sector. Titterton (1990) examined differences in residential provision for the elderly in the mid-1980s (Table 4.2).

One further difference between Scotland and England which is relevant to the development of community care is found in their different approaches to joint planning for health and social care. In England and Wales there has, since the mid-1970s, been a requirement on health authorities and local authority social service departments to establish joint consultative committees. In Scotland liaison committees developed only on a voluntary basis. Writing of the situation in the 1980s, Hunter and Wistow (1987) concluded that 'in contrast to England and Wales, the record of joint planning in Scotland has been remarkable for the virtual absence of any progress'. Partly as a consequence of this slow progress, and partly because of the sheer dominance of the hospital sector, the concept of community care has been understood differently north and south of the border. In Scotland, community care has tended to mean getting patients out of hospital, whereas in England equal emphasis is given to keeping people in their own homes.

TABLE 4.2: *Providers of Residential Accommodation for the Elderly, Scotland and England*

	Scotland (1988) %	England (1986) %
Local authorities	58	50
Voluntary organisations	25	12
Private sector	17	38

Source: Titterton, *Caring for People in Scotland,* 1990.

The significance of these Scottish-English differences is clear: the barriers to be overcome in the development of community care were more formidable in Scotland than in England, and implementation of the Griffiths-led revolution has generally been slower north of the border.

THE GRIFFITHS REPORT

In 1986 the then Secretary of State for Social Services asked Sir Roy Griffiths (of the Sainsbury supermarket firm) to examine the way in which public funds were used to support community care policy and to advise on ways of making community care more effective and efficient. The ensuing report, *Community Care: Agenda For Action* (Griffiths, 1988) was only 30 pages long but it was radical in content. Griffiths described community care as everybody's distant cousin but nobody's baby: there was a critical lack of clear-cut responsibilities between health boards, social work departments, housing departments and the voluntary and private sectors.

To achieve the required clarity and effectiveness he had three major recommendations. First, there should be a separate minister of community care responsible for the link between objectives and resources, and for monitoring overall progress towards achieving the objectives. Central government should also provide ring-fenced funds for the speedy development of community-based resources. Second, social work (or social services) departments should play the lead role in identifying need, creating packages of care and co-ordinating services. However, they should be enablers rather than monopoly providers and they should actively stimulate the private and voluntary sectors so as to maximise consumers' choice. Their role as regulators should be strengthened to allow them to inspect provision in all sectors. Third, those referred to residential and nursing homes should be assessed by social workers to ensure that residential care was appropriate and to establish their financial capacity to contribute to the costs of their care.

These proposals were not revolutionary in that they built on earlier developments in social work but they were radical in their promotion of a more mixed economy of care. As Griffiths himself stressed, 'it is vital that social service authorities see themselves as the arrangers and purchasers of care services, not as monopolistic providers'.

CARING FOR PEOPLE

The Griffiths report was published in March 1988 but the white paper, *Caring for People* (Cm 849), did not appear until November 1989. It has been widely surmised that the major reason for the delay stemmed from resistance on the part of the prime minister (Margaret Thatcher) to the proposal to give the lead to local authority social services (and Scottish social work) departments, rather than to a joint board or even to the NHS. Apparently both alternatives were examined but neither was considered practicable. The white paper proposed three key changes in service delivery. First, social work departments should become the main agency for assessing need, designing care packages and ensuring that they were delivered. Second, to achieve consumer choice and high quality services, the local authority should become an enabling body and develop a mixed economy of care. Third, to ensure a comprehensive range and seamless web of services, the local authority should collaborate with health boards, voluntary agencies, housing authorities and the private sector to produce detailed community care plans which they should subsequently monitor.

In addition to these major changes in service delivery there were two further proposals. First, a new system of inspection was to be introduced for residential care. The inspection units were to be at 'arms length' from the local authority. Second, a new funding structure was produced for those seeking financial assistance with residential and nursing care. (There had been a rapid growth in supplementary benefit/income support payments to fund residential care during the 1980s.) This was to be financed through a transfer from the social security budget to local authorities which could also be used to fund domiciliary services, thus reducing the need for residential care. While clients' ability to pay for all or some of their costs was assessed according to rules laid down by government, social workers were given the responsibility for assessing the *need* for care.

THE NATIONAL HEALTH SERVICE AND COMMUNITY CARE ACT

The 1990 act marked a watershed in the evolution of health and social care services in Britain. As well as making changes to the organisation of the NHS with the introduction of an 'internal market' (see Chapter 3), the act was the first piece of legislation to bridge health boards and local authorities: it challenged the traditional division between health and social care, and it laid the foundation for an integrated system of long-term care. But legislation is one thing and its implementation is another.

Initial responses to the proposed changes were sharply divided. Those working within the NHS were almost exclusively concerned with the implications of the internal market, both for hospitals and GP fundholding; those in local authority social work departments were equally concerned with their lead role status and the practicalities of assessment and care-management. Both the NHS and social work departments had a few enthusiasts, a larger group of sceptics and a majority who were prepared to wait and see. Within the NHS the enthusiasts were largely to be found in the steadily growing cohorts of managers and a small number of entrepreneurarily-minded GPs. The initial reaction of social workers was studied by Wistow and his colleagues (Wistow *et al*, 1994). In a sample of 24 English social services departments (broadly equivalent to social work departments), they characterised two as 'conscientious objectors', five as 'reluctant new beginners', four as 'floating voters' who were waiting to see how the changes would turn out, nine as 'incrementalists', and three as 'proven enthusiasts'. There is no directly equivalent information on the initial reaction by social work departments in Scotland but anecdotal evidence suggests that there were even fewer 'proven enthusiasts' and rather more 'conscientious objectors' north of the border.

The reaction of the voluntary sector was also equivocal. A survey of Scottish voluntary organisations (Barbour *et al*, 1990) found that just over a third viewed the proposals contained in *Caring for People* as a good opportunity for their organisation, a further third were uncertain and just under one-in-ten viewed them as a distinct threat. On the whole, national and regional organisations were more favourably disposed than those which only operated on a local basis.

From these initial reactions, it should not come as a surprise that implementation of the 1990 act has been slow and patchy, particularly north of the border. The move towards a purchaser-provider split has been even slower in Scottish social work departments than it was initially in England. A review of developments in Scotland (Stalker, Taylor and Petch, 1994) found that only three regions (Lothian, Highland and Grampian) had formally separated their provider and purchaser functions, and only two (Tayside and Grampian) had evolved care management as a separate designated function.

Given the incomplete and patchy nature of implementation, and the effects of local government reorganisation, it is still too early to attempt a final assessment of community care in Scotland. Major changes inevitably take longer to implement than their advocates would ideally like and it is as well to remember that the full title of the white paper is *Caring for People: Community Care in the Next Decade and Beyond*. But an interim assessment is possible.

There are three overriding questions: first, whether there have been any demonstrable shifts in the pattern of services, from institutional to community-based provision; second, whether there have been any demonstrable shifts in the mix of care, that is increased involvement of the voluntary and private sectors; and, third, whether there has been any demonstrable improvement in collaboration between health and social work authorities.

CHANGES IN THE PATTERN OF CARE

Having reviewed the community care legislation and its implementation, it is useful to locate these developments within longer-term trends and to summarise current provision for the main client groups: the frail elderly, people with mental illness, those with learning difficulties and the physically disabled.

Care of the Frail Elderly

The very elderly, usually defined as those 85 and over, are the main users of services. The number of Scots aged 85 and over increased by over 60 per cent between 1980 and 1994, and this increase is expected to continue until the year 2001.

FIGURE 4.1: *Residential Provision for the Elderly, 1981-95*

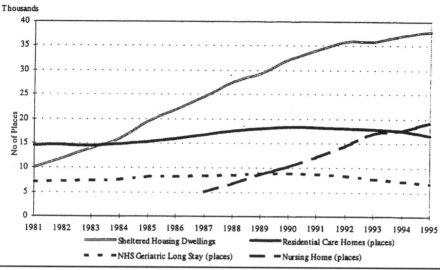

Source: Scottish Office, *Statistical Bulletin: Social Work Series.*

It can be seen that the number of long-stay NHS beds peaked at around 9,000 in 1989 and subsequently decreased to just under 7,000 in 1995 (Figure 4.1). Of course, this decrease has to be viewed in the context of the progressive *increase* in the number of the very old which makes the reduction in the number of NHS beds is particularly significant. However, in relation to community care policy objectives, the dramatic rise in nursing home places, from 5,000 in 1987 to almost 20,000 in 1995, is clearly counter-productive. Moreover, the rise has been continuous and there is no evidence of a slackening-off following full implementation of the new arrangements for community care in 1993. One obvious interpretation of the two trends so far discussed is that the achievement of a reduction in NHS long-stay beds has only been possible because of the increase in the number of nursing home places. The number of places in residential homes reached a peak of over 18,000 in 1990. Since 1993 the number of places has fallen by around 1,300, to under 17,000 in 1995.

For clearer evidence of a shift from institutional to community-based provision there is the rise in the number of sheltered dwellings (see Chapter 6). There are now almost four times as many sheltered housing units as there were in 1980. Between 1990 and 1995 the number of units grew by nearly one-fifth, to almost 38,000.

The number of day centre places and recipients of home help services have both steadily increased over the period (Table 4.3). There has been a more modest increase in meals-on-wheels while the number of meals served in lunch clubs has actually decreased. Thus, in relation to provision for the frail elderly, the evidence is of a continuation of established trends rather than a specific response to the 1990 act. It is also worth noting that this legislation has not reversed the strong upward trend in the number of nursing home places.

TABLE 4.3: *Major Forms of Domiciliary Provision, 1980, 1990 and 1995*

	1980	1990	1995
DAY CENTRES			
Number of places	3,625	7,704	8,582
Places per 1,000			
population 65 and over	4.9	10.2	11.1
HOME HELPS			
Number of clients[1]	60,703	82,183	93,471
Clients per 1,000			
population 65 and over	82.3	107.9	120.8
Number of home helps	9,685	10,323	11,272
Clients per home help	6.3	8.2	8.3
LUNCH CLUBS			
Number of meals (000s)	2,700	2,384	2,262
Meals per 1,000			
population 65 and over	3,662	3,130	2,924
MEALS ON WHEELS			
Number of meals (000s)	1,863	2,169	2,238
Meals per 1,000			
population 65 and over	2,527	2,849	2,892

Note: 1. Whole time equivalent.

Source: Scottish Office, *Statistical Bulletin: Social Work Series.*

Care of the Mentally Ill

There have been contradictory trends in the provision of NHS beds for people with mental illness: a gradual decrease in the number of beds for the working-aged population, matched by a gradual increase in the number of psycho-geriatric beds for the population aged over 65. Both these trends are long-term, but the number of psycho-geriatric beds peaked in 1992, since when there has been a modest decline. It is likely that this decline can be directly attributed to implementation of the 1990 act.

Figure 4.2 shows changes in the number of places in residential homes and day centres. Both increased over the 14-year period and the rise in the number of day centres after 1988 is particularly noticeable. Day centres have a dual function: rehabilitation/sociability for the mentally ill and respite for their carers. The needs of such carers are now well known, and the Carers (Recognition and Services) Act, 1995 will probably result in substantially increased day care provision for the mentally ill and other client groups. Thus, in relation to services for those with mental health problems, there has been a substantial decline in institutional provision, from 17,199 places in 1980 to 11,374 places in 1995. This represents a clear shift in the pattern of

FIGURE 4.2: *Places in Residential Homes and Attendances at Day Centres, 1981-95*

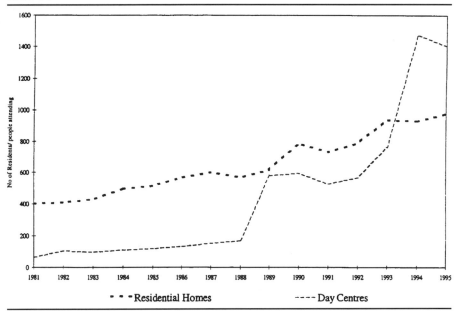

• • • Residential Homes   - - - - Day Centres

Source: Scottish Office, *Statistical Bulletin: Social Work Series.*

care and is clearly in line with the objectives of community care policy.

Care of People with Learning Difficulties

Over the period 1981-95 the number of residents in hospitals dropped by 48 per cent, and there have been corresponding increases in the numbers in residential homes and on the registers of day centres. The impact of the NHS and Community Care Act is difficult to discern in the long-term trends: paradoxically, the only departure from these trends is the flattening in 1991 of the previous increase in the numbers attending day centres.

While there has already been a substantial shift in the balance of care for people with learning difficulties (Figure 4.3), there is still a sizeable institutional population and by for the biggest share of financial resources remains in institutional care. For example, the *Greater Glasgow Joint Community Care Plan 1995-1998* (Strathclyde Regional Council *et al*, 1995) estimated that of 1,777 people with a learning disability in Greater Glasgow, 810 still lived in long-stay hospitals. The plan's priorities over the subsequent three years were to resettle in the community up to 350 long-stay hospital patients, and to increase the overall capacity of accommodation with intensive support, family placements, day activities, respite care and home-based care.

Care of People with Physical Disabilities

The main forms of provision for the physically disabled—residential care and day

FIGURE 4.3: *Care for People with Learning Disabilities, 1981-95*

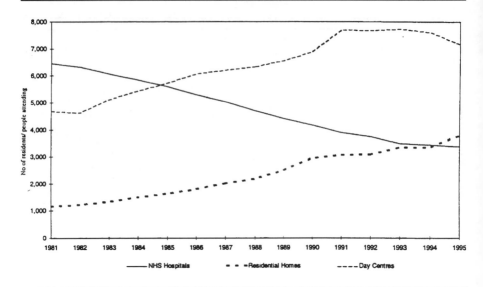

Source: Scottish Office, *Statistical Bulletin: Social Work Series.*

centres—did not increase to any great extent during the 1980s and the first half of the 1990s. The number of residential places increased by just over a 100 during the period 1990 to 1995, but there were only 762 such places in 1995. There are slightly more day centre places now than there were in 1980, but there was a decrease from 1,663 to 1,515 between 1990 and 1995.

Most local community care plans identify huge shortfalls in service availability in relation to needs. The major requirements are suitable housing, access, rehabilitation services and employment opportunities.

CHANGES IN THE CARE MIX

The Conservative government's drive to introduce markets in health and social care placed different demands on the health and personal social services. For health services the emphasis was on the creation of an internal market, and health authorities seem to have adapted to the purchaser-provider split with little difficulty. Indeed, in his contacts with health service personnel, the author is continually surprised by the strength of the 'them-us' dichotomy between the purchasers and providers. Social work departments had a dual obligation placed on them: like health boards, they had to adopt the purchaser-provider split but, in addition, they were obliged to create *external* markets by making use of external providers, that is voluntary and private, for-profit, organisations. This concept of 'enabling as market development' was new to social work and it was contentious, particularly for Labour-controlled authorities.

Even apologists for the Conservative government would admit that movement towards developing new suppliers has been rather patchy and limited. As far as social work departments are concerned, the first point to be made is that most are reluctant purchasers. They believe that they already provide good-quality services and they should be allowed to continue as the main, if not monopolistic, suppliers. This is particularly true in relation to the home help service, which seems to have achieved the status of a sacred cow, especially in the minds of elected members of social work committees. The second point to be made is that most social work departments have been preoccupied with establishing arms-length inspection units, writing community care plans and reviewing assessment procedures. In relation to all these more pressing activities (let alone statutory developments in child care), seeking out new suppliers has generally taken a back seat. The third reason social work departments generally advance for the slow progress is the underdeveloped nature of alternative suppliers, particularly those in the private sector.

Where social work departments have a willingness to look at alternative suppliers, they invariably have a preference for voluntary over private agencies. This preference is justified in terms of trust, track record and transaction costs, all of which are fairly self-explanatory.

We have seen that the initial reaction of voluntary organisations was ambivalent. This overall ambivalence stemmed from a number of considerations. First, a fear that the move to service provision would limit their traditional innovative and campaigning activities. Second, that charging for services would raise practical and ethical issues for those agencies which raise funds directly from the public and/or rely on volunteers. And third, that the move from traditional fund-raising or grant-aid introduces the need for professional management training and support. These concerns continue for smaller voluntary organisations, but the leading organisations like Age Concern, the Church of Scotland and the Archdiocese of Glasgow have overcome them and now occupy a critical position, particularly in the care of the mentally and physically disabled.

When we turn to the private sector, the first question to be asked is why it currently provides such a small proportion of the care of all client groups except the frail elderly. From the point of view of private providers, the main requirement is the creation of a level playing field. The most obvious way in which the field currently slopes is in relation to tax: local authority services are VAT exempt while private organisations—unless they operate as agents for self-employed care workers rather than as employers—are liable. As a consequence, many choose to act as agents but, in so doing, they render themselves less able to exert control over their staff and to maintain standards. The playing field also slopes in relation to the costing of services. The unit cost of local authority services rarely includes a share of the cost of centrally provided services—administration, management training and so on—all of which have to be included in the private sector's calculations. There are also claims that the playing field slopes in relation to the supply of information, consultation and involvement in community care planning: for example, few community care plans provide evidence of any serious involvement of the private sector.

Having reviewed the composition of each sector, we can turn to examine their contribution to the residential care of vulnerable people over the period 1980-95. Since these contributions vary by client groups, Table 4.4 summarises trends and current provision for the four main groups.

TABLE 4.4: *Residential Care Mix by Client Group, 1980 and 1995*

		Local Authorities %	Private Sector %	Voluntary Sector %
Frail elderly	1980	65	1	34
	1995	49	27	27
People with mental problems	1980	80	0	20
	1995	4	9	87
People with learning problems	1980	51	0	49
	1995	21	15	64
Physically disabled	1980	0	0	100
	1995	5	4	91

Source: Scottish Office, *Statistical Bulletin: Social Work Series.*

It is clear that the residential care mix varies dramatically by client group. A greater mix has been achieved in the care of the frail elderly than any other client group. But as far as overall change is concerned, the care of the mentally ill has been completely transformed, from a situation in 1980 when 80 per cent of residential care was statutory to one in 1995 where 87 per cent was provided by voluntary organisations. At the other extreme, the care of the physically disabled has changed least: it was 100 per cent by voluntary organisations in 1980 and 91 per cent 15 years later in 1995. Overall, with the exception of residential care for the frail elderly, the private sector has made few inroads, largely for the reasons already advanced.

In domiciliary care, most provision is still by the statutory sector; there have been some increases in voluntary sector provision but the private sector remains cautious. There are two sorts of private company operating: those which recruit trained nurses and can provide the full range of care at home; and those which recruit untrained staff and concentrate on personal assistance, overnight supervision, etc. Expansion by these companies beyond their currently small share of the home care 'market' is limited by the reluctance of local authority social work departments to contract out their services. There is an understandable concern to protect in-house home care services, and these have greatly increased in their flexibility. Clients can now receive local authority home care for a wider range of tasks and over longer periods, including weekends. Pressures on local government finance have led to moves to charge more, or for the first time, for these services.

Health-Social Work Collaboration

The history of collaboration between health and social work authorities has been characterised as 'stop, start and stutter' (Kohls, 1989), and few of the many commentators

FIGURE 4.4: *Greater Glasgow: Projected Resource Transfers to Community Care*

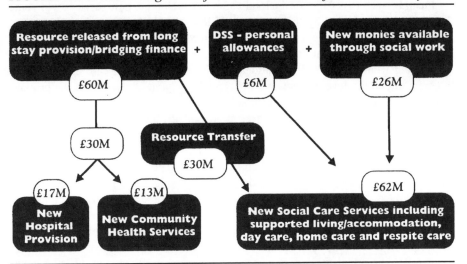

Source: *Greater Glasgow Community Care Plan 1995-1998*, 1995.

(for example, Hunter and Richards, 1990; Smith *et al*, 1993) can point to any significant and sustained progress. But the fact that the NHS and Community Care Act bridged the health-social care divide gave grounds for hoping that implementation might bring about levels and forms of collaboration hitherto unattainable.

The act required social work departments, as the lead agents, to work with health boards to produce initial Planning Agreements in 1991 as a prelude to the first Community Care Plans in 1992. Both were to include, *inter alia*, a shared assessment of need, agreed policies on assessment procedures, and arrangements for hospital discharge and care management. Despite the clear requirement of a joint approach, nine of the 15 Scottish social work departments produced separate initial Planning Agreements, and five went on to produce their first Community Care Plans independent of the relevant health board. The second generation of plans has now appeared and most departments have produced joint plans. Examination of a number of these second generation plans reveals a move from region-wide to locality planning. This change clearly anticipated the reorganisation of Scottish local government and further developments will probably follow. In due course, it is likely that many of the new authorities will want to pursue the trend towards locality planning. Such a move could be very important, particularly if it is co-ordinated with parallel NHS developments in locality purchasing. Given these complementary changes, it is at least possible that by the year 2000 health and social care needs could be planned and purchased by a single locality-based agency.

One of the main aims of the NHS and Community Care Act was to change the patterns of funding. Since 1993 this has meant a shift of resources to community-based services from three sources: long-stay hospitals, DSS personal allowances (income support) and new monies such as the Mental Illness Specific Grant. To show how these transfers are operating it is useful to look at the situation in one area (Figure 4.4). It can be seen that £30m of the total £62m to develop the new services will come from resources released by the reduction of long-stay beds, £26m in new money, mainly the Mental Illness Specific Grant, and a further £6m from DSS personal allowances. It is anticipated that these transfers will be effected by 1998.

Moving from strategic to operational levels of health-social care collaboration, the most important developments are in hospital discharge, operation of the primary care team and registration and inspection.

First, in relation to hospital discharge arrangements, the recent survey by Stalker, Taylor and Petch (1994) showed that, while the majority of health boards and local authorities had produced protocols, the status of the documents was often unclear and few appeared to have been produced collaboratively. The authors of the survey concluded that the 'absence of widespread agreement is of some concern...until this issue is resolved the smooth transition from hospital to home cannot be guaranteed'.

The unsatisfactory state of current practice is revealed in a recently completed study of discharge in a West of Scotland health board (Fitzpatrick, 1995). Of 158 frail elderly patients discharged, none reported having had a comprehensive assessment by a social worker. Other findings from the study were that 29 per cent waited for two weeks following discharge to see their GP, 30 per cent waited over three weeks to see a district nurse, and 43 per cent waited over three weeks to see a social worker.

In relation to collaboration between the primary care team and social work, the 1990 act seems to have had very little impact. Despite the fact that around one-third of referrals to social work departments come from the primary care team, there has, on the one hand, been no increase in social work attachments and, on the other, no significant involvement of GPs in community care planning. The situation is best described as a 'stand off' in which social work staff claim that GPs will not come to meetings, and GPs complain that the meetings are a waste of time. An illustration of the present state of affairs is provided in the author's recent attempt to divert a group of GPs from a proposed study in which they wanted to gather proof that social workers could not do community care assessments. Their preferred strategy was to proceed without informing the relevant social work department because, if they did so, they feared that any meeting would turn into a talking shop.

There has been a hope that, with the move to fundholding, many GPs would use surpluses to employ social workers to act as practice care managers. This has not happened, even in Grampian where fundholding has proceeded furthest. However, an interesting development in Grampian has been the alignment of care managers with general practices, which would seem to have considerable potential. In their review of strategies to improve GP-social work collaboration, Newman and Beardow (1992) concluded that the following had been the most successful: a recognised joint approach with defined objectives, allegiance to an agreed strategy to developing links, all GPs encouraged to make their views known, other partners to be seen to act on the advice of the GPs, and any questionnaires to be kept simple.

Finally, and in relation to registration and inspection, Scottish Office guidance in a circular (Social Work Services Group, 1990) encouraged health boards and local authorities to co-operate, and to work towards common standards for both nursing and residential homes. In 1991 local authority registration and inspection functions were extended to cover their own as well as other establishments. Thus, the possibility now exists for achieving common standards across the entire range of long-term institutional provision. This potential had still not been realised at the time of Stalker, Taylor and Petch's 1993 survey. Throughout Scotland, they found that health boards continued to inspect nursing homes, and local authority social work departments continued to inspect residential homes: Tayside, Highland and Western Isles were planning joint teams, but otherwise the collaboration only extended to developing joint standards. With an increase in the number of dual registration establishments, it seems inevitable that joint teams will emerge as the norm, and it is even conceivable that one authority might contract out its responsibilities to the other. These possibilities have been strengthened by the reorganisation of local government and the reduced size of most social work departments.

It is clear from this review of developments in planning, discharge, inspection and collaboration that progress towards the 'seamless web of care' has been infinitesimally slow. The situation is essentially the same south of the border. In its review of progress over the first year since full implementation, Social Services Inspectorate (1995) made four observations which merit reporting in full. First, consultation between social services, health, housing, private and voluntary providers and other key agencies had improved considerably. Second, productive joint working—joint commissioning, pooled budgets, shared success measures—would, however, require considerable additional work. Third, there was an urgent need to take action locally to align the planning cycles, commissioning strategies and resources of health, social services and housing agencies. Fourth, continuing organisational change within social services and the NHS, and uncertainties about possible changes in local government structures and boundaries, had worked against effective collaboration.

Improvements in Service Delivery

More important than the organisational and practice changes noted above are changes in the way in which services are experienced by clients. From clients' point of view the important questions are whether they get a service and its quality. Three aspects of service delivery can be examined for improvements: assessment, care management and user involvement.

Assessment: While social workers and other professionals have always regarded assessment as a core practice skill (and some have undoubtedly done it sensitively and effectively), better assessment practices have emerged as the fundamental requirement for good community care. The NHS and Community Care Act, 1990 and guidelines (Social Services Inspectorate/Social Work Services Group, 1991) have called for needs assessment which is holistic (that is covering both health and social functioning); determined by what is required rather than by what is available (that is needs-led rather than service-led); and informed by users' preferences (that is there should be some choice). The inference is clear: existing practice was deemed to have fallen short in all three respects and, particularly, in the tendency to assess for specific services rather than overall need.

Evidence of change in community care practice following the 1990 act comes from a longitudinal study of a typical social work area team which examined the effects of in-service staff training (Ford and Taylor, 1995). Following implementation of the training programme, there was a substantial increase in the proportion of users who received a 'thorough' assessment while 'superficial' assessments were eliminated. More recent findings come from interviews with 65 social work practitioners in 1994 (MacDonald and Myers, 1995). Most of the front-line workers interviewed for the study felt that the scope of assessments had widened and that they were now assessing for needs rather than for available services. This rhetorical shift notwithstanding, the researchers also detected a growing recognition of external constraints. Despite being comfortable with the language of needs-led assessment and its underlying philosophy, front-line staff reported that their attempts to put it into practice were constantly frustrated by a lack of resources. Indeed, some regarded the entire needs-led assessment exercise as positively harmful since it raised expectations which could not be met. The main gaps identified by the front-line workers throughout Scotland were 24-hour and seven day a week home care; transport to and from day and respite care; conveniently located and homely residential and nursing care; residential, day and home care for those with dementia; community-based accommodation; and services for the mentally ill.

We clearly have to be careful with evidence based solely on perceptions of service gaps since they could reflect a lack of creativity on the part of the practitioners, one of the defects which the practice guidelines have sought to remedy. However, it does seem likely that the modest but real improvements in assessment are threatened by a dearth of new resources.

In its review of the implementation of the 1990 act in England, the Social Services Inspectorate (1995) highlighted a further problem: that of determining the 'right' ratio between simple and complex assessments. This is not an issue on which much has been published, but every social work manager is aware that the recommended assessment procedures apply to complex cases. But if a frail elderly client wants an extra couple of hours of home care or a ramp or financial assistance to pay the TV licence, it may not be necessary for the social worker to conduct a full-scale assessment. If it is not, then it is useful to know what proportion of clients are likely to present with such simple needs, and to devise an alternative and quick assessment. The ratio of simple to complex assessments is potentially an important datum for planning, but, as the inspectorate has reported, this ratio varies too much from department to department for it to have credibility. This is clearly an issue on which more research is required.

Care Management: Early experiments in community care (Challis and Davies, 1986) produced some evidence to suggest that care management with a devolved budget and a reduced care load could keep frail elderly people in their own homes for longer and with higher levels of satisfaction than traditional social work services. Despite initial enthusiasm for case management (later called care management), progress has been extremely slow. The guidelines on case management (see above), like most community care directives, were permissive rather than prescriptive. Thus, while it was insisted that assessment should be separated from service provision, practitioners were allowed to play a dual role, alternating between their traditional one as, for example, social workers or occupational therapists, and their new role as care managers. This duality in the guidance literature is reflected in the emerging pattern across Scotland.

In her overview of care management in Scotland, Buglass (1993) identified three models: care management as a separate job, care management as a task within a social work agency, and care management as a joint social work-health task. Of the 12 social work departments before local government reorganisation, only two (Tayside and Grampian) had chosen to develop care management as a separate task. Both departments advertised for care managers and both appointed non-social workers, mainly occupational therapists, to the posts. In a further four departments (Orkney, Dumfries and Galloway, Shetland, and Western Isles) the joint agency model was either in operation or planned. The most clearly articulated example of this joint agency model was the Primary Assessment Team in Dumfries and Galloway. These teams operated on the basis of regular meetings between local adult care teams and primary health care teams. Care co-ordinators (they preferred this term to care managers) were appointed from either team, as considered appropriate, but the local authority retained control of the financial arrangements.

The majority of departments (including Strathclyde and Lothian) chose to define care management as a social work task. In this interpretation, care management is not a separate job and there are no dedicated care managers. This can and has been called a minimalist approach, in the sense that it involves social workers and their agencies in least change to established practice. It may also turn out to be a temporising approach until the merits and defects of the more distinctive models can be assessed.

There is another and more important sense in which the Scottish approach to care management can be described as minimalist. A key feature of the English pilot projects was a decentralised budget (Challis and Davies, 1986): care managers had a specified weekly budget (for example one-third of the weekly cost of a residential place) with which to purchase individualised packages of care. In Scotland there has been a strong reluctance to devolve budgets to individual care managers. Indeed, throughout most social work departments, budgets were only devolved as far as district managers. In their survey, Stalker, Taylor and Petch (1994) noted that some departments were considering further devolution to the level of team manager, but only one (Western Isles) was even contemplating devolution to care managers.

Overall, then, care management has still to develop and not even its most enthusiastic supporter could claim that it had yet been successful in Scotland. Indeed, as long as it is conceived as an integral part of the social work task ('something we have always done'), it is difficult to see how the care manager can possibly evolve into the social care equivalent of the fundholding GP purchaser of care. It is noteworthy that most progress in this direction was made in Grampian and some of the more rural areas.

The Social Services Inspectorate (1995), in its review of the implementation of the 1990 act in England, made only one comment on care management, yet it speaks volumes:

A variety of models of care management was being tested, which would require some time to assess. Most authorities had concentrated on the assessment component of the care management process.

User and Carer Involvement: The principle of user involvement is paramount and unchallenged. It operates principally at the level of individual assessment though there is also the expectation that users will become involved at the planning level. The 1989 white paper, *Caring for People,* is admirably clear and realistic: it instructs community care workers to 'take account' of the wishes of the users and carers and, *where possible,* to involve them in decisions relating to their care. In response, both local authorities and health boards have made policy statements on users and carers, many have produced users' and/or carers' charters and others have established liaison groups. Generally, the response from social work departments has been greater; for example, Stalker, Taylor and Petch reported that none of the Scottish health boards had produced a carers' charter and few provided literature specifically geared towards community care users and carers.

But the greatest activity, again more prominent in social work departments than health boards, has been the design of new assessment proformas. Virtually every professional group involved in community care has had to struggle with the practical problems of incorporating users' and carers' perceptions and preferences. They have had to decide on such issues as at what stage users' and carers' views should be solicited: how much space should be allocated for users and how much for carers; and whether they should always be assessed separately. In their review of these assessment proformas, Stalker, Taylor and Petch found that, on the whole, they devoted more space to recording the needs of carers than of users. This suggestion of over-reaction to carers will be taken up later but it is first necessary to assess the extent to which front-line community care staff have increased their responsiveness to users.

In their study of community care implementation, Ford and Taylor (1995) found that the proportion of clients who felt that their views had been taken into account in assessments increased from 48 per cent to 68 per cent after the staff training programme. However, when it came to user choice, it was necessary to distinguish between choice about what services were made available, choice between services and choice within a service. In relation to the first, users felt they had absolutely no choice about the range of services available to them. This was entirely determined by managerial and professional decisions about the best use of available resources which were almost exclusively those provided by the statutory agencies. Indeed, interviews with social work staff suggested a general reluctance to inform users about non-statutory provision which stemmed from a number of considerations. First, most staff were badly informed about what was available outside the statutory sector. Second, some were unwilling to suggest a non-statutory service in case something went wrong and they were held accountable. Third, there was a generalised feeling that statutory services *should* meet all needs, and advice about other services, particularly those assumed to be profit-making, was viewed as a mild form of treachery. Wistow and his colleagues reported similar reactions in a number of the social services departments in England (Wistow *et al,* 1994). For all these reasons, choice *between* services was also largely non-existent: it was just not available to most clients.

However, while there was no evidence of choice in the first two senses, there was in relation to the third: choice *within* a service. In the post-intervention cohorts many clients reported favourably on the increased flexibility of service delivery. They felt they had a choice over, for example, the time or day of the week when a home help was available. The efforts of workers were appreciated: indeed, for many clients, flexibility compensated for shortages.

Turning specifically to carers, their discovery as a risk group and caring as a new social problem could yet be hailed as Griffiths's major achievement. The subsequent legislation and activities of campaigning groups have given carers a high profile, and there can be few social work practitioners who are unaware of the requirement to assess carers' needs. But exhortation and awareness is not all, and it is entirely an empirical matter to determine if their needs are taken into account in routine community care assessments. If the presence of a carer section in an assessment proforma is any indication, it is clear that most Scottish social work departments are already thinking about carers. Indeed, as we have already seen, many assessment proformas now devote more space to record the needs and views of carers than they have given to users.

Further evidence of the high level of awareness of carers' needs comes from a recently completed study (Watson and Taylor, 1996) which presented a sample of front-line community care workers with hypothetical examples of carers and invited them to identify what needs if any were present in each. The research found strong evidence that community care assessors, mainly social workers, were systematically underestimating the needs of high dependency carers but overestimating the needs of those with low dependency. The study concluded that front-line workers should be more discriminating in their assessments of carers so that they can target resources on those most in need rather than dissipate them on those with minimal or no needs.

In line with this conclusion, there is increasing evidence that carers vary greatly in their characteristics and circumstances. Some care for long hours with little help and report high levels of strain, while others care for shorter periods with a good deal of outside assistance and report no strain. In a sample of middle-aged carers, Taylor, Ford and Dunbar (1995) calculated that one in ten were particularly vulnerable or at risk. In a subsequent study of carers of all ages, Taylor and Ford (1995) employed three risk criteria: caring for 20 hours or more per week, providing personal or nursing care, and reporting no helpers/confidants. They found that some ten per cent of carers did not fall into any of these categories and were defined as the 'no risk' group; 30 per cent were at risk on one criterion, the 'low risk' group; 36 per cent were at risk on two criteria, the 'medium risk' group; but 25 per cent were at risk on all three criteria and were defined as the 'high risk' group. The study concluded that practitioners should make every effort to adopt a more discriminating approach.

CONCLUSION

The social care provisions of the NHS and Community Care Act, 1990 were not fully implemented until 1993, so it would be unreasonable to expect that a great deal should already have been changed by it. Structural changes, like renaming departments or substituting a new assessment form for an old one, can be achieved by the stroke of a pen. Cultural changes, like assessing need rather than eligibility or thinking of patients or clients as customers, require longer. It is likely it will only be in the next millennium that we are able to assess the full impact of what some have called the

Griffiths revolution. But perhaps the term 'revolution' is inappropriate: a review of changes in the pattern and mix of care suggests continuity rather than abrupt change. The changes which have occurred since 1990 are relatively modest and, for the most part, continuations of trends over the last two decades.

Following the election of a new Labour government, the proposals of the party in opposition are likely to be relevant to the future shape of the health and social services. To the extent that these intentions were revealed in *Renewing the NHS: Labour's Agenda for a Healthier Britain* (Labour Party, 1995), we can expect continuity rather than further radical change. The purchaser-provider split will stay in the health service although 'comprehensive agreements' will replace annual contracts, while fundholding general practices are to be phased out and replaced by 'locality commissioning' (see Chapter 3). In relation to community care, the Labour party document was modest: it acknowledged that there are no easy answers and proposed a royal commission.

There could be merit in a concerted attempt to go beyond the foundation laid by the 1990 act and establish a national system of community or long-term care. Which term is used may be important. One of the recurring weaknesses of the attempt to develop community care is that it is defined as non-institutional care. This creates a problem for institutions, and those who work in and from them, and it is becoming increasingly clear that we will always require them in some measure. For this reason alone, the term long-term care may be preferable to community care. The second compelling reason for an examination of long-term or community care is the urgent need fully to involve the medical profession, particularly GPs. For obvious reasons they have, up till now, been more concerned with internal changes within the NHS; they are only beginning to realise the enormity of the potential changes stemming from the lead role of social workers. In care planning an accommodation has to be reached which respects the contribution each group of professionals can make towards the establishment of a truly integrated system.

NOTE ON SOURCES: In addition to references in the text, statistics are from *Scottish Office, Statistical Bulletin: Social Work Series.*

5
CHILDREN AND THEIR FAMILIES

INTRODUCTION

Children and their families use a wide variety of services, including practically all those discussed in this book – social security, health care, the personal social services and education – as well as facilities such as libraries, parks, swimming pools and youth clubs. Many of these are universal, in the sense that they are open to anyone of the appropriate age. This chapter is concerned with a more restricted set of services, namely those provided by social work departments and other child care organisations, together with the associated legal system. Most of these services are selective, in that they have eligibility criteria and gate-keeping processes for deciding who should have access to them. They include day nurseries, and children's and family centres; home support; counselling; many kinds of youth, community and group work; and residential care, fostering and adoption. In some circumstances, the 'service' may be imposed for the sake of the child or wider society, so we shall be concerned with issues of social control as well as social support.

The distinction between selective social services for children and more universal provision is not clear cut, but the main rationale for the former is their intention to meet the particular needs of some children and their families, rather than needs of children generally. Even when there is widespread demand for a service (as in relation to day-time care for pre-school children), central or local government may decide that there are only sufficient resources to offer limited provision for those deemed to have special needs. In practice, this targeting tends to be directed towards children and families with significant difficulties and problems, which in turn may lead to stigmatisation of the service and its users.

The services respond to both perceived needs (for example, of children with learning difficulties) and social problems (for example, family conflict, child abuse, juvenile offending). The main service providers are local authorities and voluntary agencies. Some of the latter are small local organisations, others are Scotland-wide (for example, Aberlour Trust; Children 1st), whilst a few are part of large UK-wide organisations (for example, Barnardos, National Children's Homes Action for Children). Recent demographic trends mean that the types of households in which children grow up have become increasingly diverse, with consequences for the range of needs. Poverty has grown, and now about a quarter of Scotland's children live in families dependent on Income Support (Long, 1995a). About one in five children are in lone parent households and each year thousands of children experience the divorce or remarriage of their parents (Tisdall with Donaghie, 1995).

Services also respond—and change—according to prevailing approaches. Often, these approaches are the current winners of debates, which may later be reversed. Four themes are described below, which have influenced the development of services examined later in this chapter.

Rights: Children, Parents and the State

The children's rights movement has grown in the past century, culminating with the United Nations' Convention on the Rights of the Child which was ratified by the UK government in 1991. The convention identifies three key principles:

All rights guaranteed by the convention must be available to all children without discrimination of any kind.

The best interests of the child must be a primary consideration in all actions concerning children.

Children's views must be considered and taken into account in all matters affecting them.

Children's rights are sometimes mistakenly seen as referring to children being able to choose or even control what happens. But the convention outlines several different kinds of rights, and choice is only one of them. Parents and society have responsibilities to provide and protect children's rights. Consequently, children, parents and the state form a complex triangular relationship that lies at the heart of many issues and dilemmas. Several writers have devised classifications of different perspectives (Adler, 1985; Harding, 1991). Three main types can be recognised, depending on which corner of the triangle is emphasised :

Paternalist: stresses the right of state agencies to intervene to protect children from neglect or harm at home.

Parentalist: argues that normally parents are in the best position to decide on children's interests and to meet them. Either the state should leave parents alone or give them support, but not remove children except in extreme circumstances.

Liberationist: believes that children's wishes should normally be paramount and they should have similar rights to self-determination as adults.

In practice most people and most legislation seek to balance these competing interests and have varied responses according to the circumstances, so that it is not so much a matter of belonging to one camp as of reconciling the different considerations in a particular situation.

Child Rescue Versus Prevention: The shifting balances between paternalist and parentalist approaches is exemplified by the long-standing issue of the breadth or narrowness of circumstances where it is justified or beneficial for children to be taken away from home, especially on a compulsory basis. Both Hendrick (1992) and Heywood (1978) suggest that, at certain times, the emphasis has been on 'rescuing' children from adverse circumstances to give them a fresh start in life. At its most extreme, from Victorian times until as recently as the 1960s, this involved shipping children to the colonies. During other periods, policy has shifted towards supporting children at home and preventing the need for a 'rescue' mission, or else putting maximum effort into a quick return home. Holman (1988) observed that law and practice moved in this direction for 20 years after the second world war, but then there was a reversion. Fuelled by alarm about child abuse, a tendency developed to 'play safe' by removing children, when support services to the family might have enabled them to stay at home. The Orkney affair is a recent example in which children suspected of having been sexually abused were 'rescued' by professionals, in a manner which the subsequent inquiry indicated was unfortunate and precipitate (House of Commons, 1992).

Welfare Versus Justice: Debates between welfare and justice models have been long-standing in Scotland, particularly for young people who offend. In the welfare model, the children's interests should be central to all services and decisions. Any measures taken in relation to an offender are thus not necessarily proportionate to the scale of offending, but are appropriate to the child's needs. A child who offends may have the same needs as a child in need of 'care and protection', and thus should be dealt with in the same type of legal proceedings and with the same array of disposals. Such a model has largely dominated the approach to children in Scotland since 1968, in the children's hearing system (see below).

Critics suggest that the welfare philosophy is paternalistic, unfairly groups together the innocent with the guilty and disregards consequences of behaviour (for a discussion, see Murray, 1992). Many other countries use what is described as a justice model, in which 'troublesome' and 'troubled' children are dealt with separately, where there is an emphasis on due process and proportionality. England and Wales moved towards a more welfare-oriented system in the 1970s (though not as far as Scotland) but have subsequently reverted to a more sharply segregated approach, which is also common in North America.

Welfare Pluralism: Possible providers of children's services include statutory, voluntary and private organisations, which may have a variety of relationships with one another. For example, statutory organisations may contract with voluntary or private organisations to provide a service for which the former are legally responsible. Voluntary and statutory organisations can join together to provide a joint service, jointly funded from charitable and statutory sources.

The role of voluntary organisations and the private sector was furthered by the promotion of a 'mixed economy of welfare' by the Conservative government between 1979 and 1997. This encouraged local authorities to become 'enabling authorities', purchasing services from outside agencies to fulfil statutory duties. The voluntary sector has expressed some concern about the resulting 'contract culture,' with the risk of becoming wedded to the priorities of local and central government, and thereby losing their innovative and advocacy roles (Francis, 1995).

Services for Children

In the remainder of the chapter, we consider in turn legal and service provision in Scotland for children and their families, concentrating on social work services. After a brief glimpse at relevant history, we outline the key features of the law, policies and systems established by the Social Work (Scotland) Act, 1968 and changes introduced by local government reorganisation in 1996 (see also Chapter 1). The Children (Scotland) Act, 1995 was also being implemented at the time of writing. An account is then given of the unique Scottish children's hearings and their role in juvenile justice. Next, issues of child abuse and protection are considered, followed by a review of services to support families. Finally, services for children away from home are discussed.

A BRIEF HISTORY

Since the time of the poor laws formal welfare intervention has gradually increased for children and their families (Hill, Murray and Rankin, 1991). The poor law authorities tended to respond when poor people became destitute or came before the courts, rather than actively intervene to protect and safeguard children's welfare. The prime responsibility for children lay with their parents. From the eighteenth century, organised charities and institutions took on a more active role and supplemented the poor law through 'philanthropic' works; they were often driven by concerns to instil morals and to remove children from undesirable influences. Specialised philanthropic organisations were established to work with particular groups of children and their families, and many forerunners of major charities today were founded in the nineteenth century.

Several of these 'child-rescue' charities set up residential institutions. Those intended to reform older children became the forerunners of 'approved schools', established under the Children and Young Persons (Scotland) Act, 1932. While such schools would appear rigid and overly disciplinarian by today's standards, they did focus on training rather than punishing children. The rise of philanthropic organisations thus increased intervention in the lives of families, widened the range of services and encouraged the focus on the needs of children.

Scotland had a relatively low level of institutional care for children in the nineteenth century compared to England. Many children were kept out of institutional care because of the tradition in urban areas to 'board out' children with families in the countryside, so they could benefit from the 'better environment'.

The state began to take on a more active responsibility for the care and welfare of all children in the second half of the Victorian era, and penalties were introduced for ill-treatment. But services remained fragmented between health, welfare and education departments, and a flourishing voluntary sector. The Children Act, 1948 brought together public child care services into unitary children's departments, and the Children Act, 1963 allowed these departments to provide material ('in kind') or financial help. The 1963 act also placed a duty on local authorities to provide advice, guidance and assistance so as to reduce the need to receive children into, or keep them in, local authority care.

The first substantial acknowledgement that children had separate rights as citizens independent from their parents, which the state had the duty to protect, came in the Children Act, 1908. The act underlined the need to treat children who offended differently from adults, in providing rehabilitation rather than punishment; it separated juvenile courts, which would deal with children in need of care and protection as well as young people who offended, from adult courts. The Children and Young Persons (Scotland) Act, 1932 furthered this separation by allowing for specially constituted juvenile courts, with the welfare of the child expressly stated as one of their major considerations.

Despite the organisational changes in juvenile courts, by the time that Lord Kilbrandon was given the remit of reviewing arrangements for dealing with young people in need of care or protection and juvenile delinquents in 1961, the justice system showed considerable fragmentation. Only four specialised juvenile courts had been established in Scotland, and young people's cases were heard in a number of different courts with staff who could have little knowledge of their welfare needs.

Kilbrandon and the Social Work (Scotland) Act

The Kilbrandon committee reported in 1964 (Cmnd 2306). It began with the assumption that all children appearing before juvenile courts—whether for care or protection, or for offending—were exhibiting symptoms of the same difficulties. 'The distinguishing factor was their need for special measures of education and training, the normal up-bringing process having, for whatever reason, fallen short'.

Young people who offended usually pleaded guilty in court, so that decisions about a case's facts were rarely required. Instead, the courts were making decisions on what should happen to these young people, as well as the children who were in need of care and protection. But the courts were usually making such decisions without appropriate training, and with few means by which to supervise or modify their decisions.

The committee therefore proposed a radical separation of decision making: decisions on guilt and innocence would remain with the judiciary but a separate system of 'juvenile panels' would make decisions on care. Cases were to be referred to the panel only by an official called the reporter. A 'matching field organisation' would provide care and supervision for the children judged to need it by the panel; since the process was seen as an educational one, these functions were to be performed by a new social education service department set up within the local education authority.

The white paper, *Social Work and the Community* (Cmnd 3065, 1966), accepted Kilbrandon's recommendations but with a notable difference. Rather than a social education service, a separate and comprehensive social work department would be created. The new department would not only service the children's hearings, but bring together personal social services for people of all ages. The white paper thus went far beyond Kilbrandon's mandate to consider children: it incorporated the growing belief that professional social work had common principles, objectives, and methods for working with individuals and families. Further, the state would have a statutory responsibility to provide and co-ordinate the personal social services, thus shifting the balance of responsibility away from voluntary organisations.

The Social Work (Scotland) Act, 1968, provided the legislative foundation for social work departments, with the requirement for local authorities to have a social work committee and a director of social work. The new departments were made responsible for 'fieldwork' and a range of services: residential, day-care and domiciliary. In Part III of the act, the new system of children's hearings was implemented in 1971, largely as suggested by Kilbrandon.

Beyond the children's hearings, a revolutionary feature of the 1968 act was the wide-ranging 'duty of every local authority to promote social welfare by making available advice, guidance and assistance'. This duty was further specified for children (that is, under 18 years), to diminish the need for taking in or keeping a child in local authority care, or for referring a child to a children's hearing. Local authorities had the power to provide not only assistance 'in kind' but also in cash. To many observers, this positive promotion of welfare in the 1968 act was indeed revolutionary, and notably absent from parallel legislation in England and Wales (see, for example, Cooper, 1983; Martin, 1983; Younghusband, 1978).

Scottish local government was reorganised in 1975 (see Chapter 1); apart from the three all-purpose islands councils, a two-tier system was established with nine regional and 53 district councils. Services with key responsibilities for children and their families were divided between the tiers: while the regions were responsible for the key services of education and social work, the districts dealt with housing and recreation.

For over 20 years the Social Work (Scotland) Act, 1968 remained the foundation of child care services in Scotland, although the Children Act, 1975 and the Adoption (Scotland) Act, 1978 made significant changes in planning for young people in local authority care and in adoption. Early year reviews and childcare inspections were added to Scottish local authorities' duties by the Children Act, 1989. However, most of this 1989 act only applied to England and Wales, and there was a growing sense that Scottish child care also needed a searching review and new legislation.

The Decade of Review, Reports and Scandals

In 1988, the Secretary of State appointed the Child Care Law Review Group to consider 'options for change and improvement in child care law which would simplify and improve arrangements for protecting children at risk and caring for children and families in need' (Scottish Office, 1991). The child care law review found that existing law was 'fundamentally sound and met the main needs of children and their families.' The review saw no need for wholesale change but made 95 recommendations designed to clarify and define inter-agency co-operation and to ensure the social needs of, and pressures on, children and their families were met.

The smooth path of child care policy revision, however, was shaken by a series of scandals, inquiries and reports in the 1990s. In child protection, the removal of children from their homes in Orkney became the subject of a major scandal and Lord Clyde's inquiry report (House of Commons, 1992). In residential care, scandals from England underlined the needs for change identified in the report produced by the Scottish

Office's Social Work Inspectorate, *Another Kind of Home* (1992)—the Skinner Report—and the report by the Convention of Scottish Local Authorities et al, *Caring for the Future* (1992). The children's reporter's system was reviewed in 1992, while the child care policy in Fife was subjected to an inquiry by Sheriff Kearney (House of Commons, 1992). Meanwhile, other reviews of law affecting children were taking place. The Scottish Law Commission published a report in 1992, and a consultation paper, *The Future of Adoption Law in Scotland,* was issued the following year (Social Work Services Group, 1993).

Five years after the Child Care Law Review was established, a white paper, *Scotland's Children* (Cm 2286, 1993), was published. Despite the long wait—or perhaps because of it—the white paper was seen by some as disappointingly modest and lacking specific details about what could be expected from children's legislation. Legislation was finally enacted in the Children (Scotland) Act, 1995 which largely replaced the 1968 act as far as child care services are concerned. The legislation brings together aspects of private, child care and adoption law that affects children. Much of the Scottish Law Commission's report was incorporated, including a fundamental conceptual shift from parental rights to parental responsibilities.

The act is being implemented within the new local government structure (see Chapter 1). The same authority which provides social work and education services is now also responsible for housing and many hope that this will aid inter-agency co-operation between these services. Most new authorities will be smaller and hence have smaller social work and education budgets than their predecessors. This has raised concerns for specialist services reliant on economies of scale. Joint working is permitted through joint committees or joint boards, although some authorities may wish to preserve their autonomy and not voluntarily join in such partnerships. While joint boards or committees may make the lines of democratic accountability weaker, such arrangements provide a possibility of ensuring that specialist services can be maintained.

Social work and education committees, and directors of education and social work, are no longer legally required. These changes have paved the way for consolidated housing and social work departments, which at least three new authorities (Clackmannanshire, East Lothian and Stirling) have set up. They may herald improved inter-professional co-operation or, on the other hand, they may undermine the social work services and erase clear lines of democratic accountability.

THE CHILDREN'S HEARINGS SYSTEM

Three key principles are embodied in the children's hearings system. First, the 'best interests of the child' is the sole criterion for decision-making; other considerations, such as retribution and deterrence, are excluded. A recent exception, however, has been introduced: when the public is judged 'at risk of serious harm', a child's welfare is no longer the paramount consideration. Second, the child and family participate fully in the discussion and, as far as possible, the decision-making. Particular attention is now given to enabling children themselves to express their views. There is also a new emphasis on the privacy of the proceedings and the importance of keeping the numbers of people attending to a minimum. Third, the principle of lay involvement is of major importance. This acknowledges that communities have a part to play in managing their own disturbances, and cuts across the widespread tendency to assume that all problems must be handled by professional specialists.

Structure and Operation of the Children's Hearings System

Children's Panels: At the heart of the children's hearings system is the work of nearly 1,700 members of children's panels. The panels are composed of lay people who are appointed by the Secretary of State from a list of applicants nominated for an area. The nominations are made by the children's panel advisory committee, a local authority committee created for the main purpose of recruiting and selecting panel members. Panel members are selected on the basis of procedures intended to identify such desirable personal attributes as open-mindedness, ability to communicate and freedom from extreme degrees of permissiveness or punitiveness, and also to ensure a reasonably balanced representation of age-groups, the sexes and broad socio-economic categories. Panels vary in size from 11 in Shetland to nearly 500 in Glasgow.

Since the inception of the system, considerable importance has been attached to the training of panel members: all are required to attend a period of part-time training before commencing service and are encouraged to undergo regular in-service training thereafter.

Three members (including at least one female and one male) of a children's panel constitute a children's hearing. The hearing is responsible for making decisions concerning children who in earlier times would be—or, in most other countries, are now—dealt with by juvenile courts or similar bodies. Cases reach children's hearings through the reporter to the children's panel, the gatekeeper to the hearings system.

The Principal Reporter: Since the abolition of the regional councils, the reporters' service is administered from a central office, the Scottish Children's Reporter Administration, where the Principal Reporter is based. Although no official requirements have so far been laid down, the 117 reporters' posts are filled largely by personnel with legal or social work backgrounds.

A child may be referred to his or her area reporter by any agency or any individual who believes that the child may be in need of compulsory measures of supervision. In practice, referrals come from the police and procurators fiscal (77 per cent), from education departments (ten per cent) and social work departments (ten per cent), and also from other sources such as voluntary bodies and private individuals.

After investigating the referral by inviting reports from the social work services, from the child's school or from other specialist services, the reporter can decide:

- to take no further action;

- to ask the social work department to advise, guide and assist the child and family on a voluntary basis;

- or to bring the child before a children's hearing if (i) he or she is satisfied that there is sufficient evidence of at least one ground for referral, and (ii) it appears to the reporter that the child is in need of compulsory measures of supervision.

Reporters refer only one-third of all referrals they receive to a children's hearing.

There are 12 official 'grounds of referral' to a children's hearing. These can be encapsulated into four main types: if the child is alleged to have committed an offence; if the child has been truanting from school; if the child needs 'care and protection', for reasons such as parental neglect, substance abuse, falling into 'bad associations' or risk of harm in a household; or if the child is 'out of control' of the parent, or whomever is looking after the child. A child can be referred to protect others' interests, under certain circumstances when the local authority is 'looking after' them.

Local Authorities: Social work departments provide background reports on children and undertake the supervision of those judged by the hearings to be in need of 'compulsory measures of supervision'. Some children are also supervised on a voluntary basis. Reporters send about ten per cent of all children referred to them to the social work department for voluntary supervision.

Jurisdiction and Powers of Hearings: Jurisdiction is generally limited to children under 16 years. Young people between 16 and 18 who are already subject to a supervision requirement imposed by a hearing may be dealt with by a hearing in the event of a further referral. The Lord Advocate retains the power to direct the prosecution of children of any age in serious cases. These cases are taken in the sheriff court or High Court and generally involve offences against the person except where a court hearing is technically necessary for proof (as in some cases where offences have been committed jointly with adults). At present fewer than 1,000 children are proceeded against in the adult court annually; this represents a considerable fall since the early 1970s when three times that number appeared in court each year. (Martin *et al*,1981)

The chairman has the duty to state the grounds of referral at the beginning of the hearing and to ensure the child and parents understand them. The hearing is not competent to consider questions of guilt or innocence and, if the grounds of referral are denied or not understood, the case cannot be discussed further. Then the hearing can decide either to dismiss the case or to send it to the sheriff court for proof; in practice the latter option is the one generally adopted. The reporter also has authority to abandon the referral at this stage.

In 1993 some 45 per cent of care and protection cases and six per cent of offence cases went to the sheriff court to establish the grounds of referral. The majority of these cases were based on the child's inability to understand the grounds and the remainder arose from the denial of the grounds of referral. If the sheriff finds the grounds established, the case returns to a hearing for consideration. In general, sheriffs have confirmed the grounds for referral in nearly all those cases where the child has failed to understand but, where grounds have been denied, sheriffs have found these established in rather more than half the cases. Under the 1995 act, the child or parents can apply for a review of the sheriff's decision. The applicant must have new material evidence that is likely to be credible and reliable, which for specific reasons could not be used at the original application for proof.

Also under the 1995 act, in almost all proceedings related to children's hearings or child protection, every hearing or sheriff must now consider whether it is necessary to appoint a 'safeguarder' who has the specific mandate to safeguard and promote the interests of the child. Formerly this power was restricted to those cases where there was a conflict of interest between the child and parents but it was used in fewer than one per cent of cases (Lockyer, 1994).

Before reaching a decision, the hearing considers details related to the grounds for referral and reports obtained from the social work department and other sources. After discussion with the family, the hearing must decide on the course of action that is in the best interests of the child. The decisions open to a hearing are:

- to discharge the referral (that is, the child goes home and no further action is taken);
- to make a supervision requirement with or without residential or other conditions; or,
- in prescribed circumstances, to place a child in secure accommodation.

The child or parents may appeal to the sheriff against the decision of a hearing. Under the 1995 act, a sheriff has a range of choices: not only to remit the case back to the hearing for reconsideration or discharging the case, but also to substitute his or her own disposal for that of the children's hearing. An appeal can also be made from the sheriff to the sheriff principal or to the Court of Session on a point of law or irregularity.

It is standard practice for all supervision requirements to be reviewed routinely within a year. In addition, a review may be arranged at the request of the children's hearing which made the supervision requirement, or on the recommendation of a local authority. A child or parent may also ask for a review after a period of three months from the date of making a requirement.

Statistical Patterns: Although the children's hearings system has since its inception made provision for the referral of children on a variety of grounds other than delinquency, the intake of cases has in each year been numerically dominated by offenders. During recent years, however, there have been significant shifts in the scale and distribution of referrals. Referrals on offence grounds, after rising steadily for the first five years of the system's operation, have since declined somewhat more steeply. On the other hand, neglect, ill treatment and risk of abuse have appeared more frequently as grounds of referral in each successive year, rising from 600 in 1972, to 1,700 in 1980, and dramatically increasing to 13,535 in 1993. This trend no doubt reflects an increasing public and professional awareness of the problems of child abuse.

Research Findings

Since its inception, the children's hearings system has given rise to extensive debate in Scotland and at the same time has aroused sympathetic interest on an international scale (Fox, 1991). During the first decade, discussion of principles and practice was largely based on tentative knowledge gained by experience. Thereafter, information derived from systematic research contributed an increased understanding of how the system operates and a framework of empirical findings within which the case for developments in policy, practice and training could be argued. (For further discussion, see Lockyer, 1992 and 1994; Martin *et al*,1981).

A major aspect of the debate has been whether the welfare-based children's hearing system adequately meets justice standards. Research has revealed that a significant proportion of hearings fall short of the standard of legal procedures laid down in the 1968 act and the Hearing Rules, which is by no means exacting. But research evidence shows also that hearings are capable of maintaining the rights of children to know the case against them, to deny the grounds and to participate in the proceedings. Indeed those hearings that adhere to the rules of procedure are very often the most successful in achieving a high level of family participation (Martin *et al*, 1981).

Full involvement of children and parents in the proceedings of the hearing is an important goal of the system (Lockyer 1994; Martin *et al*, 1981). Research findings show clearly that a notable measure of success is achieved in involving family members in the hearing discussion. Most young people feel able to communicate their views although some feel excluded and alienated (Freeman *et al*, 1996). Children and parents in general respond very favourably, and see the panel members as genuinely interested in what they have to say, as trying to help them and as treating them with courtesy and respect (Erickson, 1982). However, for the most part, this discussion is contained within limits that exclude highly emotive areas. Anxious to avoid what they see as stressful and potentially damaging confrontation with parents, panel members shift rapidly from references in reports about domestic problems of a serious nature, to the safer topics of school attendance and leisure pursuits (Martin *et al*, 1981).

Future Prospects

It is now a quarter of a century since the hearings system was introduced and during this time a good deal has been achieved. Despite the spate of criticism in its early years, the system has acquired a significant national and international reputation, and has developed a strength of loyalty among those who are responsible for making it work. That the Scottish system should have been allowed to remain virtually unaltered while juvenile justice in England and Wales was being steered in a more punitive direction is evidence of the effectiveness of key participants in the shaping of public policy. In the next few years, the hearings system may well encounter new challenges as it confronts the changes in legislation, the reform of local government, a new administrative structure for the reporters' service and greater involvement with the courts.

CHILD WITNESSES IN CRIMINAL PROCEEDINGS

The prosecution of children in Scotland for all but the most serious of offences has virtually disappeared, as a consequence of the introduction of the hearings system. The protection of children from abuse is largely accomplished by establishing the abuse within the hearings system rather than prosecuting the alleged offender. Nevertheless, prosecutions of abusing adults, especially where the abuse is serious, is still necessary from time to time.

Concern about duplication of inquiries organised by the police and social workers has meant that joint investigations have become normal. Indeed, such importance is placed on gaining evidence in order to prove abuse in court that it may be difficult to offer help to the child for fear of appearing to 'distort' his or her evidence. If the case does go to court, children—who are very often key witnesses in these cases—may be required to speak about distressing and embarrassing events not only in front of a judge and lawyers but also in the presence of the accused. As a result of widespread concern that some children might be harmed by this experience, the law has recently developed so as to facilitate the giving of evidence by children, whilst at the same time ensuring that there is no prejudice to the rights of the alleged offender to a fair trial.

Evidence from Children

The most radical measure introduced to protect children in the court room is the use of a live closed circuit television link. Since 1991, in certain circumstances, a child under the age of 16 years is permitted to give evidence from a room adjacent to the courtroom by means of a television link. After considering the findings of a two-year monitoring and evaluation, the government decided to extend the provision to every sheriffdom in Scotland (Murray, 1995).

Other measures introduced more recently have been the use of screens in court to shield the child from the accused, and the video recording of evidence in advance in lieu of the child appearing at all. This last provision is different from the provision in England and Wales where the child's video-recorded interview is admissible at trial in place of the child's examination in chief, but the child is still required to appear for cross-examination.

Research in both Scotland and England has concluded that, while these reforms are useful tools for enabling children to give evidence less stressfully, they do nothing to shorten the delays in coming to court and to improve the standard of legal questioning, nor to make the courts a more sensitive environment for children (Cashmore and Haas, 1992; Davies and Noon, 1991).

CHILD PROTECTION

Cases of child abuse and neglect have come increasingly to dominate the work of both the hearings system and social work services. The definition of abuse is a complex matter, but it is clear that what constitutes abuse varies from place to place and time to time (Saraga, 1993). Severe beatings were once thought acceptable, but are no longer so. Sexual abuse was thought to be rare as recently as the early 1980s, but is now known to be quite common. Disagreements remain about what counts as sexual abuse and how to measure its incidence. In the main, official agencies other than the police only become involved when a child is abused by a family or household member. It is generally assumed that parents will act to protect and comfort children in relation to abuse by strangers, although schools and others have important educational and surveillance roles.

Official categorisations of child abuse change from time to time, but the main types are as follows:

- *Neglect*: for example, not feeding a child properly, leaving young children unattended, failure to ensure proper medical care.

- *Physical abuse*: causing physical injury to a child.

- *Sexual abuse*: engaging children in sexual activities.

- *Emotional abuse*: damaging a child's emotional development or sense of self-worth.

This last category is the most recent and ill-defined.

Actions are generally considered abusive only when they are intentional. Thus, physical abuse is sometimes referred to as 'non-accidental injury'. However, it can be argued that hitting a child in anger is impulsive, whilst neglect may sometimes result as much from lack of understanding of children's needs as deliberate ill-will. Moreover, much evidence connects physical abuse and neglect with poverty, stress, depression, drug and alcohol misuse (Corby, 1993). This is not the case for child sexual abuse, where the most significant factor is that the great majority of abusers are men (Gillham, 1991).

The triangular relationship between children, parents and state is particularly problematic in the area of child abuse. It has been acknowledged for centuries that the state has a quasi-parental duty to safeguard children's welfare *(parens patriae)*. At the same time, strong norms of parental responsibility and family privacy mean that the state should not interfere in family life unless there are significant grounds for doing so. An inherent tension exists between these two principles. It is very difficult for professionals representing the state to monitor children's daily lives in order to detect ill-treatment or to respond when situations of harm or risk are identified, without being perceived by individual families or the public at large as intrusive. Yet children have a right to be protected from such harm. By turns, there have been major criticisms of both insufficient and excessive action to protect children (see below).

During the late 1980s, the term 'child protection' gained currency to describe actions by official agencies to prevent, respond to or alleviate child abuse. Even more specifically, child protection has come to denote the investigation processes in relation to suspected child abuse. Suspected abuse should be reported to local authorities, who have a duty to cause enquiries to be made and, if necessary, inform the children's reporter. In turn, the reporter will investigate whether there are sufficient grounds to refer the matter to a children's hearing for consideration and determination. Referrals on child abuse grounds mostly come via front-line professionals like teachers, health visitors and GPs or from relatives, friends and neighbours (Birchall and Hallett, 1995; Waterhouse and Carnie, 1989). Unlike the United States and some other European countries, there is no legal duty for professionals to report suspected abuse, but local authority workers and the police are obliged to do so.

In an emergency, an order can be sought from a sheriff without recourse to the hearings. A sheriff may make three types of order:

- *Child Assessment Order:* enables medical and other assessments to be made when it is suspected that a child is suffering or is likely to suffer harm, but it is not possible to establish this for sure. This applies in circumstances when parents or carers deny access, or refuse to take a child to a doctor for examination.

• *Child Protection Order*: provides for a child to stay in or be taken to a 'place of safety', which is normally a hospital, residential establishment or foster home. It covers situations when it is believed that a child has been, or is at risk of being, 'significantly harmed'.

• *Exclusion Order*: excludes an alleged abuser from the child's family home, if necessary for the protection of the child and a better safeguard of the child's welfare than removing the child.

An exclusion order means that a child can be protected from the threat of abuse without having to leave home and suffer the further distress of separation from familiar people and surroundings. This represented a major innovation of the Children (Scotland) Act, 1995 and was derived from a similar provision to protect women from violent partners.

Inquiries in both England and Scotland have consistently highlighted the importance and difficulty of different agencies and professions collaborating effectively when abuse is suspected (Hallett and Birchall, 1992). As a result, several mechanisms have been set up to improve co-ordination. Child Protection Committees consist of senior members of the key agencies who meet to plan overall strategies in their particular areas. For dealing with particular cases, two key mechanism are the Case Conference and Child Protection Register.

Case conferences are multi-disciplinary meetings of the professionals involved, with the family. They meet shortly after suspected abuse is revealed and thereafter as needed. Their purpose is to share information, establish the degree of risk or harm and co-ordinate plans for further action. For a long time, parents and children were excluded from Case Conferences, but now they often are involved (Directors of Social Work in Scotland, 1992).

Registers were set up to improve identification and information sharing. They are held by local authorities and contain the names of children deemed to have been abused and details of agencies involved. The decision to register a child or not is normally made at an initial case conference. Likewise de-registration should follow a case conference. The categories of registration for Strathclyde Region in mid-1994 were: physical injury 48 per cent; physical neglect 25 per cent; sexual abuse 24 per cent; and emotional abuse three per cent (Strathclyde Social Work Department, 1995).

Referrals of physical abuse and neglect involve similar proportions of boys and girls, but, in relation to sexual abuse, girls outnumber boys considerably (Galbraith, 1994). Referrals, 'conferencing' and registration have differed considerably by localities (Directors of Social Work in Scotland, 1992). Generally rates of registration per thousand children are higher in urban areas. A register of abusers is now being proposed to enable perpetrators to be traced and, it is hoped, deterred from further abuse.

As already indicated, many criticisms have been levelled against agencies and individuals dealing with children at risk. These have led to modifications in the law and procedures, with central government providing close prescriptions of what to do. During the 1980s, a series of well-publicised inquiries suggested that professionals were too reluctant to intervene when there were strong indications of risk of injury or death for a child. As a result, governmental and legal pressure reinforced a tendency towards 'child rescue', that is, removing children from home to make sure they were safe. Cases of child sexual abuse were also increasingly discovered and a similar approach was adopted. This was witnessed in the Cleveland affair in England, when in a short space of time over 100 children were taken into care because of suspected sexual abuse. The subsequent inquiry (Cm 412, 1988) indicated that a proportion of the children had indeed been seriously abused, but also argued that the removals had been precipitate and not always necessary. Moreover, children were sometimes treated not as people but as 'objects of concern'. Yet very similar action was taken with respect to nine children in Orkney just a few years later. The Clyde report (House of Commons, 1993) on the Orkney case reiterated many of the lessons of Cleveland, including the seemingly obvious point that children's wishes and feelings should be carefully considered. Lord Clyde also recommended greater involvement of sheriffs in decision-making and earlier rights of appeal for parents.

Research has shown how uncomfortable most innocent family members find investigations and their aftermath. Children who have been sexually abused are commonly distressed by multiple interviews and medical examinations or negative comments from peers and adults (Roberts *et al,* 1993). Despite this, few regret having revealed their abuse. Pitcairn and Waterhouse (1993) found parents feared their children would be removed from them and often felt their own concerns were misunderstood.

Voluntary agencies do not usually play a part in child abuse investigations, unlike in England where a number of local authorities have contracted out this task to the National Society for the Prevention of Cruelty to Children. The Royal Scottish Society for the Prevention of Cruelty to Children (now renamed Children 1st) has largely withdrawn from this kind of work, and it now concentrates on helping sufferers of abuse and their families. A valuable and distinctive role is played by ChildLine Scotland, which offers a confidential 24-hours telephone contact for any child; in 1994 it handled 500 calls a day. Many of the children had multiple concerns, but the most frequently reported problems were abuse and bullying.

Children are affected not only by aggression towards themselves, but violence by men to their mothers. Not uncommonly, the two go together and even when the children themselves are not physically harmed they experience distress in witnessing the violence and insecurity about its consequences (NCH Action for Children, 1994; Saunders *et al*, 1995). Women's Aid in Scotland accommodated nearly 3,000 women and over 4,000 children in 1994.

FAMILY SUPPORT

The Providers

Local authorities have been able to assist families in kind or in cash since 1963, and this power was strengthened in the 1968 act. Local authorities provide a number of non-financial services to families, such as domestic help or counselling. For the most part, cash assistance has been used to help families in crisis buy food in an emergency or to pay off debts to avoid eviction or ensure heat, light or cooking (Davidson, 1993; Fowles, 1988).

Voluntary organisations provide a wide range of specialist services for children in a variety of circumstances, including those with disabilities, those who have been sexually abused, persistent offenders and the homeless. Services are also provided for families. A number of projects seek to empower people to tackle issues such as inadequate employment opportunities and racism. Many of them benefit from collaboration between local authorities and voluntary organisations.

Besides their own fund-raising, voluntary organisations may obtain grants, loans or assistance with premises and equipment from central and local government, as well as the European Union. Some voluntary bodies rely mainly on unpaid volunteers—for example, certain schemes enable experienced parents to befriend families who would like support and assistance (for instance, Homestart)—while others run fully funded and professionally staffed services.

Early Years Services

Few areas exemplify welfare pluralism as well as early years services. Agencies in both the private and voluntary sector are key providers of early years services, as well as statutory agencies. In the past, there have been three main types of provision:

- nursery schools and classes run by education departments;
- voluntary, private and self-help playgroups; and
- day nurseries, run by social work departments, voluntary agencies, employers or private individuals.

Strathclyde Region was unusual in having unified services between social work and education, under its Pre-Five Unit.

Nursery education is a free, part-time service for children aged three to five. Playgroups typically admit children aged two to five years and parents often contribute time and money. Many playgroups receive grants from local authorities. Originally set up as an alternative to nursery school provision, they have increasingly become seen as a prelude to it (Hill, 1987). Day nurseries admit a wider age range from babyhood onwards and are typically open for a full day. Local authority places are usually free, but may be means-tested. There has always been a shortage of places, which are therefore allocated according to priority systems based on risk and special needs.

Private or voluntary day nurseries must be registered with local authorities and meet defined standards. Childminders are private individuals offering a daytime and after-school care service for working parents. They too should be registered if caring for an unrelated child for more than two hours a day (MacLeod and Giltinan, 1992). Some are supported financially by local authorities, usually to assist families with parenting difficulties.

Recent years have seen the development of multi-purpose children's centres and family centres. Holman (1988) observed that there are three main types:

- *client-focused*: which provide counselling, advice and support, mainly to parents with identified difficulties;
- *neighbourhood-focused*: which offer a range of groups and classes open to anyone from the local area; and
- *community development-oriented*: which seek to engage and empower local people, so that they help develop and run their own services.

Mothers are usually more involved than fathers and many are lone parents. Mothers value the social opportunities and respite provided by the centres, but some centres also stress the importance of enhancing women's educational and employment potential (Long, 1995a; Wilkinson and Stephen, 1994).

Within resource constraints, local authorities aim to provide accessible de-stigmatised services that involve parents and promote equal opportunities (for example, Central Regional Council, 1993), but there are limitations. Publicly funded childcare services are provided for only two per cent of children under three, and 35-40 per cent of children from three to five years in Scotland (Tisdall with Donaghie, 1995). Only Portugal and other parts of the UK have such low rates of publicly funded childcare in the European Union. Most of the services for pre-school children are part-time. Thus, while perhaps meeting some of the social and educational needs of children, such services do not necessarily help parents in balancing full-time work and family responsibilities. Availability of provision is geographically uneven so that, for example, rural communities tend particularly to be under-provided (Cohen, 1995).

The Conservative government introduced nursery vouchers for four year-olds in 1997, valued at some £1,100. But Labour opposed the scheme and the new government is ending it after the first year. In 1997-98, however, parents could exchange vouchers for places in establishments of their choice, whether an education authority nursery school or class, a private nursery, or a playgroup. If they provided appropriate education, vouchers could also be used for day nurseries (Scottish Office Education Department, 1995). Parents who already pay for childcare would have been better off, but the value of vouchers was barely enough to allow low-income families access to private childcare. Concerns were also raised about the quality of some provision and loss of revenue to local authorities where vouchers were used in the private sector (Long, 1995b). The government is replacing vouchers with extended local authority provision from 1998.

Local authorities are required to undertake an inter-agency review of early years services for children under eight. The first reviews were submitted by local authorities in 1992. While the review process encouraged inter-agency working, analysis of the reviews suggested that working relationships between statutory, voluntary and private sectors were not yet based on real equality. Consultation with parents, children and local councillors was particularly lacking and difficult. Information about special interest groups (such as children with special needs, from ethnic minorities, from lone parent families, or living in rural communities) was largely absent (Martin, 1994).

Services for Children with Special Needs or Disabilities

Services for children with special needs or disabilities has also been an area where voluntary organisations have been heavily involved, providing a range of support groups, information, and practical help. A number of agencies provide expert advice and foster mutual assistance in relation to specific disabilities (for example, Epilepsy Association of Scotland; ENABLE, formerly Society for the Mentally Handicapped). The larger, more general, child-care organisations run special centres and respite services for a more diverse clientele.

Social work departments offer a range of services for children, such as respite services, occupational therapists' advice, aids and adaptations, and home helps. Children with special needs are specifically mentioned in education legislation and social work personnel are typically involved in the formal process of establishing a Record of Special Educational Needs. Once a recorded young person reaches school leaving age, a transfer is required between education and social work through a process called the Future Needs Assessment. Queries have been raised, however, about whether social work involvement and knowledge is adequate to meet the needs for young people leaving full-time education (Hubbard, 1992).

The Children (Scotland) Act, 1995 introduced specific duties for local authorities towards children with disabilities for the first time in mainstream Scottish child care legislation. The act also went further than its counterparts in the rest of the UK, by also including children *affected* by disabilities (thus including siblings of disabled children or children of disabled parents). The duties include:

- minimising the effect on the child of a disability;

- giving children affected by a disability an opportunity to lead lives which 'are as normal as possible';

- providing an assessment of the child in order to decide on services; and

- providing an assessment of the carer's ability to care for such a child.

The 1994 Carers National Association Survey showed that 91 per cent wanted a legal right to respite services. At present, provision is extremely patchy across Scotland and has been concentrated in the larger (former) regions. Despite extensive attempts made in parliament, the provision of respite services was not specified in the legislation. Reference to respite services, however, will have to be included in local authority children's service plans.

Older Children and Young People

Young people may receive social work services at home through children's hearing supervision orders or on a voluntary basis. This can take the form of individual or family counselling. Some social work offices make use of volunteer befrienders to assist young people who lack close social relationships or are believed to require a positive role model (Triseliotis *et al*, 1995).

In many local authorities, group work is considered most appropriate for this age range, and it may be referred to as Intermediate Treatment or Intensive IT. Usually IT offers a combination of activities, discussions and structured exercises, and also can involve individual and family work. Aims include social education, development of skills and self-esteem, and diversion of motivation and energy from anti-social activities. Although a children's hearing may make attendance at an IT programme a compulsory condition of a supervision requirement, usually the young person attends on a voluntary basis. For youngsters at serious risk of removal from home, there are also day care services, which combine education, group work and counselling. Besides local authorities, voluntary organisations like Barnardos and the Aberlour Child Care Trust also run IT and alternatives to custody projects.

After the age of 16, few young people who offend are dealt with by the children's hearings system. Most go to court, but may still have considerable involvement with social work departments. For example, social workers supervise both probation and community service orders. In recent years, central government strengthened attention to this area of work by 100 per cent funding of work with adult offenders and by introducing National Standards and Objectives in 1991.

Certain regions in Scotland established youth strategies, primarily to encourage systematic co-ordination between social work, education and other agencies to tackle school-based or offending problems (Kendrick, 1995b). Like family centres, these strategies may be case-oriented, have a community development approach or combine both.

'Children in Need'

The legislative framework behind these family support services was dramatically changed by of the Children (Scotland) Act, 1995. The local authorities' previous 'general welfare duty' was replaced with a duty to safeguard and promote only the welfare of 'children in need'. The government saw categorisation of children in this way as necessary to target resources and avoid unnecessary intervention (House of Commons, 1995). According to the act, a child is 'in need' when:

- the child is unlikely to achieve or maintain, or to have the opportunity of achieving or maintaining, a reasonable standard of health and development unless services are provided;
- the child's health or development is likely significantly to be impaired, or further impaired, unless such services are provided;
- the child is disabled; or
- the child is affected adversely by the disability of another family member.

This unexpected import from the Children Act, 1989 was firmly opposed by Scottish children's agencies as the legislation went through parliament, because of concern about the individualisation of the category 'children in need', which could work against the kinds of open-access family and youth centres described above that assist 'communities in need'.

The experience in England and Wales of the category 'children in need' has not been positive, in part owing to lack of resources, but also because the category has proved to be, at the same time, both too broad to be defined consistently and too narrow, so that it marginalises and stigmatises social services (Cm 2144, 1993; Cm 2584). Research in England has also indicated that 'children in need' has been too closely translated to mean only 'children at risk' and, in fact, the 'children at risk' register is being used as means to gain access to services. Consequently, many families whose children are not registered receive no services despite having similar needs to those who are registered and do receive services (Department of Health, 1995).

SERVICES FOR CHILDREN AWAY FROM HOME

For many years, children placed away from home under local authority auspices were described as 'in care'. For some, this description has had stigmatising connotations. The Children (Scotland) Act, 1995 introduced new legal terminology that brought Scotland into line with England and Wales. Children are no longer 'in care', but are 'looked after' by a local authority. The change intends to emphasise that local authorities are looking after the children in partnership with parents, as much as possible, rather than taking over from parents. It remains to be seen whether the new terminology does reflect or encourage new attitudes.

Children can be placed away from home ('accommodated') at their parents' request or their own request. Children may be placed away from home by a supervision requirement from a children's hearing. Four-fifths of the latter group are in their teens, whereas voluntary admissions are more evenly spread across the age range.

Children nowadays are rarely orphaned with no family to look after them. They are therefore more likely to be 'looked after' because of the temporary or permanent inability or unwillingness of parents and other family members to care for them, or after having broken the law. Thus the main precipitating factors are parental illness, abuse or neglect, family conflict, offending and school non-attendance. The great majority of children looked after away from home come from families on very low incomes living in areas with high scores on indicators of multiple disadvantage (Freeman and Montgomery, 1988). Poor families experience high stresses and are also more subject to contact and 'surveillance' by professionals.

The numbers of children 'in care' at any one time fell steadily during the 1980s, following a period of substantial increase in the previous 30 years from some 10,000 in 1980 to 3,500 in 1991. This decline well exceeds what would be expected from the decline in the birth rate and is attributable, in part, to policies and services that have emphasised supporting children at home and helping those away to return home quickly or, if need be, to be adopted.

Residential Care

Residential care consists mainly of children's homes (now often referred to as residential units) and residential schools. The latter, as the name implies, combine both care and educational functions on the same premises. Secure accommodation is provided for young people who are considered a danger to themselves or others, usually on account of serious offending. Safe refuges and 'crash pads' offer short periods of respite and support for young people experiencing a family crisis (Swanson, 1988).

The number living in different types of establishment in 1991 was some 2,300, made up as follows:

Local authority homes or units	1087
Residential schools	598
Voluntary organisations' homes	147
Other	481

The total represents a drop from over 6,000 in 1976. The large institutions which existed up to the mid-twentieth century are now largely a thing of the past, but most residents still live in homes with nine or more children, and about a third in units of 26 or more. There are small numbers of young people, mostly males, in prisons and other secure facilities.

Residential care has largely become a service for young people in their teens. At one time there were residential nurseries for pre-school children and family group homes for primary aged children, but it has become the prevailing view that younger children away from home should normally be looked after in family settings. In 1994, less than 10 per cent of children living in residential homes and schools were aged under eleven.

Boys are over-represented in residential care (unlike foster care). Most young people in residential care have educational difficulties and serious emotional or behavioural problems. Many do not attend mainstream schools, some as a result of exclusion (Kendrick, 1995a; Triseliotis *et al*, 1995).

During the 1970s and 1980s, the residential sector was something of a backwater, seen as a last resort when all efforts had been made to keep children in their own families or to place them in alternative families. Most staff were untrained, poorly paid and perceived to have low status. Ironically it took a series of scandals involving extreme instances of poor care in residential establishments to provoke a fresh look at their role, with an emphasis on the positive functions (Berridge, 1996). In Scotland, an investigation was initiated which led to the Skinner report (Social Work Services Inspectorate, 1992). This proved very influential, and its proposals for action received government backing and prompted additional funding.

The number of staff working in residential care has grown in recent years, in spite of the reduced numbers of children, so staff-resident ratios have increased. Children experience a high turnover of people they are living with, because not only do many residents move in and out, but one in ten staff leave each year. In 1993 about 90 per cent of residential staff had no professional qualification. Following recommendations by the Skinner Report and the findings of the CoSLA/trade union report on residential care staffing, the government has provided additional funding for training and funded the Centre for Residential Child Care at the University of Strathclyde.

Fostering

Foster care involves children being looked after in a family by people other than their parents. This may be arranged on a 'voluntary' basis with parental agreement, or compulsorily (for example, as a result of a supervision requirement from a children's hearing). The people looking after foster children were, until recently, called 'foster parents' but now are usually called 'foster carers' in recognition that their role is not to imitate or usurp that of the original parents. Most often, foster carers and children do not know each other before placement, apart perhaps from brief introductions. In some circumstances, however, relatives, friends and neighbours become foster carers. About one in ten children fostered in Strathclyde in 1993 were placed with relatives (Strathclyde Social Work Department, 1993).

The great majority of foster carers are recruited and supported by local authorities, which are responsible for most children who are fostered. The only voluntary agency involved is Barnardos, which has a special scheme for children who are difficult to place. Parents can pay another couple or individual to look after their child, without involving an agency at all. This is known as private fostering and is subject to regulation and local authority supervision.

Similar numbers of children are in public foster care as are in residential care (about 2,400 in 1991), but the age distribution is quite different: foster children are spread quite evenly across all age bands, while residential care tends to have older children. Although fewer children are now fostered than 20 years ago, the *proportion* placed in foster care is higher than it used to be, as a result of the much reduced usage of residential establishments for younger children.

Particularly over the last 20 years, the perceived role of foster carers has been transformed, with accompanying organisational changes in fostering services. Professionalisation and specialisation are two key elements in this process. Fostering is increasingly seen as a skilled task for which training, support and remuneration are both needed and offered. Often foster carers are expected to work with a child's family, giving advice and help to parents in particular. They often have to deal with parents' complex or stressful problems (for example, domestic violence or alcoholism). The children, too, often have major emotional or behavioural difficulties or health problems, which can place significant demands on foster carers' time, skills and patience well beyond those required for daily care of the child.

Whereas formerly foster carers might take any child in need of a home, nowadays most specialise according to the nature of the child and family or the expected duration of placement. Many different labels are used, but distinctions are usually made between:

• *emergency fostering:* admissions at short notice for brief periods;

• *short-to-medium term fostering:* care of a child for days, or months up to about two years with the expectation of the child returning home;

• *long-term or permanent fostering:* looking after a child for most of all of the rest of his or her childhood; and

• *professional or specialist fostering:* time-limited placements with planned agreements and specific goals to be achieved, mostly with respect to teenagers or children with disabilities.

Growing difficulties in recruiting foster carers have encouraged more realistic allowances and greater willingness to pay for work done. This recruitment problem can be attributed in part to changing social expectations, since fostering has largely relied on the willingness of women to devote their time to childcare activities. Nowadays, women are more likely to be pursuing paid employment outside the home. In addition, the changed demands of fostering mean that it has become less attractive to those who simply want to look after children, some of whom may be less suited to the task.

The Rights and Views of Children and Young People

At all levels, commitments have been expressed to improve participatory rights. A national organisation, Who Cares? Scotland, represents young people with experience of being 'looked after'. It receives financial support from central and local government, as well as the voluntary sector.

Several regions established Children's Rights Officer posts during the early 1990s. In Lothian, these posts covered education and health services, as well as social work. Most agency policies now include complaints mechanisms and clear entitlements for children to have written information about their rights. Strathclyde Region held a phased consultation with young people in residential units and IT groups, partly to allow them to influence the Regional Child Care Plan (Freeman et al, 1996). These developments, and similar ones concerning representation in the hearings or rights at school and elsewhere, have, however, been piecemeal.

Leaving Care

Most short-term placements end with children returning home. This is often the case with longer placements, too, but some of these last until the child reaches the legal age limit or the upper age for the particular establishment, usually at age 16-17. By then, relationships with their families may have broken down completely or not be viable as a base for the transition to young adulthood. In such cases significant numbers of young people face major problems of homelessness, poverty, unemployment and social isolation (Bannister et al, 1993). Realising this, most authorities have developed preparation programmes and have also sought to provide after-care, but many youngsters still struggle with little support at an age when most of their more advantaged peers are still living at least partially at home. Their difficulties are exacerbated by restricted access to income support and shortage of accommodation for young, single people. Local authorities have a duty to provide after-care for young people who are in care at school leaving age until they are 19 years old. After that, the local authorities have a power to provide such help, until the young person is 21 years old.

Adoption

In adoption, all the legal rights and responsibilities of a child's original parents are transferred to the adopters and legally the child becomes part of the adoptive family. Adoption is regarded as such a fundamental change in the status of a child that it is dealt with by the courts and not children's hearings. Socially, too, it has been customary to view adopted children as fully belonging to the adoptive family, with an expectation there would be no contact at all with the original family.

This 'closed-book' approach, however, is now being questioned. A growing trend in adoption has been towards greater 'openness', that is, some continued communication between adoptive and birth families. Most commonly it involves sharing information between adoptive families and birth parents, especially at the time of placement but also on a continuing basis. Increasingly, adoptive and birth parents (usually mothers) may meet once or twice prior to placement (Paterson with Hill, 1994; Stone, 1994).The number of adoptions has declined dramatically, from 2,268 in 1969, to 1,084 in 1983 and 786 in 1992.

Adoption is commonly thought to involve childless couples providing a home for infants. This still occurs, but adoption has greatly diversified since the 1960s. Most children of unmarried mothers now stay with their birth families. Adoption services have shifted from meeting the needs of adult couples for babies and instead seek permanent substitute homes for children who need them. Previously, it was thought children who were older, or had disabilities or behaviour difficulties were not adoptable, but experience has proved that homes can be found for such children. Higher proportions of children are now over five years old when adopted, some by step-parents or their foster carers, and others from residential or foster care. About half of adoptions in the early 1990s involved step-parents.

At one time, most adoptions were arranged by voluntary agencies. A few of these are still to be found in Glasgow and Edinburgh, but nowadays the majority of adoptions (apart from the special case of step-parent adoptions) are dealt with by local authorities. It is the duty of each authority to provide an adoption service, to arrange placements and to offer counselling and support after placement and for adults. Post-placement services have been developed since the mid-1980s, in recognition of the continuing identity issues for all adoptees and the additional challenges which can occur when children are placed well beyond infancy (McGhee, 1995; Triseliotis, 1988 and 1991).

Adoption agencies have shown greater willingness to place children for adoption instead of keeping them in residential or foster care, if return home seems unlikely or inadvisable (Borland, 1991; O'Hara, 1991). This represents the paternalist strand in the constant tensions over child-parent-state rights discussed in the introduction to this chapter. Adoption allowances were introduced in 1982 to enable people to adopt who otherwise could not afford it or to assist with special costs, usually in relation to physical disability (Hill et al, 1989). There has also been an increased readiness to arrange adoptions even though birth parents objected (Lambert et al, 1990). These trends have been criticised for favouring adopters and punishing birth parents (Ryburn, 1992; Teague, 1989).

CONCLUSION

A wide range of social services for children and their families have been explored in this chapter, ranging from early years services to child protection. Such services have experienced radical changes since their origins in the poor laws and philanthropic organisations, and they continue do so. In the introduction, four approaches and debates were described as key influences on services: rights and the triangular relationship between children-parents-state; 'child rescue' versus prevention; welfare versus justice; and 'welfare pluralism'. Where do Scottish services for children and their families today stand in relation to these influences?

Rights: Children, Parents and the State

For several decades after the second world war, the language of legislation and professionals concerned with children mostly emphasised their welfare and interests. What these might consist of in any particular case were largely determined by adults, albeit seeking to act in favour of children. Over the last few years, the children's rights movement has encouraged a more child-centered approach, with children having rights not only to protection and provision but also participation. In Scotland, considerable progress has been made in recognising children's rights: for example, the establishment of children's rights officers in local authorities; greater involvement in decision-making by children who are 'looked after'; and the legal requirement to consider the views of children in matters affecting them, introduced in the Children (Scotland) Act, 1995.

Although the 1995 act has been held up by the government as implementing the UN Convention on the Rights of the Child, this claim seems somewhat rhetorical. For example, while the act supports the right of children to have their views considered, this right does not apply when courts, children's hearings or local authorities judge the public to be at risk of 'serious harm'. Neither has translating the rhetoric of children's rights into practice been unproblematic. For example, the UN convention requires preservation of a child's identity, and that the child's best interests should be the primary consideration in adoption. The adoption and fostering of children, with particular religious and ethnic backgrounds, by adopters and foster carers who do not share these backgrounds has raised considerable debate. Arguably, adoption and fostering services should seek to have adopters and foster carers from a range of backgrounds, and many services are trying actively to recruit such carers, but too few may be available.

Balances within the triangular relationship between children, parents and the state have changed over the years. Beginning with the 1908 act, children have increasingly been seen as having their own rights, rather than being the 'property' of their parents. Parents now have responsibilities to their children, and rights only in order to fulfil these responsibilities. Parents can now be excluded from children's hearings, recognising that a child may feel unable to speak in their presence. A parent can be excluded from a child's home, as one option in child protection procedures. No longer are children's rights and parents' interests always assumed to be synonymous.

The powers of the state to intervene in families has ebbed and flowed. While the poor laws allowed for intervention in extreme cases, the philanthropic organisations of the Victorian era encouraged considerably more active intervention. Many of the responsibilities of such organisations were eventually taken over by the state, through local authority social work services' duties and powers to protect children, even if that meant removing the children from their parents. The 1980s were a high point for paternalist policies, with a higher emphasis on compulsory placements of children away from home, whereas the 1990s have seen a strengthening of attention to both children's and parents' wishes. Most recently, social work services have been encouraged to have a 'partnership with parents', as exemplified by the intention behind the new terminology of 'looked after'.

Child Rescue Versus Prevention: The scandals around child abuse, and child protection procedures, that erupted in the past few decades have greatly influenced the approach of services to child protection. Considerable resources are now dedicated to the assessments of children who may be 'at risk', and to the inter-agency work required. Crisis protection work is now accused of eating up social work resources, and such work of heavily emphasising assessment of risk rather than providing services, either to prevent re-abuse or to prevent abuse in the first place. The demand to shift the balance further towards prevention has grown stronger. Yet social work services to children and their families are arguably moving further away from preventive work, as the duty to promote the welfare of all children has been replaced by duties toward a specific category, 'children in need'.

Welfare Versus Justice: Considerable public attention has been focused on persistent young offenders; in England and Wales recent legislation and policies have encouraged a harsher, more punitive, approach, something that Scotland has so far largely avoided. Scotland has retained its welfare-based approach to children who offend, as well as children in need of care and protection, through the children's hearing system. Procedurally, however, justice arguments have had more influence in both child protection and children's hearings. For example, appeal procedures to emergency child protection orders have been strengthened in the 1995 act. The new power of a sheriff to alter the disposal of a children's hearing, on appeal, has been justified by the need to apply justice procedures to a welfare decision. This power, however, is seen by many as a possible threat to the welfare model of the children's hearing system.

Welfare Pluralism: Informal networks, philanthropic organisations and private agencies have played an important part in child welfare provision for many years. This plurality was furthered more recently by the promotion of a 'mixed economy of welfare' by the Conservative government of 1979-97. Such pluralism is readily evident in such areas as early years services, where voluntary and private agencies provide a great deal of such services. Local government reform may well further encourage welfare pluralism. Many of the new smaller unitary authorities are unlikely to be able on their own to provide the necessary range of services. Contracting out to voluntary and private organisations is thus a logical choice.

Children's services plans, a new statutory requirement on local authorities, provide one means by which to plan and manage services. Such plans could aid greater transparency of local authorities' intentions not only to voluntary and private agencies, but also to children and their families as well. Used effectively, the plans could also encourage local authorities to work together, perhaps to commission jointly a specialised service requiring economies of scale.

Challenge and Opportunity

Services to children and their families face immense change. The Children (Scotland) Act, 1995 introduced new duties on, and powers for, local authorities. While arguably inconsistent and insufficient, the act underlines certain key principles of children's rights, and, most notably, the right of children to have their views considered. The 1995 act has been implemented under the new local government structures which provide both opportunities and challenges. The smaller size of most councils compared with the regions they replaced may encourage greater co-ordination of services but, on the other hand, lead to increased differences in service provision between areas.

The UN Convention on the Rights of the Child provides a set of standards by which to judge services to children and their families, demonstrating the strengths of core principles that, for the past 25 years, have been at the heart of Scotland's response to vulnerable children and young people: principles such as working with families, listening to children, and the primacy of their welfare. Furthermore, current changes to law and practice provide new opportunities for creating still better services for children. Courts, children's hearings and social work services are, however, only some of the services that can address problems such as child abuse, homelessness of young people, and crime by young people. Arguably, the UN convention requires change not only in the services considered in this chapter, but also in areas such as housing, education, employment and social security. Only then can the full range of children's rights to protection, participation and provision be met.

NOTE ON SOURCES: In addition to references in the text, statistics are derived from Scottish Office, *Statistical Bulletin: Social Work Series*.

6
HOUSING

The need to deal with the deplorable conditions and acute shortages which character-ised housing in Britain was once seen as one of the most important goals of social policy, and it bulked large in party programmes and at general elections. This was particularly true of Scotland where housing conditions were on the whole worse than south of the border. Today, however, most—though not all—households are adequately housed, and housing has slipped down the political agenda. It is difficult to imagine housing as the leading issue in election campaigns which it was as recently as the 1960s. The purpose of this chapter is to examine the objectives of housing policy and how far they have been achieved; and to see how, as some problems have been solved, others have come to the fore. Scottish housing can of course be dealt with only com-paratively briefly in a single chapter, but a recent book, *Housing in Scotland* (Currie and Murie, 1996), covers the topic at much greater length.

Housing policy, like most social policy with the major exception of social secu-rity, is the responsibility of the Scottish Office, and is to some extent distinctive from that in other parts of the UK. But only to some extent: although there are different emphases, the direction of policy is dictated by the party in power at Westminster and it has always been at least broadly similar. Thus owner occupation or council housing have been favoured at different times, slum clearance vigorously promoted and then largely abandoned, and the right to buy (RTB) introduced, to give random examples of a similar approach on both sides of the border. Though owner occupation has differ-ences, for example through the working of the separate Scottish legal system, Scot-tish distinctiveness is on the whole greater in the case of council and other public rented housing where policy is developed in Edinburgh by the Scottish Office Devel-opment Department, albeit within parameters set by London.

Scottish Homes, which was set up in 1989, in addition to its responsibilities for funding and overseeing the operation of housing associations, and managing the re-maining houses it inherited from the Scottish Special Housing Association, has a role in commissioning research and analysing housing needs and problems. Each of the 32 local authorities in Scotland has important housing responsibilities. Scottish councils for many years built and managed large numbers of houses, and some undertook enor-mous slum clearance programmes which swept away a great deal of very inadequate urban housing. But these traditional functions have become much less important: they build very few houses now and their existing stock is being eroded by council house sales and possibly in the future by large-scale transfers to housing associations. But their strategic role in taking a broad view of local housing needs has been emphasised since the 1970s. They have to submit housing plans to the Scottish Office Development Department every four years looking five years ahead at, for example, capital expenditure programmes for council house improvements and improvement grants for the private sector.

Scottish housing was historically marked by two features, its physical inadequacy and a distinctive tenure structure, but both have become very much less pronounced. Scotland long favoured flats, at any rate in towns, and they still constitute nearly two-fifths of the housing stock, twice the proportion in England. Flats tended to be built at high density and they were often small: hence severe overcrowding used to be a characteristic Scottish problem. To some extent housing quality and building type were linked to tenure: inadequate housing was a major factor in the development of a very large council housing sector in the half century after the first world war, whilst owner occupation was slower to replace renting in tenements than in houses south of the border.

THE SCOTTISH HOUSING STOCK

In 1917 the Royal Commission on the Housing of the Industrial Population of Scotland (Cd 8731, 1917) drew attention to the deplorable housing conditions which were widespread, in rural as well as urban areas. Houses were often insanitary, badly built and in a poor state of repair; and many were far too small for the families which lived in them. Nearly a quarter of the population was living at a density of more than three persons per room, and nearly a half at more than two persons per room. (Today less than four per cent live at more than one per room.) The Ballantyne commission stated that urgent replacement and reduction of overcrowding to no more than three persons per room required an increase of 25 per cent in the housing stock. The majority of the commissioners believed that, as commercial enterprise had failed over a long period to provide an adequate supply of decent housing, the state should subsidise council building.

The adequacy of the housing stock has improved enormously over the last 80 years, both in terms of the number of dwellings and their quality. Widespread severe shortages and overcrowding, and lack of basic amenities such as WCs inside the dwelling and bathrooms have been overcome. Nevertheless, problems still exist, in part because of rising expectations. One reason why homelessness, for example, is now a problem is because it has come to be accepted that the state, through local authorities, should provide a safety net for those in difficult housing circumstances, something which is comparatively new. Then there are unpopular and socially deprived council estates which reflect both badly designed developments and the inherent difficulties of managing housing for the most disadvantaged households. Both these problems will be discussed later.

Successive governments since the second world war have had an objective for housing policy which was summed up in one white paper as 'a decent house for every family at a price within their means' (Cmnd 4728, 1971), though between 1979 and 1997 it seemed at times as though more importance was being given to increasing the level of owner occupation. Housing policies such as slum clearance, improvement

TABLE 6.1: *Population, Households and Dwellings in Scotland, 1921-95*

	Population (000s)	Average Household Size	Households (000s)	Dwellings (000s)	Dwellings: Surplus (deficit)[1] (000s)
1921	4,883	4.4	1,099	1,058	(41)
1951	5,096	4.5	1,436	1,375	(61)
1961	5,179	3.3	1,570	1,627	57
1971	5,229	3.1	1,686	1,809	123
1981	5,180	2.8	1,854	1,987	133
1991	5,107	2.5	2,052	2,160	108
1995	5,137	2.4	2,121	2,232	111

Note: 1. Crude surplus or deficit of dwellings compared with number of separate households.

Sources: *Scottish Housing: A Consultative Document*, Cmnd 6852; and Scottish Office, *Statistical Bulletin: Housing Series.*

grants and council house building have, of course, been important but in the final analysis housing standards largely reflect the prosperity of the economy: rising real GDP has been crucial in the achievement of better conditions throughout the twentieth century. Although housing problems still exist—and no doubt always will in some form—a great deal of progress has been made. Even in the 1960s a substantial minority of the population was clearly inadequately housed, but that is much less the case today: the badly housed minority is a lot smaller and its problems are different—for instance a damp council flat in a not very pleasant area rather than a two-roomed tenement flat with no bathroom and a shared WC.

Achieving the objective of a decent home for every family involves both the size and the quality of the housing stock, and these will be discussed next; later some aspects of housing finance and subsidies, which affect affordability, will be examined.

Size of the housing stock

One aspect of adequacy is the number of dwellings (houses and flats) in relation to the size of the population and the number of households. Some data on population, households, their average size and dwellings are given in Table 6.1. While there was only a small increase (about five per cent) in the size of Scotland's population between 1921 and 1995, the number of households (basically defined persons living alone or as a group) almost doubled. As a result average household sizes fell from 4.4 to 2.4 persons. The number of dwellings more than doubled, and as a result instead of a deficit of dwellings a crude surplus emerged in the late 1950s. It can be seen that this surplus has continued at something over 100,000 dwellings.

But this apparent surplus should be treated with caution for a number of reasons.

First, some houses are always empty on a particular day because they have recently been completed or the previous occupants have moved out. Second, the balance of households and dwellings varies from area to area depending on population shifts, which tend to be linked to availability of jobs. Central Clydeside, for example, has continued to lose population whereas more prosperous areas gain it. Furthermore, vacant dwellings are often of poor quality, for instance in unpopular council estates.

The process whereby only slightly more individuals have formed a much larger number of households is the result of social change, greater life expectancy, and increased prosperity. Families are having fewer children, many marriages now end in divorce, and young people are leaving home earlier. There has been a large increase in the elderly population. Finally, individuals have been encouraged by rising incomes (and the availability of housing benefit) to set up or maintain separate households. One manifestation of these trends is the growth in the number of one-person households which now constitute over 30 per cent of the total.

As a result of the reduction in household size (and the building of new houses) there has been the dramatic reduction in the overcrowding mentioned above. Even between the 1981 and 1991 censuses, households living at a density of more than one person per room fell from 14 per cent to under four per cent (OPCS, 1993).

Quality of the Housing Stock

Housing standards have also greatly improved during the last 50 years. Less than a quarter of the existing housing stock was built before the 1920s (since when virtually all new dwellings have had basic amenities) and nearly all have been improved with bathrooms, etc. if these were lacking. Three-fifths of the stock has been built since 1945. In 1951 about half of Scottish households did not have a fixed bath or shower, by 1991 less than one per cent. This enormous change is the result not only of new building, but of slum clearance and improvement. Together with shortages and overcrowding, amenity deficiency dominated housing policy down to the 1960s; now it is an almost insignificant problem.

A different, and in principle more severe, criterion of unsatisfactory housing is failure to meet the statutory tolerable standard (or before 1969 unfitness for human habitation). A dwelling is Below Tolerable Standard (BTS) if it lacks an inside WC or a hot and cold water supply, but amenity deficiency is no longer very significant. The number of BTS dwellings fell steadily until it reached some 50,000 in the early 1990s. This figure was based on estimates made by local authorities which, on the whole, had reasonable knowledge of their older stock; there was an assumption, however, that dwellings built since the 1920s, including council houses, were unlikely to be BTS. In England and Wales central government had undertaken national house condition surveys since the 1960s, and in Scotland some local authorities started doing their own surveys. Glasgow carried out a survey in 1985 which led to the estimated BTS stock being almost quadrupled. Finally, in 1991, Scottish Homes conducted the first Scottish House Condition Survey on behalf of the Scottish Office. The survey was the first national estimate of BTS dwellings derived from a standard methodology. It was estimated that nearly five per cent of the occupied stock or some 95,000 dwellings failed the tolerable standard. The survey was repeated in 1996 when it was estimated that the number of BTS dwellings had fallen by two-thirds, to between one and two per cent of the stock; it can be argued, however, on the basis of local surveys done by some local authorities that the actual reduction has been less than this (Scottish Homes, 1997). In a reversal of the traditional relationship when amenity deficiency was widespread, there are now six times as many BTS dwellings as those lacking basic amenities.

The most striking finding of the 1991 survey was that over one-third of BTS dwellings were in the public rented sector (mainly council houses) where nearly five per cent of the stock was affected. Very few of these dwellings lacked basic amenities; virtually all council houses have had these from the start. Nearly two-thirds of the public sector BTS dwellings failed on the ground of not being substantially free from rising and penetrating damp. The problems of unsatisfactory council housing will be discussed below.

Almost two-fifths of the BTS stock was owner occupied, but the proportion of owner-occupied dwellings which were BTS was below the average for all tenures. Owner occupation is now the largest tenure in Scotland and it still contains some unimproved older houses and flats and rural cottages which were once privately rented. Over 20 per cent of BTS dwellings were privately rented and these constituted as many as one in six of what is a very small and largely moribund tenure where there had been little new building for many years.

There used to be a very heavy concentration of BTS housing in central Clydeside and other major urban areas, but major slum clearance and improvement programmes mean that this is now less marked. Although the majority of the BTS stock is still in urban areas its incidence is actually higher in rural areas. One factor in this is cottages in the Highlands and Islands which, for example, lack an adequate water supply or sewerage system.

HOUSING TENURE

The distinction between the different tenures is of great importance in housing policy. They are characterised varying terms of access, availability of assistance with housing costs and types of accommodation, and they tend to be used by different groups in the population. The main tenure categories have traditionally been owner occupation, public authority renting and private renting. These categories can, however, usefully be refined and updated. Owner occupation is essentially clear cut (except for a small amount of 'shared ownership' which combines ownership and renting). Public authority renting includes, as well as council housing, dwellings owned by Scottish Homes, the new towns and government departments. Then there are housing associations, essentially not-for-profit providers of rented housing. Rented accommodation, provided by non-profit landlords, including local authorities and housing associations, and allocated on the basis of need mainly to lower income households, is now increasingly referred to as social (rented) housing. This is a useful category because the function of public renting (including council housing) and housing associations is very similar; there is, for example, little difference in the characteristics of households living in each sector, and the 1979-97 Conservative government favoured provision by the latter rather than the former. Finally, a substantial proportion of private rented housing is occupied

TABLE 6.2: *Housing Completions in Scotland, 1971-94*

	Private Sector[1]	%	Public Sector[2]	%	Housing Associations[3]	%	Total
1971-76 (*annual average*)	11,475	(35)	21,057	(63)	581	(2)	33,200
1976	13,704	(38)	22,279	(61)	544	(1)	36,527
1977	12,152	(44)	14,642	(54)	546	(2)	27,320
1978	14,443	(56)	10,189	(40)	1,127	(4)	25,759
1979	15,175	(64)	8,063	(34)	544	(2)	23,782
1980	12,242	(59)	7,488	(36)	881	(4)	20,611
1981	11,021	(55)	7,062	(35)	1,928	(10)	20,011
1982	11,523	(70)	3,733	(23)	1,167	(7)	16,423
1983	13,166	(73)	3,492	(20)	1,271	(7)	17,929
1984	14,115	(75)	2,647	(14)	2,076	(11)	18,838
1985	14,449	(79)	2,828	(15)	1,048	(6)	18,411
1986	14,870	(80)	2,301	(12)	1,466	(8)	18,637
1987	13,904	(78)	2,634	(15)	1,169	(7)	17,707
1988	14,179	(78)	2,815	(15)	1,278	(7)	18,272
1989	16,287	(81)	2,283	(11)	1,620	(8)	20,190
1990	16,461	(81)	1,992	(10)	1,963	(9)	20,416
1991	15,333	(79)	1,732	(9)	2,264	(11)	19,529
1992	14,389	(78)	1,010	(5)	3,044	(17)	18,443
1993	17,735	(82)	958	(5)	2,826	(13)	21,519
1994	17,315	(83)	657	(3)	3,007	(14)	20,979

Notes: 1. Nearly all for owner occupation.
2. Local authorities, new towns, SSHA/Scottish Homes and government departments.
3. Not including SSHA.

Source: Scottish Development Department, *Scottish Housing Statistics*; and Scottish Office, *Statistical Bulletin: Housing Series.*

by tenants in receipt of housing benefit which may meet the whole of their rent. In a sense, therefore, part of this small sector functions as a sort of quasi-social housing for low income households.

Table 6.2 shows housing completions by tenure, and it can be seen that overall output more or less halved during the 1970s; to a large extent this reduction was related to the end of major slum clearance and consequent rehousing needs. The public sector had a dominant position in Scotland after 1945 but its contribution fell drastically from the 1970s, and in recent years the public sector has come near to ceasing to build new houses, but to a limited extent the output of social housing has been maintained by housing associations. They started from a low base but have been responsible for seven to 17 per cent of completions since the early 1980s; it might be

TABLE 6.3: *Housing Tenure in Scotland, 1961-95*

	Number of Dwellings (000s)	Owner Occupied %	Public Rented %	Housing Association %	Private Rented %
1961	1627	26	43		32
1966	1710	29	47		25
1971	1822	31	52		17
1976	1921	33	54		13
1981	1970	36	52	2	10
1986	2050	43	47	3	8
1991	2160	53	38	3	7
1995	2232	58	31	4	7

Sources: Department of the Environment, Scottish Office and Welsh Office, *Housing and Construction Statistics*; and Scottish Office, *Statistical Bulletin: Housing Series*.

said that the Conservative government was unenthusiastic about social housing of any sort but it was better disposed towards housing associations than council housing. The corollary of the decline of the public sector has been the achievement of a dominant position by owner occupation which since the mid-1980s has accounted for around 80 per cent of completions.

The tenure structure of Scottish housing has changed radically over the years as a result of new building, slum clearance and purchase of both private and public rented housing for owner occupation. Scottish housing before the first world war, as in other part of Britain, was dominated by the private rented sector (PRS) which accounted for perhaps nine out of ten dwellings. Then a divergence began which reached its maximum extent in the 1960s and 1970s but is now unwinding quite rapidly (Table 6.3).

There are still, however, significant differences in Scottish housing tenure compared with that in England and Wales but they are smaller than 20 or 30 years ago; public renting remains substantially more, and owner occupation less, important than south of the border. Scotland has seen an even greater decline in the PRS than in England and Wales (where there has recently been a modest revival) so that this difference has actually increased (Table 6.4).

For many years home ownership grew much more modestly in Scotland than in England and Wales; conversely the public sector became much larger. As a result, by the 1960s owner occupation as a proportion of the Scottish housing stock was some 20 per cent less important, and public renting about 25 per cent more important than south of the border. The growth of Scottish owner occupation accelerated to some extent at the end of the 1970s with the reduction in public sector building mentioned above, but the tenure was also expanding south of the border. The gap between the rates of both owner occupation and public renting persisted into the mid-1980s, since when they have diminished, mainly because of the higher rate of RTB sales in Scotland.

TABLE 6.4: *Housing Tenure in Scotland and England and Wales, 1995*

	Owner Occupied %	Public Rented %	Housing Association %	Private Rented %
Scotland	58	31	4	7
England and Wales	68	18	4	10

Sources: Department of the Environment, Scottish Office and Welsh Office, *Housing and Construction Statistics*; and Scottish Office, *Statistical Bulletin: Housing Series.*

Between 1981 and 1995 the number of owner-occupied dwellings in Scotland grew by about 80 per cent compared with a third in England, albeit from a substantially smaller base. The difference in levels of owner occupation had fallen to about ten per cent and in public renting to about 13 per cent in 1995 though it should be noted that the Scottish public sector, at 31 per cent, was still as significant as its counterpart south of the border at its maximum extent in the late 1970s. Whereas in England and Wales owner occupation grew only very slowly between 1990 and 1996 with the slump in the housing market (though growth may now resume), the sector continued to expand in Scotland.

The reasons for Scotland's distinctive housing tenure during most of the twentieth century are too complex to discuss in detail, but causal factors included a legacy of very poor conditions resulting in a higher level of council building from the inter-war period (partly for slum clearance); also a tradition of low private sector rents (reflecting poor quality accommodation) spilled over into the public sector, thus shifting some demand, which would have otherwise have been for owner occupation, towards council housing. Home ownership grew fastest in the south of England and was linked to economic prosperity, and no doubt indifferent economic performance was a factor which delayed its expansion in Scotland. Other factors include the Scottish system of owners' rates which existed until 1956 and had to be paid by developers on unsold houses, so discouraging speculative building; and the large amount of tenement property in Scottish towns and cities where owner occupation was rather slower to take over from private renting than in the terraced housing characteristic of England.

Owner Occupation

Owner occupation has been the largest tenure in Scotland since the end of the 1980s, and the Conservative government's objective of 60 per cent home ownership by the end of the 1992 parliament was almost achieved by the 1997 election. The number of RTB sales will be crucial to the rate at which the level of home ownership continues to increase in Scotland where the recent growth in home ownership has been particularly dependent on council house sales. In part this reflects the larger public sector which was always likely to make sales more significant in tenure change than south of the border; but also a high proportion of the public sector stock has been sold in Scotland. After a somewhat slow start when the RTB started in 1980, Scottish sales picked up momentum which did not fall away after their peak in the mid-1980s to the same extent as in England. Increased discounts on flats bought under the RTB, introduced in 1986, were more significant in Scotland than south of the border because of the large number of four-in-a-block flats, many of them in comparatively high status estates. By the end of 1995 sales were equivalent to over one-third of the Scottish public sector stock in 1979 compared with a quarter in England. Between 1980 and 1995 some 16 per cent of all Scottish dwellings existing at the latter date had moved from the public rented to the owner-occupied sector as a result of the RTB compared with six per cent. In Scotland well over half of the expansion in the number of owner-occupied dwellings came from sales (the remainder being newly built apart from some transfers from private renting); the comparable proportion for England was around two-fifths. In a sense RTB sales have replaced those from private renting which fuelled the growth of owner occupation for many years; but given the large size of the public sector in Scotland they have done so with particular effectiveness.

The rate of home ownership in Scotland, as in the rest of Britain, is greatest among the higher socio-economic groups. In 1991 some 87 per cent of households headed by professionals were home owners, and 80 per cent headed by employers and managers, proportions only slightly lower than those south of the border. But in England owner occupation is the largest tenure among all socio-economic groups and includes almost half unskilled households; in Scotland by contrast owner occupation falls off much more sharply, and decreases steadily through the skilled and semi-skilled to the unskilled where less than one-fifth are home owners.

A high proportion of Scottish households aspire to owner occupation; for example, a recent survey found that more than 80 per cent of Scottish households would like to be home owners, though the proportion among manual workers was rather lower (Scottish Homes, 1996). Apart from the RTB which has obviously been extremely successful, a number of smaller scale schemes have been developed to promote owner occupation. In 1989 a lot of publicity was given to a new rent-to-mortgage scheme whereby public sector tenants unable to afford an ordinary RTB purchase could convert rent into mortgage repayments and buy part of the equity in their home. This initiative has been disappointing with fewer than 1,000 sales over the six years to 1995; most tenants are either ineligible because they are receiving housing benefit or they can afford the straightforward RTB with higher discounts. While the new Labour government cannot afford to be seen as being hostile to owner occupation, there is likely to be a rather less single-minded enthusiasm for its promotion than under the Conservatives, and some of the schemes to extend low-cost home ownership with special grants and through housing associations are likely to be scaled down.

Given the strong preference of most households for home ownership, in an important sense its continued growth is desirable, though this can have drawbacks. Most owner occupiers are happy with their tenure choice but, other things being equal, the greater the number of modest income and economically less secure households living in the tenure, the more likely are problems to occur. The more 'marginal' owner occupiers that exist the greater will be the incidence of, for example, mortgage default and repossession, and inadequate repair and maintenance. As was pointed out in the discussion of housing conditions, a small but significant minority of owner-occupied dwellings are defective. This largely reflects the fact that the tenure includes some old property, not all of which has been modernised; the owners involved tend to have low incomes and are often elderly. Local authorities can provide improvement grants though constraints on expenditure mean that these are not always readily available.

Many aspects of owner occupation, such as mortgage interest tax relief, are a matter of UK-wide policy and are not the responsibility of the Scottish Office; and almost all the building societies and banks which lend for house purchase operate throughout Britain. But the Scottish housing market does have some particular characteristics: above all it tends to be less volatile than in England. House prices rose less in Scotland during the boom of the late 1980s and subsequently did not experience sharp falls. Consequently negative equity—when purchasers have outstanding loans which exceed the current value of their houses—which was a serious problem in much of England among households that bought at the height of the boom was never of great significance in Scotland. The house price to income ratio is lower in Scotland than the UK average, even excluding the large number of RTB purchasers: in other words, Scottish housing is more affordable. Consequently Scotland suffered less from the effects of high interest rates in the early 1990s, and repossessions were at a lower level than in the UK as a whole. But as Scottish house prices, and therefore loans, are smaller, a greater proportion of housing debt falls within the £30,000 limit for mortgage interest tax relief; as a result its phased reduction has a proportionately greater effect on buyers' outgoings than south of the border.

Private Renting

The private rented sector was not much less important than in England at the beginning of the 1980s but now it is significantly smaller at less than seven per cent, compared with ten per cent. Just as slum clearance once removed large numbers of private rented dwellings, during the 1970s and 1980s tenement improvement in housing action areas, particularly in Glasgow, tended to result in transfers to housing association ownership. The PRS declined faster in Scotland and then failed to share in the sector's modest revival south of the border from about 1990. Whether that revival will be sustained is debatable but the most that can be said about Scotland is that the long-term decline may have ended. This is perhaps to be expected because the PRS does cater for some niche markets, and if it got much smaller it would practically disappear. The virtual abolition of rent controls on new lettings in 1989 applied throughout Britain and no doubt boosted private renting to some extent, but commentators also point to the slump in the owner-occupied market south of the border, which scarcely affected Scotland, as another factor.

To make some rough and ready distinctions, the PRS can be seen as catering for three markets. First there is a small unfurnished sub-sector with regulated rents, essentially left over from when the PRS was much larger; households tend to be elderly and many will soon be dissolved through death. Landlords will often then decide to sell the property which may become owner occupied. Second, a more or less up-market sub-sector is occupied by reasonably affluent households for limited periods before they move to owner occupation as their long-term tenure. Renting can be convenient when, for example, someone moves to a new area. People working away from home on a temporary basis may rent (sometimes at their employer's expense). Third, households dependent on housing benefit may rent (often more down-market) accommodation, again usually on a temporary basis but in this case as a stop-gap until social housing in either the public or housing association sector is obtained. This sub-sector was referred to above as quasi-social housing; although it is provided on a for-profit basis it functions as a significant supplement (at considerable cost to the tax-payer in housing benefit) to social rented housing proper. The PRS accommodates a wide variety of households reflecting the different sub-sectors, but, given its small overall size, it has no more than a modest share of any category. Households with retired heads are now somewhat under-represented in the sector, which is a fairly recent change, as are semi-skilled households though curiously (and unlike England) not unskilled ones. Younger households, as might be expected, are comparatively frequent users of the sector though this means, for example, only one in five households with heads under 25.

Social Housing

The category of social housing (or social rented housing) is a fairly new one, which was coined in academic books and articles but has now gained official acceptance. A recent (non-Scottish) housing act, for example, uses the category of registered social landlords to encompass housing associations and local housing companies. It was pointed out above that social rented housing is characterised by provision on a not-for-profit basis and allocation on the basis of need (rather than ability to pay). Before discussing the current role of social renting, it is useful to look briefly at the development of council housing which became so important in Scotland.

Council Housing since 1919: Local authorities have been landlords for more than 100 years, although their building was on a very small scale before the first world war. The significance of council housing was vastly increased with the introduction of exchequer subsidies in 1919, and local authorities were responsible for the majority of new houses built in Scotland for almost 70 years. The results in terms of housing tenure have already been discussed. Although council housing has been considerably more important than south of the border, the sector has passed through broadly similar phases (see, for example, English, 1988). In the 1920s the emphasis was on general needs housing which was intended to relieve the severe overall shortage of accommodation rather than directly to assist those in the worst housing conditions. Most of the new council tenants came from the skilled working class who could afford to pay the comparatively high rents. Pleasant low-density estates but comparatively few tenement flats were built; these areas (with the houses generally modernised internally) are usually very popular today and have seen a lot of RTB sales.

By the 1930s it was felt that council housing should be made available to people living in slums and severely overcrowded conditions. Previously they had only benefited from 'filtering' into privately rented houses vacated by council tenants. Provision for general needs was drastically cut back, and most new council houses were used for rehousing as part of the first large-scale slum clearance programme. Council housing built in the 1930s was much more likely to consist of tenements, rents were lower and tenants poorer. Many Scottish towns and cities have bleak and unpopular housing schemes dating from this time, often with severely deprived populations and problems such as high unemployment and drug abuse. For many years local authorities maintained a more or less formal categorisation of estates; bluntly, general needs housing with its higher rents and more pleasant environment was for the 'respectable' working class whereas rehousing schemes were (and in practice still are) for the poor.

When building restarted after the second world war, council housing went through not dissimilar phases. Initially, the Labour government concentrated on the public sector, and the new houses were of a generally high standard and, as in the 1920s, were intended for general needs. But by the mid-1950s building for owner occupation was recovering (though much less so than south of the border) and large-scale slum clearance was restarted. As a result, new council housing moved (to a considerable extent even in Scotland) from meeting general needs to clearance rehousing while at the same time space standards were reduced and flats became more common. Then in the 1960s, in a commendable though disastrous attempt to speed up slum clearance, local authorities were encouraged to build large blocks of high rise and, even worse, deck-access, flats using prefabricated systems. A great deal of this housing suffers from dampness, may be as unpopular as the rehousing schemes built in the 1930s and shares their high level of social deprivation.

In addition to council housing, public rented housing is also provided by Scottish Homes which took over the Scottish Special Housing Association (SSHA) stock in 1989. The SSHA was a government agency, with over 90,000 houses in the early 1980s, rather than a housing association in the ordinary sense. It was set up in 1937 to supplement local authority house building, particularly in depressed areas; later one of its functions was to build housing to assist economic development. The landlord function of Scottish Homes is now being run down.

In 1995 some 35 per cent of the Scottish housing stock was socially rented and most—31 per cent—was rented from public authorities. In turn the bulk of public housing—29 per cent of the overall stock—was council housing, rented from local authorities. Most of the remaining public rented stock—and the category has no counterpart south of the border—was rented from Scottish Homes. Much of the ex-SSHA stock has been sold through the RTB, and the remainder is in the course of being sold to housing associations (see below). Very much smaller than public rented housing but becoming increasingly significant in the social rented sector is housing association accommodation which constituted about four per cent of all dwellings.

Stock Transfer: This term includes various procedures whereby public rented housing is transferred to new landlords, usually housing associations or analogous bodies, on a more or less large scale (as opposed to individual RTB sales). Stock transfer has become significant though so far it is much less important than the RTB. In England there have been over 50 large-scale voluntary transfers (LSVTs)—voluntary in that the process is initiated by the landlord—where a housing association takes over the whole of a council's housing stock after a ballot of tenants. So far the transfers south of the border have involved local authorities with comparatively small numbers of houses and amount to little more than one per cent of the overall council stock in 1995. The councils concerned have essentially endorsed the government view that social housing is better provided by housing associations than by local authorities. Only one Scottish local authority, the former Berwickshire district council, which transferred the whole of its stock in 1995, has completed a LSVT.

Stock transfers on a piecemeal basis have been taking place since the 1980s and are more significant than LSVTs in Scotland; over 16,000 houses had been transferred to housing associations (or co-operatives) by the end of 1995, more than half in Glasgow, mainly in run-down estates. The incentive for transfer is that investment in much needed repair and improvement can be undertaken fairly quickly by housing associations, whereas local authorities are constrained by the limited size of their capital programmes. Recent legislation for England and Wales allows local housing companies (as well as housing associations) to become registered social landlords; but local housing companies may become significant in Scotland even in the absence of new legislation. Housing companies are not-for-profit social landlords with a good deal of similarity to housing associations; but they are likely to be particularly concerned with taking over individual estates which are in poor condition and may have a negative value, so that special grants are needed to finance their rehabilitation. Another difference is that they normally have a much more substantial number of local authority representatives than housing associations, which tends to be an attraction to councils considering stock transfers. In addition, some empty stock has been sold to developers for rehabilitation and subsequent owner occupation.

When Scottish Homes took over the SSHA stock in 1989, the government made it clear that its landlord role would be transitional. The first large-scale transfer, to Waverley Housing in the Borders region, led to a major row over procedural improprieties and a failure to obtain a proper price, and the House of Commons Public Accounts Committee issued a critical report. This no doubt held up further disposals to some extent, but the stock transfers are now going forward within an elaborate procedural regime, mainly to housing associations. Interestingly, the generally abortive tenant's choice scheme—intended to allow tenants to opt for a new landlord over the heads of their existing public sector landlord—has been used to transfer some Scottish Homes stock to co-operatives formed by tenants in Grampian in what amount to LSVTs. The development corporations of the five Scottish new towns (Cumbernauld, East Kilbride, Glenrothes, Irvine and Livingston) have been wound up, and their remaining rented stock (after RTB sales of two-thirds of the total) is being transferred to new landlords, though in their case the government reluctantly conceded, in the face of the weight of tenant preferences, that local authorities might be involved.

Social housing is of special interest to social policy, in that it interacts particularly closely with other social services. A high proportion of households is dependent on social security benefits, including housing benefit which is received by around three-quarters of the total. Social housing has a crucial role in community care by providing accommodation for vulnerable groups. Indeed, one of the advantages of the new unitary local authorities may be that housing and social work are now the responsibility of the same councils. Social housing (increasingly so as owner occupation expands) is a safety net for those in need, who cannot obtain satisfactory accommodation through the market. It might be said that, although all the housing tenures are in one way or another the concern of social policy, social housing is most obviously and deeply part of the 'welfare state'.

Residualisation: To be slightly aphoristic, it could be said that while public sector housing once accommodated the working class, it and housing associations now cater predominantly for the non-working class. In 1991 less than one-third of social rented households had employed heads, over a fifth were unemployed or long-term sick and disabled, and more than a third were retired. Among households with employed heads there is a very strong bias toward the semi-skilled and unskilled, the corollary of the opposite bias in the case of owner occupation mentioned above. Only a quarter of households with heads in employment were social tenants in 1991 compared with two-fifths of all households.

There are in a sense two causes of the changing socio-economic profile of social tenants. First, some long-standing tenants who were once employed have dropped out of the labour market because of economic change or ill health (often in combination), while others have simply reached retirement age. These kinds of households tend to have been less able than those in employment to use the RTB so are less likely to have left social renting through that route. Second, non-employed households have been moving to social housing. Substantial numbers of older people moved from private renting to housing associations as a result of major rehabitation programmes in housing action areas. Now that the PRS is small and rarely provides permanent housing, social renting is very much the tenure for low income groups. Some of these households are unemployed when they move into the sector; and there is the rapidly growing number of households headed by single parents, four out of five of which were social tenants in 1991.

These trends have been referred to as the 'residualisation' of council housing, which has a number of aspects including the changing socio-economic profile of households, the deterioration of the stock as RTB sales cream off the best houses in the best areas, and the increasing dependence on means-tested benefits. It could be said that housing associations have not been residualised because most of them are fairly new and have never been very different; but they are certainly residual in terms of their tenants' socio-economic status and dependence on benefit if not quality of accommodation. With its still substantially larger size than in England, social rented housing in Scotland clearly tends to accommodate, other things being equal, a somewhat broader range of households; it may be a bit less residual than south of the border but the same process of residualisation is taking place.

In some respects residualisation can be seen as the fault of local authorities and central government in that some very unsatisfactory housing has been built and not replaced or properly maintained. But more generally the process is the result of broader social and economic changes. Owner occupation has become the preferred tenure of most households, the government has encouraged its growth, for example through subsidies, and on the whole people have found it financially advantageous. The RTB has clearly accelerated residualisation, especially in Scotland, but it would be unrealistic to suppose that council house sales have caused the process. Residualisation would have occurred anyway, and council house sales can be seen, at any rate in urban areas with large public rented sectors, as the only feasible way of adjusting the tenure structure nearer to the demands of households. The overwhelmingly public sector housing stocks in some central Clydeside areas in 1979 came nowhere near meeting the tenure preferences of local households; in the absence of sales there would have been a lot of empty council houses. This is not to suggest, however, that residualisation and RTB sales do not have significant costs, but, as with most aspects of social policy, change throws up both gainers and losers.

One indicator of the effect of sales on the public stock is the different levels of houses and flats sold, given that the former are generally seen as more attractive. About 70 per cent of RTB sales have been houses, nearly half the 1979 total, whereas less than one-in-five flats have been sold. There have also been major variations both between and within local authority areas. On the whole it is urban areas with large public sectors which have seen the lowest proportions sold, and rural areas which always had fewer council houses where the RTB has been most popular. Furthermore, house prices in these areas tend to be relatively high so that when former council houses are resold they may be outwith the reach of local people. Parts of rural Scotland now have a shortage of housing to rent. In urban areas the effect of RTB is more in terms of the quality of rented housing. As well as the difference between houses and flats noted above, there are enormous variations between estates: in some of the more pleasant and sought-after ones a majority of the stock has been sold whereas in others there have been very few sales. While there may not be a shortage of public rented housing, much of it is of indifferent or poor quality. Dwellings possess basic internal amenities but they may be damp and have a poor environment.

Council House Subsidies and Rents: Subsidies for council housing can only be mentioned in outline but it is important to note the major changes which have taken place, particularly since 1979. Initially exchequer subsidies were calculated on the basis of annual deficits, but from 1923 until the 1970s, they were fixed at the time a house was built and paid to local authorities for 40 (or later 60) years. The subsidies together with substantial contributions from local rates were largely used to reduce rents in general rather than to give assistance specifically to poorer tenants. Rent rebates were not very significant until a national scheme was introduced in 1972 (incorporated in housing benefit since 1982) as part of a highly controversial and abortive attempt to reform council housing finance. Scotland had a tradition of a low rents and high subsidies which the government had occasionally made a half-hearted attempt to change. Rents met only a minority of the cost of council housing, that is the servicing of building loans and management and maintenance expenditure.

After a confused period when the Conservative 1972 reforms were largely abandoned after a change of government in 1974, Labour introduced housing support grant (HSG) in 1978. HSG, which applied from 1979-80, meets the deficit, if any, between income from rents and expenditure, both of which are notional amounts set by central government; in particular each year the government announces the average rents which local authorities are expected to charge. When the Conservatives returned to power they found the new HSG a reasonably effective means of imposing their own housing finance policies. By specifying assumed rent increases well above the inflation rate, the average proportion of costs met by rents has grown from about half in 1979 to about 90 per cent. In 1984 the government took powers to phase out rates (later general) fund contributions to housing revenue accounts (HRAs), and these have now been eliminated, while HSG is only paid to a handful of authorities (four in 1996-97) with exceptionally high costs; it is equivalent across all councils of only about two per cent of outgoings. The government has announced that it intends to eliminate the need for HSG by taking over an appropriate amount of housing debt from the few high-cost authorities still eligible for it.

Initially during the 1980s Scottish council rents rose faster than those in England, increasing from about two-thirds to over 90 per cent of those south of the border in 1989; the traditionally lower Scottish rents had been largely eliminated. But then the gap widened again and by 1995 Scottish rents had fallen to some 75 per cent of the English average; Scottish rents increased by 52 per cent in cash terms as against 85 per cent, and dropped well behind Scottish Office guidelines. The reason is that when a local authority ceases to be eligible for HSG, as most areas have, there is nothing to withdraw and central government loses its leverage over rent levels. Rents only have to be increased to the extent needed to balance HRAs. South of the border, however, since 1989 housing benefit costs have been included in HRAs—in other words only rents net of housing benefit are now credited to HRAs—so that all areas again became eligible for subsidy. This could then be withdrawn in line with rent guidelines, thus restoring the central government leverage. To do this in Scotland would require legislation.

Rent rebates (later housing benefit) were already significant in 1979 but all council tenants whatever their incomes benefited from general assistance, from central government and local rates, which effectively halved their rents. Highly subsidised rents undoubtedly shifted some demand away from owner occupation. Now there is very little general assistance, and rents have approximately doubled in real terms, meeting virtually all HRA outgoings. Much higher rents, together with continued residualisation which means that fewer tenants are in employment, have resulted in the high level of dependence on housing benefit mentioned earlier.

Housing Associations: The origins of housing associations go back into the nineteenth century, even before council housing started to be built, but until comparatively recently they had a very minor role in social housing. Expansion of housing associations was promoted in the 1960s; the idea was that they would provide rented housing for people who could not afford owner occupation but were not in sufficient need to qualify for council housing. The notion that there was a gap which needed filling turned out to be misconceived; by that time most households with a reasonable income preferred to get some sort of owner-occupied accommodation. Then the government radically changed the role of housing associations, and in 1974, by providing generous subsidies, made them providers of social housing to supplement council housing. There was concern that, with the decline of the PRS, local authorities were becoming monopoly landlords. As well as building new accommodation, housing associations were given a major role in the improvement of older housing—which had come to be seen as preferable to slum clearance—in housing action areas. This function was particularly important in Glasgow where community-based housing associations undertook the bulk of tenement improvement.

Local authorities, as their housing stocks grew over the years, were increasingly able to cross-subsidise the high costs of new houses by pooling rents. But as most housing associations had little or no existing stock, there was no scope for cross-subsidisation; consequently exchequer subsidies had to be very large if rents were to be anywhere near affordable by social tenants. Housing association grant (HAG), which was introduced in 1974, provides a lump sum to meet that part of the capital cost—typically a high proportion so that HAG levels of over 90 per cent have not been unusual—that cannot be covered by rents. Although there have been modifications, HAG continues (in England and Wales renamed social housing grant). The proportion of capital costs met by HAG (and now SHG) south of the border has been reduced but Scottish HAG levels have remained comparatively high.

The Housing Corporation had been set up to supervise housing associations, and it was given responsibility for paying HAG. The Housing Corporation in Scotland had a considerable degree of autonomy, and in 1989 its functions were transferred (together with those of the SSHA) to the newly created Scottish Homes (see above). There are some 270 registered housing associations in Scotland; on average they are smaller than those south of the border, few having more than 1,000 dwellings. Scotland has a greater emphasis on community-based associations serving a particular locality than on regional or national organisations. Housing co-operatives are essentially similar but their membership consists of all their tenants. The higher level of HAG in Scotland means that there has not been the same financial pressure on smaller associations to merge as south of the border.

Access to Social Housing: One of the characteristics of social housing is that it is allocated on the basis of need; local authorities and housing associations have considerable discretion about the detail of their allocation policy though the criteria used are basically fairly similar (English, 1987). Current housing circumstances—sharing, overcrowding, lack of basic amenities, insecurity of tenure and so on—are of central importance, together with health or other personal circumstances which may be exacerbated by inadequate accommodation. Some priority is usually also given in respect of time on the waiting list. Many landlords now use points schemes whereby different aspects of need are given numerical values, the total of which determines priority. In the case of some applicants there may not be a great deal of difference between urgent need assessed under an ordinary allocation scheme and homelessness which is discussed below.

Allocation of social housing raises many issues, but one aspect which should be emphasised is that the crucial question is often not so much who gets access to the tenure—who is eligible to be allocated a dwelling of some sort—but who gets which dwelling. This was not previously the case when there was a healthy demand for all council housing, and the majority of available lets were in any case newly built. Indeed, gaining access to the sector as a whole rather than to a particular house is probably still the more important hurdle with housing associations (and those local authorities with a small number of houses). But in most areas lengthy waiting lists co-exist with estates where demand barely keeps pace with vacancies and it may be difficult to ensure that all the houses are occupied; this phenomenon of difficult-to-let estates emerged in the 1970s. Houses are available in unpopular estates more or less immediately even without much specific housing need. The point is, however, that by and large only applicants in severe and urgent need are willing to consider moving to an unpopular estate; most prefer to wait for somewhere more attractive. Those who do move to unpopular areas tend to be poorer and in difficult circumstances or even homeless—that is why their need is urgent—and they reinforce deprivation in these estates.

Deprived Estates: Social housing as a whole is being residualised, but some council estates have long been residual in both socio-economic and physical terms; the two tend to go together. Thirty or more years ago the bulk of the worst housing, economic deprivation and social problems were to be found in their traditional location, inner city private rented tenements. But almost all these areas have been demolished or rehabilitated, and the bulk of deprivation is now to be found in unpopular council estates; many are slum clearance estates dating from the 1930s but others are comparatively new blocks of systems-built flats. Analysis of the 1991 census indicated that over 70 per cent of the most deprived ten per cent of Scottish enumeration districts contained mainly public rented housing. Over two-fifths of mainly public rented enumeration districts were among the 'worst' ten per cent (Duguid, 1995).

Unpopular and deprived estates, with high rates of unemployment and long-term sickness, above average numbers of single-parent households, generally low incomes, drug abuse, anti-social behaviour and crime are a major problem for housing policy; but they are also a problem for other aspects of social policy including social work, health care, education and policing. There have been a variety of initiatives in an attempt to counter urban deprivation. The Glasgow Eastern Area Renewal (GEAR) project in the 1970s and 1980s was concerned with the regeneration of the east end of the city, and involved a number of participants including the regional and district councils, the SSHA and the Greater Glasgow Health Board. GEAR had considerable success in improving housing conditions and the environment, and in attracting new business to offset the loss of jobs in traditional manufacturing industry though the new ones did not necessarily go to local people. But GEAR was concerned with the 'traditional' problems of an inner urban area which had only pockets of council housing. In the late 1980s the Scottish Office turned its attention to the comparatively 'new' problems of large peripheral council estates with the publication of *New Life for Urban Scotland* (Scottish Office, 1988) and established four 'partnerships'. There had been previous attempts to tackle difficult-to-let estates but the partnerships were on a much larger scale than anything which had been done before.

The partnerships were set up with a ten-year life in Castlemilk (Glasgow), Ferguslie

Park (Paisley), Wester Hailes (Edinburgh) and Whitfield (Dundee) to 'plan and direct the regeneration' of the estates. There was to be 'a comprehensive approach based on tackling a number of social, housing and environmental objectives' with a long-term strategic plan of up to ten years (Scottish Office, Central Research Unit, 1996). In principle the partnerships were supposed to involve not only various public sector bodies but also the private sector such as developers, and local people; in practice the first have been predominant. Staff are seconded from various Scottish Office departments, local housing departments and so on to each area. Housing and the environment are a major, though by no means the only, concern of the partnerships; reduction in unemployment levels, for example, through measures such as training, is also a major, though more difficult to achieve, objective. An important housing objective is tenure diversification, through the transfer of council stock to housing associations and building for owner occupation (with the support of grants to reduce selling prices).

The high level of expenditure has resulted in major physical improvements to the estates; the issue is not whether success of this kind can be achieved but the enormous cost of taking similar action in run-down council estates generally. In fact the distribution of expenditure, for example, by Scottish Homes and in capital programmes allocated to local authorities, has been skewed in favour of the four partnerships, and other areas with pressing problems of their own have tended to have less spent on them as a result. The more interesting question, however, is how far the partnerships will succeed in dealing with the many other problems of the estates—for example, high levels of unemployment and long-term dependence on disability benefits, single-parent households and drug abuse as well as low educational attainment. It is difficult to disentangle the effects of a specific programme from wider trends—a worsening problem might, for instance, have increased even more without an intervention which can therefore be seen as a 'success'—but the levels of benefit dependency in three of the partnerships actually increased in the first years of their existence. A fundamental problem is that the estates are among the least acceptable in their respective areas—few except the more or less desperate are willing to accept houses in them—which is a matter of reputation and location as well as quality of the housing itself. But unless the estates do become more acceptable, tackling their economic and social problems will be extremely difficult. If, however, they manage to recruit less desperate and deprived households, there must be a danger that their problems will be displaced to other estates.

HOMELESSNESS

The growing problem of homelessness at a time when the housing stock has never been so large or of such high quality might seem paradoxical. The availability of housing clearly is important—if there were a plentiful enough supply of low-cost accommodation there would presumably be very little homelessness—and an area such as London with high house prices and a shortage of social housing has a particularly severe problem. But homelessness is not simply a matter of availability of housing; it is also related to lifestyles, household formation and break-up, job opportunities and so on. Homelessness, rather like other much-used concepts in social policy such as poverty, in itself has no precise meaning and has to be defined before it is of much use. Like poverty, most people would accept that homelessness exists but may disagree about how it should be defined; while some equate it with literal rooflessness (in other words not having a bed to sleep in) others—for example Shelter—include anyone who is not adequately housed, perhaps because of dampness or sharing a dwelling. The official definition comes somewhere in the middle and includes not only those without accommodation of any kind but those who are likely to lose it within a short time. Local authorities have responsibility towards some categories of homeless people, notably families with children, but not to others, including most single people. Therefore it is necessary to distinguish statutory homelessness and provision by local authorities from non-statutory, mainly single, homelessness which is catered for, if at all, mainly by the voluntary sector.

As far as local authorities are concerned, their responsibilities were greatly extended by the Housing (Homeless Persons) Act, 1977, which also transferred them from social work to housing departments. The legislative framework can be seen as a series of hurdles; if an applicant gets over them all he or she will be provided with accommodation. First, an applicant has to be accepted as homeless or threatened with homelessness; this means that he or she (or someone who normally lives as a member of the family) has no accommodation or is unable to use it (for example because of a threat of domestic violence). In fact, few applicants are actually roofless, and in reality it is often difficult to say that they are literally forced leave their existing accommodation when, as so often happens, it is shared with friends or relatives. Very often people are not so much homeless as living in inadequate or overcrowded housing. Second, the local authority has to decide whether the applicant is in 'priority need'. If he or she is in priority need the local authority must secure at least temporary accommodation; if not it is only required to provide advice and assistance in finding accommodation. Third, the applicant may be deemed to be intentionally homeless; but if he or she is unintentionally homeless the local authority will secure (though not necessarily itself provide) permanent accommodation.

Although there is a detailed Code of Guidance issued by the Scottish Office, and a substantial number of judicial review cases have defined local authority responsibilities, they still have some discretion in making decisions about applicants. A local authority which is under pressure from a large number of applicants and has little social housing may have a tough approach at each stage; unlike some London boroughs, however, this rarely seems to happen in Scotland where only about one in five lets (excluding transfers)—though no doubt predominantly in less popular areas—are allocated to the homeless compared with twice that proportion in England.

Some of the priority need categories are clear cut, and the local authority has little or no discretion in the case of households which contain dependent children or a pregnant woman or are homeless because of an emergency (such as fire or flood). Discretion does arise, however, in deciding whether someone is 'vulnerable' because of old age, physical disability, mental illness or handicap or, especially, 'other special reason'. Vulnerability could very well encompass a great many homeless single people, but most local authorities have been somewhat reluctant to accept them as being in priority need.

The intentionality provision was included in the legislation to deal with cases of blatant irresponsibility or unreasonable behaviour. No doubt if the circumstances of applicants were carefully investigated many could be classified as intentionally homeless, in that the problem is rarely unrelated to their actions of one kind or another. In the past, some housing departments tended to deem a sizeable proportion of applicants as intentionally homeless but in recent years the average for Scotland has been around ten per cent of those in priority need.

The number of applications to local authorities in Scotland had risen to 20,000 a year by the mid-1980s, remained fairly constant at about 25,000 for some years and then increased substantially to over 40,000 in the early 1990s (though some of the change is likely to have been due to earlier under-recording). It is clear, however, that the number of non-priority applicants has increased faster than those in priority need, more than tripling between 1989-90 and 1994-95.

Reasons recorded for homelessness by local authorities are somewhat arbitrary in that they refer only to applicants' immediate circumstances, but the main ones are that friends or relatives are no longer willing or able to provide accommodation (about 40 per cent) and dispute with spouse or cohabitee (about 25 per cent). Mortgage default has tended to become more important but is still a comparatively minor cause of homelessness.

Local authorities secure accommodation for nearly all priority need applicants, apart from those who return to their previous accommodation or do not pursue their applications; this is most often social housing. There has been some increase in the use of bed and breakfast accommodation but this is still on a small scale compared with London. Local authority short-stay hostel accommodation has become much more significant. Non-priority applicants, as required by the legislation, are most likely to be found short-stay accommodation.

Although the single homeless are much more visible than homeless families—the seemingly ubiquitous *Big Issue* sellers have perhaps replaced rough sleepers as the public image of the homeless—a good deal less is known about them because, except to the extent that they approach local authorities, there is no direct source of information about their numbers and circumstances. Estimates of their numbers can be no more than informed guesses. Local authorities, notably Glasgow, make some provision for the single homeless but voluntary organisations are also involved, in some cases supported by government grants.

HOUSING FOR SPECIAL NEEDS

Housing has a particularly close inter-relationship with other social services in meeting the needs of the growing numbers of vulnerable groups such as the dependent elderly, people with physical disabilities and the mentally ill. These groups have become increasingly important for housing with the move away from institutional care towards care in the community. The implementation in 1993 of the National Health Service and Community Care Act, 1990 has (or should have) made housing for these groups a priority. Community care is discussed in Chapter 4, but here the implications for housing are briefly examined.

A difficulty with community care is the number of agencies which are involved—housing bodies, both local housing departments and housing associations, social work departments, the National Health Service and voluntary organisations—whose activities need to be co-ordinated. In a circular to housing and social work authorities and health boards (Scottish Office, 1994b) central government emphasised the need for effective working partnerships in the planning and delivery of community care and support services. 'Housing authorities and other housing bodies need the support of health and social work services in providing for customers with community care needs …within the field of community care the three sectors are mutually dependent, and must co-operate to succeed.'

A distinction can perhaps usefully be made between the elderly and other vulnerable groups. First, the majority of the elderly continue to live in their own homes without any special help; but the growing number of the very elderly in their eighties and older are more likely to need specialised accommodation and support. Second, local housing departments have long made special provision for the elderly whereas that for other groups (except to some extent the physically disabled) is much more recent and on a smaller scale. Third, whereas other vulnerable groups are heavily dependent on social housing, increasing numbers of the elderly are home owners and they generally wish, if possible, to retain that status. Private sheltered housing can meet the needs of the better off elderly, but it is expensive and in practice they have to own reasonably high value houses which can be sold. For the most part, however, social landlords, both local authorities and increasingly housing associations, will have to bear the brunt of providing housing for special needs. Conversely, as social housing as a whole contracts with the growth of owner occupation—as fewer 'ordinary' households are social tenants—people with particular needs and problems of one sort or another are likely to become dominant. Some of these households—the long-term unemployed and sick and single parents for instance—will not generally be the clients of community care; but the vulnerable groups mentioned above will also bulk large. Thus the role of social landlords is tending to move from the straightforward, essentially 'bricks and mortar', management of large housing stocks to a more intensive and personalised relationship with a smaller number of tenants.

Sheltered housing for the elderly combines specially designed and accessible accommodation with a warden service and an emergency call system linked to the warden or central office. Very sheltered housing provides more support with full-time warden cover and one main meal a day. Responsibility for meeting the cost of wardens, incidentally, has sometimes been a matter of dispute between social landlords and social work departments. Amenity housing on the other hand does not have a warden (though local authorities have become somewhat reluctant to build new units as they are subject to the RTB). There are over 50,000 socially-rented amenity and sheltered housing units for the elderly, more than a third provided by housing associations. Mainstream housing can also be adapted, and community alarm systems, linked to mobile support services, make it more feasible for the elderly to remain in their own homes (and are a cost-effective form of provision). Another initiative is Care and Repair, a charitable organisation now administered by Scottish Homes, which gives advice and help to older owner occupiers whose homes require improvement and repair.

Local authorities have for some time provided housing for the physically disabled, both specially designed (sometimes suitable for wheelchairs) and adapted accommodation; there are now over 30,000 units. Involvement with other special needs categories is more recent and often involves group housing projects in which housing associations have a major involvement. The run down of long-stay mental institutions, in particular, requires appropriate housing provision, and health boards have given financial support for new schemes. There is no doubt that appropriate accommodation will have to be provided on a considerably larger scale to meet the needs of people for whom mainstream housing is not suitable if community care is to mean an improved quality of life for everyone who would once have been institutionalised.

CONCLUSION

Scottish housing has undergone profound change over the years: the historic shortage of accommodation has been largely eliminated; space standards have vastly improved and almost all dwellings have amenities such as bathrooms. This does not mean, however, that there are no problems, but ironically these often affect council housing, which was built primarily to eliminate bad conditions. By no means all the tenure is unsatisfactory but some estates suffer from dampness and poor environment, and have severely deprived populations. Housing policy, through improvement (and in some cases demolition and rebuilding) and better management, can deal with physical deficiencies, but this is unlikely to be enough. Whereas housing problems could once very largely be solved by building new houses—often housing estates—this is much less the case today. Difficult-to-let council estates, and homelessness for that matter, in part reflect social problems, to whose solution housing measures can do no more than contribute. On the other hand, social housing has a major role in broader social policy, particularly in its contribution to community care.

The greatest changes affecting housing during the 1980s and 1990s, however, have not been the expansion and improvement of the stock, which used to be the focus of policy, but the transformation of tenure. Between 1979 and 1987, by raising council rents and introducing the RTB, the Conservative government powerfully reinforced the growth of home ownership. Scotland has already lost the deplorably poor housing conditions once suffered by so many households; it is now losing its distinctive tenure structure as the public rented sector contracts and owner occupation expands towards a position almost as dominant as south of the border. But housing policy must also be concerned with those who are not able to enjoy good quality home ownership, including the homeless and tenants of run-down council estates. For them the availability of decent social housing is crucially important.

NOTE ON SOURCES: In addition to references in the text, statistics are from Scottish Office, *Statistical Bulletin: Housing Series*; Department of the Environment, Scottish Office and Welsh Office, *Housing and Construction Statistics*; Scottish Homes, *Scottish House Condition Survey 1991*; Wilcox, *Housing Finance Review, 1995/96*.

7
EDUCATION

INTRODUCTION

This chapter describes the dominant features the educational provision in Scotland and traces some of the more important changes introduced during the 1980s and 1990s. The education system in Scotland traditionally has been, and remains, distinct from that in England and Wales, but charges that there has been an 'Englishing' of the system, while not new (McCrone, 1990), appear to have increased in frequency during the 1990s. The system south of the border has also been the subject of sweeping reforms, in terms of a marked trend towards *centralisation, privatisation, vocationalisation* and *differentiation* (Chitty, 1989); and it can be argued that recent suggestions of a loss of Scottish educational distinctiveness relate to the effects of these reforms.

The Scottish System

Accounts of, and claims about, the distinctiveness of the Scottish education system and its traditions abound (see particularly Scotland, 1969; Humes and Paterson, 1983; McPherson and Raab, 1988; McPherson, 1990; McCrone, 1992). But for present purposes the key elements of this distinctiveness are the different age for enrolment in Scottish secondary schools; differences in curriculum and assessment in both primary and secondary schools and in further education colleges; differences in university degree structures; and differences in the loci of control over educational practice and the genesis of policy. To these differences one should add that the introduction of the comprehensive system of secondary education was much more uniform and widespread than in England (McPherson, 1990), and that rates of entry into higher education in Scotland have been and remain higher than those in the rest of the UK (McPherson, Munn and Raffe, 1991). These distinctive features have largely survived the sweeping changes described in this chapter.

The main characteristics of education reforms in Scotland during the last two decades, however, are more or less indistinguishable from those in England and Wales: the primacy accorded to the ideology of the free market; the identification and treatment of parents, students and business as consumers; the wresting of control from local authorities and professional educators; and the assertion of centralised control over the direction and administration of schooling. The Conservative government asserted that its policy was to devolve powers to local institutions and to consumers, particularly in relation to the management of schools and colleges, parental involvement in school management, and business involvement in the design of vocational syllabuses; but at the same time it massively increased its own powers and reduced the autonomy of both local government and educators, principally through its sweeping reforms of school curricula. The effect of these changes has been to change drastically the nature of education provision in Scotland during the 1980s and 1990s, although their full impact will not be clear for some time to come.

Patterns of Change

The major forces propelling changes in education in Scotland can be reduced to four. First, the major demographic trends which became evident in the later 1970s and in the 1980s, of a falling birth rate and consequent reductions in the numbers of pupils entering the system, have continued into the 1990s. The dominant changes that have taken place and responses to them in terms of educational provision will be described on the basis of statistics produced by the Scottish Office. Second, there is the rise in unemployment, particularly for young people, which began in the 1970s, continued throughout the 1980s, and is still evident in the 1990s. This has had an impact at different levels and in diverse types of institution, particularly on patterns of enrolment, staying-on rates and curricular innovation. Third, there have been associated changes relating to broader social trends, such as the increased demand for further qualifications, including a return to education and training by adults, which have affected enrolment. And fourth, there has been the political thrust emanating from both Whitehall and Edinburgh to make education and the qualifications it entails more closely geared to what government perceives to be the 'needs' of industry and the economy more broadly.

Changing School Rolls

Over the last decade the effects of falls in the birth rate in the 1970s and 1980s continued to be felt right through the school system. In 1981-82 there were nearly 977,000 pupils attending school in Scotland. Of these the vast majority, over 941,000, attended schools run by local education authorities. A decade later, in 1991-92, the respective figures were nearly 826,000 and 791,000, representing a net decline of over 150,000 occupied school places. In other words, there were 15 per cent fewer pupils overall, and 16 per cent fewer in local education authority schools. But this decline in the school population was by no means even across the age range.

The decline in the 1980s was most marked among 12-15 year-olds who fell by 30 per cent. The number of secondary school pupils aged 16 also showed a decline of nearly 18 per cent. Over the same period the number of pupils in primary schools also fell, but at a much lower rate of a little less than 10 per cent. There had, however, been an earlier decline in the size of the primary school population, with a 30 per cent fall in school rolls between 1976 and 1987, roughly corresponding to the fall in secondary school rolls in the 1980s.

In most other categories, however, there was an overall increase in the number of pupils. Those under the age of five receiving pre-school education rose from 43,000 to 56,000, although this was mainly among pupils attending part-time. There was also an increase in the numbers of school students of 17 years and older, from 21,500 to

23,400; and by 1991-92, over 14,000 adults were recorded as attending school. The overall decline in pupil numbers also did not apply to the private sector, which registered an increase from 34,000 to nearly 35,000 pupils.

Recent estimates suggest that the numbers of pupils over five will rise by about seven per cent from the 1993 level, to about 828,000 in 2004; but this will still be well below the level of the school population in the 1970s and will not be sustained. It is projected that there will be another decline, by five per cent of the current level, to fewer than 740,000 pupils by the year 2015. Such figures, however, can only be very approximate, given the possibility of fluctuations in the numbers of pupils staying on beyond 16 and of adults returning to school.

SCHOOL PROVISION

Provision for Pre-School Children

For many years it has been recognised that various forms of pre-school educational provision can be of enormous benefit to children, both for their later academic performance and more generally in terms of their social development. The Plowden report recommended that nursery education should be a priority (Central Advisory Committee for Education, 1967). Some of its recommendations were recognised in two white papers in 1972: the first proposed that by 1980 there should be enough nursery school places for 50 per cent of all three year-olds and 90 per cent of all four year-olds (Cmnd 5174, 1972); and the second referred specifically to Scotland (Cmnd 5175, 1972). Steps were taken to implement some of Plowden's recommendations, most notably through increases in nursery school places in designated Educational Priority Areas; but actual provision fell far short of the increases proposed. In Scotland nursery school places rose from about 10,000 in 1972 to nearly 37,000 in 1983, catering for over 28 per cent of the three to four-year old population. The next decade, however, was marked by economic constraints on local education authorities, and the rate of increase slowed. By 1993 there were just over 48,000 nursery school places, catering for 37 per cent of the relevant age group. The number of nursery schools actually fell during this period, from 245 to 240, although the number of nursery departments in schools rose, from 300 to over 500.

Nursery school provision is predominantly on a part-time basis, with 94 per cent of pupils attending in either the morning or the afternoon, or for part of the week. The vast majority of pupils are four year-olds, and boys marginally outnumber girls. Nursery provision also tends to be in relatively small units, with over half the schools or departments catering for fewer than 60 pupils each.

There is considerable geographical variation in provision. Generally there is a tendency towards greater provision in urban as compared with rural areas, with nearly 52 per cent of three to four year-olds in Glasgow attending nursery classes, as against 32 per cent in (the former) Strathclyde region as a whole. Levels of provision also vary, however, on the basis of policy differences between the regions before 1996. For example, whereas in Lothian nearly 52 per cent of the relevant age groups attended nursery classes, in the Borders the figure was under 20 per cent, and in the Highlands 17 per cent.

There are over 3,000 full-time equivalent staff employed in local education nursery schools in Scotland, mainly made up of trained nursery nurses (2,000) and teachers (nearly 1,000). The percentage increase for all staff since 1983 has been over 10 per cent, while that for teachers has been much higher, at over 22 per cent. If this increase is related to the numbers of children attending nursery schools, there has been a slight increase in the ratio of children to staff, from almost seven in 1983 to nearly eight in 1993. It should be added that while there is little geographical variation in the overall ratio of staff to children, there are marked variations in the availability of teachers, with some areas employing comparatively few.

In addition to nursery school provision, a further 5,700 places are now provided for children requiring full-day care in day nurseries, an increase of 55 per cent over 1983. Local education authorities also recognise provision for nearly 50,000 pre-school play group places and list over 8,000 registered child minders catering for nearly 20,000 children. Local authority lists of both pre-school play groups and child minders indicate marked increases.

The Conservative government introduced a system of pre-school education vouchers shortly before it lost office; following pilot schemes in four areas, it was to have operated throughout Scotland from 1997-98, all parents of four year-olds receiving a voucher which could be used in either local authority or private nurseries. The Labour party was opposed to nursery vouchers, and the new government has announced that they are to be discontinued after the first year.

Primary school provision

It has already been noted that the number of primary school age children in Scotland fell sharply in the 1980s: in the early 1980s there were over half a million children between the ages of five and 11; by the early 1990s the number had fallen by nearly 50,000 to about 450,000, almost all of whom attended local education primary schools. The number of primary schools has been affected by this decline in pupil numbers. In 1993 there were 2,341 education authority primary schools in Scotland, 120 fewer than in 1983; but the number of primary school teachers was slightly higher. These changes were reflected in figures for pupil-teacher ratios, which fell from over to under 20.

There is considerable regional variation in the size of primary schools, directly linked to their urban or rural location. Over 60 per cent of the primary schools in the Western Isles, Argyll and Bute, and Shetland had rolls of fewer than 50 pupils each, whereas in Lothian fewer than nine per cent fell into this category and none did so in Glasgow. The average roll for primary schools in Scotland was 187, with very few exceeding 300.

Scottish education authorities budgeted for a total outlay of nearly £728m on primary schools in 1994-95, averaging £1,652 per pupil, but figures vary widely from school to school, largely depending on the size of the school roll. A large primary school's running costs per pupil may be as low as £1,200, while those of some of the smaller schools in the islands exceed £4,000 or even £5,000. The regions with the lowest average running costs per pupil were Dumfries and Galloway, and Strathclyde. At the other end of the scale are Shetland and the Western Isles. While the size of the school roll is the key factor determining the level of running costs, other factors come into play. Some authorities also provide extra staffing and resources for schools in areas designated as multiply deprived; and some schools put additional funds into special units and secondary departments.

Secondary School Provision

As noted above, the fall in school enrolments during the 1980s was most marked in secondary schools; in 1983 there were nearly 400,000 pupils in secondary schools run by local education authorities, but by 1993 the figure had fallen to just over 300,000, representing a decrease of 20 per cent over the period. In response to this decline local authorities attempted to reduce the number of secondary schools through mergers and closures, particularly in urban areas. Such plans, however, were often faced with concerted campaigns by the managements of the threatened schools themselves, supported by teachers' associations, parents and community groups opposed to the loss of school amenities in a given locality. The result was a modest decline in the number of secondary schools, from 444 to 408, a decrease of eight per cent. Generally speaking, secondary schools became smaller in size often with considerable unused capacity, although some schools managed to maintain and even increase their rolls, largely as a result of increases in school placement requests (see below). There was also a reduction of about 13 per cent in the number of teachers employed in local authority secondary schools; the teacher-pupil ratio fell from 14 to just under 13.

Over 180 secondary schools had rolls which exceeded 800 and another 140 had rolls of between 400 and 800. In Strathclyde and Lothian regions, schools tended to be relatively large, with very few having rolls of less than 100, unlike the islands where the majority of secondary schools have fewer than 100 pupils and some have fewer than ten.

The budgeted expenditure for Scottish secondary education in 1994-95 was £831m, and the average cost per pupil £2,658 (about £1,000 more than those for primary schools). As with primary school costs, the figures vary widely since they are largely dependent on the size of the individual schools. In the Borders and Fife the cost was £2,600 whereas in Orkney it exceeded £3,800 and in the Western Isles £4,500. Costs were also affected by regional policies concerning schools in urban areas of multiple deprivation, which may receive extra staffing and resources.

Special School Provision

Since the publication of the Warnock report on special education (Cmnd 7212, 1978), government policy has tended to place greater emphasis both on identifying children with special educational needs and on integrating special needs provision into mainstream schooling. Some schools have been adapted to cater for pupils with such needs, but there is still a demand for educational institutions which cater exclusively for pupils with particular needs. There was a total of 333 schools catering exclusively for children with special educational needs in 1992-93, a net increase of 19 since 1982-83; 136 are funded directly by local authorities and these cater for nearly 6,500 pupils out of a total of about 10,000 attending special schools and classes. The schools vary widely in the type of educational provision they provide, by expenditure per pupil and in the size of their rolls, from as few as two to nearly 200.

Post-School Provision

There is a wide variety of post-school provision of further and higher education in colleges and universities in Scotland. The distinction between the two is not always clear, and is further complicated by recent changes in the status of some of the institutions and by curricular reform. The term 'higher education' is sometimes reserved for institutions with degree-awarding status, whereas the Scottish Office, for example, uses it to denote courses leading to 'advanced' qualifications, including Higher National Certificates and Higher National Diplomas.

The Scottish Office draws a three-fold distinction between colleges of further education, higher education colleges and universities (the last two being grouped under the heading of higher education institutions). There are currently 46 colleges of further education situated throughout Scotland, running vocationally oriented courses, mainly at a non-advanced level. Then there are the colleges of higher education offering vocationally oriented degree courses, which either have the power to award their own degrees directly or have validating arrangements with other higher education institutions. Of these, four are colleges of education providing courses in teacher training, social work, speech therapy, community education, and recreation and leisure. Another, Glasgow's Jordanhill College, merged in 1993 with Strathclyde University. The other higher education colleges comprise three Colleges of Art and the Royal Academy of Music and Drama, together with Queen Margaret College, the Scottish Agricultural College and the Scottish College of Textiles.

Finally, there are now 13 universities in Scotland, a dramatic increase in recent years, but stemming in part from changes in status of existing institutions. Four—St Andrew's, Glasgow, Aberdeen and Edinburgh—date back to medieval times. The other universities have more recent origins: Stirling was founded, and Strathclyde, Heriot-Watt, Dundee and Stirling were granted university status, in the 1960s while Robert Gordon, Napier, Glasgow Caledonian, Paisley and, most recently, Abertay became universities in the 1990s. The Open University also has its Scottish headquarters in Edinburgh and offers degrees to students throughout Scotland.

In part as a result of this expansion in university provision, but also because of the rise in the number of pupils achieving school-leaving qualifications (see below), a desire for additional training, a perceived lack of employment opportunities, and reforms to further and higher educational curricula, many more young people are continuing in formal education after leaving school, and many adults are also returning to the classroom. Although opportunities to enter higher education are currently expanding, this was not the case for much of the 1980s, when provision of places was outstripped by demand in terms of the numbers of qualified school leavers.

The proportion of appropriately qualified people enrolling in higher education in Scotland has traditionally been greater than in England and Wales (McPherson, Munn and Raffe, 1990; 1991); by 1990 some 23 per cent of young Scots qualified for higher education and 21 per cent enrolled, as against 16 per cent south of the border. About two-thirds of S6 leavers enter further full-time education, mostly higher education;

and about one third of S5 leavers continue their full-time education, mostly enrolling in non-advanced courses in colleges. In addition, increasing numbers of adults who have been away from school for some years are now resuming their formal education at both college and university.

SCHOOL ATTENDANCE AND AGE OF LEAVING

Schools and local authorities have always kept records of pupil attendance during the years of compulsory schooling, but the Conservative government announced in 1993 that from the session 1994-95 each school must make this information available to the parents of its pupils. It is also now government policy to publish regular annual reports. For primary schools the average attendance on a sample day in 1993 was just over 90 per cent. Only in Strathclyde was the figure below 90 per cent; this was largely due to the comparatively low attendance rates in Glasgow (under 82 per cent) and Lanark (under 87 per cent). Figures for secondary school attendance were generally lower, at just over 84 per cent; the lowest were again for Strathclyde (82 per cent), with schools in Glasgow recording an average of only 75 per cent.

The census of attendance was conducted in January and therefore is unlikely to give an accurate reflection of attendance patterns over the school year. But on the basis of this and other analyses one can say that average attendance rates will tend to be around 90-95 per cent in primary schools and 85-90 per cent for pupils in the compulsory years in secondary schools. Over the last ten years average attendance rates appear to have fallen. They also tend to be higher in schools located in rural areas and in those in more affluent urban neighbourhoods.

Attendance figures such as these give no indication as to the causes of absence, which in many cases will have been authorised by the schools concerned. Rates of truancy—unauthorised absence from school, for any period, as a result of premeditated or spontaneous action on the part of the pupil, parent or both (Scottish Education Department, 1977a)—are lower, although they tend to follow the same broad pattern. There is and has always been considerable debate about both the definition of truancy and its causes (Carlen, 1992), and the Conservative government's decision to publish figures for non-attendance rates by school has intensified the debate.

Age of Leaving

The last few years have witnessed a significant changes in patterns of school leaving; the proportions of pupils staying on into S5 and S6 are much higher than they were a decade ago. In the early 1980s pupils leaving school from S4 formed 44 per cent of all school leavers, but by 1992-93 this figure had fallen to less than 25 per cent. Whereas in 1982-83 more than one pupil in three left from S4, by 1992-93 only one pupil in five left from S4.

Clearly, many of the pupils staying on into S5 are doing so in order to take Highers, more Standard Grades or National Certificate modules. Many also now stay on into S6: whereas in the early 1980s those leaving from S6 comprised about one in five of all leavers, this has risen to two in five. This is even truer for girls: those staying on into S6 comprised nearly half of all leavers in 1992-93. There are also geographical variations in these patterns. In Argyll and Bute, for example, 20 per cent of all school leavers in 1992-93 left at the minimum leaving age, while 53 per cent of leavers did so from S6. Highland and Lothian also had relatively high staying-on rates. In Glasgow, by contrast, 35 per cent of all leavers left at the minimum age, and fewer than 36 per cent did so from S6.

SCHOOL LEAVING QUALIFICATIONS

McPherson, Munn and Raffe (1991) identify two features distinguishing Scottish school leavers from those in the rest of the UK, both related to the one-year Higher system compared with the two-year A level system: the greater proportion who leave with Higher passes; and the greater proportion with passes in maths and physics.

Historically speaking, as more pupils have chosen to stay on at school so the levels of school leaving qualifications have risen. In terms of examination passes at least, pupils leaving school in the 1990s had much higher qualifications than their counterparts in the early 1980s. But comparison is rendered difficult by changes in the type and nature of school examinations, principally the introduction of National Certificate modules, the replacement of Ordinary by Standard Grades, the move from 'traditional' to 'revised' Highers, and the introduction of the Certificate of Sixth Year Studies. These and other curricular innovations will be discussed shortly, but first the changing profile of Scottish school leavers is considered.

The impact of recent curricular innovations, when coupled with the rise in the staying-on rate, is remarkable. From the later 1970s the proportion of school leavers with no qualifications at all fell rapidly, reaching just over 25 per cent by 1982-83. By 1992-93 it had fallen further to a little more than 10 per cent. Some of the gains were modest, however: a further 15 per cent only gained one or more Standard Grade pass in a low grade (4-7). In addition, the proportions of school leavers with various numbers of Standard or Ordinary passes in grades 1, 2 and 3 did not alter much over the decade. But at Higher level the proportions increased significantly: 43 per cent of all school leavers in 1992-93 had acquired at least one Higher at grades A to C, in contrast with 33 per cent in 1982-83. Over 28 per cent obtained three or more Highers, against 21 per cent in 1982-83; and nearly 16 per cent five or more Highers, against less than 11 per cent in 1982-83.

The proportion of leavers taking the Sixth Year Studies Certificate increased from under 8 per cent in 1982-83 to nearly 13 per cent in 1992-93; but as a proportion of S6 leavers, those taking the examination fell over the same period, from 33 per cent to 30 per cent.

The fact that many of those now sitting Highers do so over a two-year period, staying on to repeat or take new Highers in S6, has undoubtedly contributed significantly to the increased numbers and proportions of school leavers with passes. Universities now often take the longer period into account in establishing their admissions criteria, demanding more Highers passes at stipulated levels from those leaving S6. It could also be argued that the move from a traditional, exclusively examination-based, qualification to a revised syllabus incorporating an element of course work assessment into the award has made the acquisition of Highers more accessible and attractive to a broader school population. But this does not necessarily mean that Highers require today a lower academic standard of attainment than they did in the past. Comparing boys' with girls' performances, the data suggest clearly that girls not only stay on at school for longer than do boys, but also tend to achieve more qualifications and at higher levels. This is true for both the 1980s and 1990s. In 1992-93 some 12 per cent of boys as against nine per cent of girls left school with no qualifications, and nearly 30 per cent of the boys against 21 per cent of the girls left with no Standard Grade passes above grade 4. Fewer girls than boys also left school with only one to four Standard Grades. But turning to school leavers with five or more Standard Grades, we find that percentage among girls was higher than that among boys, and this superiority grows more marked as we move up the ladder of academic attainment. The percentage of girls leaving school with at least one Higher award in 1992-93 was 48 per cent, while that for boys was 38 per cent; 32 per cent of girls achieved three or more Highers as against less than 26 per cent boys; and 17 per cent achieved five or more Highers as against 14 per cent of boys.

Although the figures for scholastic performance indicate that girls' rates and levels of qualification have risen more than they have for boys, and generally surpass them, one cannot infer that the sex inequalities for so long characteristic of formal education have now been obliterated. Riddell (1992) argues that qualitative research indicates the continuation of 'sexist' practices in schools, and Croxford (1994) demonstrates some of the forms these take. Subject choice is often still related to gender, as is enrolment in further and higher education (Durndell and Lightbody, 1993).

In terms of geographical comparison, Strathclyde's school leavers tended to leave with lower and fewer qualifications than the average: in 1992-93 some 19 per cent of the leavers in Glasgow had no qualifications, against the regional average of 12 per cent and the Scottish average of 10 per cent; at the other end of the range, 23 per cent left with at least three Highers (grades A-C), against the regional average of 27 per cent and the Scottish average of 29 per cent.

These findings require interpretation. It has long been recognised that there is a close correlation between pupils' formal educational attainments and the socio-economic status of their parents. Holding ability constant, children from materially deprived neighbourhoods tend to 'underachieve'. There is considerable debate as to the causes of such achievement differentials, with researchers variously identifying factors in the home environment (especially material conditions and the educational experience of close family members), in the neighbourhood and in the schools themselves. Currently the debate has become focused on levels of school effectiveness, given government pressure to make schools more accountable, partly through the publication of examination results. McPherson (1990) writes that the improvement in the quality of schooling he identifies in Glasgow 'must be understood against a background of social change in the last decade which has seen the social disadvantage of the Glasgow school population increase relative to the rest of Scotland'. Noting the correlation between single-parent families and low attainment, he goes on to cite the relatively high and growing incidence of one-parent families in Glasgow, as well as its levels of 'social deprivation on a wider front'. McPherson treats such changes as part of a broader trend towards the polarisation of income in Britain today.

Two other points need to be made in any discussion of examination results. First, according to recent research, the social class gap as well as the gender gap in attainment has narrowed. McPherson and Willms (1987) have demonstrated that since secondary education was reorganisation in the early 1970s on a comprehensive basis 'there has been an equalisation of educational attainment between social classes. This equalisation is apparent among males and females alike. Improvements in attainment have occurred across the full range of attainments and for virtually all groups defined by gender and social class.' Second, as some of the critics of the policy of publicising examination results in their present form have pointed out, one danger in so doing is to highlight formal, measurable performance at the expense of more general, social objectives and achievements. Schooling comes to be treated as a pragmatic instrument of certification and training rather than a means of social development.

The performance of school leavers in independent schools in comparison with that in local education authority schools shows considerable differences. Forty-two per cent of the leavers from private sector schools achieved five or more Highers passes at A-C grades as against 14 per cent in the state sector; and additionally seven per cent gained passes at A level which is not included in education authority school syllabuses. Sixty per cent of private sector school leavers achieved at least three A-C grade Highers against 26 per cent in the state sector; and 73 per cent gained one or more A-C grade Highers in comparison with 41 per cent. If, however, we look at trends in these results over the 1980s we find that the rate of increase in the attainment of qualifications has been much more rapid for leavers in the state sector; while the proportions of leavers from independent schools with more and higher qualifications has increased, the increases are far less marked.

Since 1992 the Scottish Office has published figures for examination performance by school for the whole of Scotland. The publication of examination results, particularly in their current form, has caused widespread debate and considerable adverse criticism. While the government argues that parents have the right to know how pupils in the school attended by their children perform, school management, local authorities and teachers' organisations have been more or less unanimous in condemning what amount to crude league tables which, they argue, are seriously misleading and liable to excerbate the problems faced by many schools. Various alternative schemes are now being devised, based on 'value-added' criteria which seek to calculate the relative inputs of schools in relation to the levels of educational attainment pupils bring with them to school. The aim is to reduce the stigmatising effect of the publication of examination results on schools located in socio-economically disadvantaged neighbourhoods in which examination performance tends generally to be lower.

SCHOOL LEAVERS' DESTINATIONS

Of more than 50,000 pupils who left local authority schools in 1993-94, some 42 per cent continued with full-time education at either further or higher levels, 27 per cent went into full-time higher education and 15 per cent into full-time further education. Twenty-two per cent went into employment and 18 per cent into training. The destinations of the remaining 18 per cent were either unknown or classified as 'other'.

If we look at the regional figures, there are significant variations in the proportions of leavers continuing in full-time education. The Western Isles had the highest percentage of such students at 61 per cent, with Borders, Orkney, and Dumfries and Galloway all recording 50 per cent or more; in contrast Lothian had 37 per cent and Strathclyde—which accounted for nearly half of all Scottish school leavers—40 per cent. Within Strathclyde, only 30 per cent of all leavers in Glasgow enrolled in further and higher education. The proportion of those entering full-time *higher* education also varies, with Orkney recording 46 per cent against Glasgow's 15 per cent. Within Glasgow, however, there are major variations in the destinations of leavers by individual school.

Two other related aspects of further and higher education provision which need to be considered are the increase in the numbers of 'mature' students (those over 21 on enrolment) and the development of a variety of 'non-traditional' means of access to universities in Scotland.

Traditionally there has been a very close relationship between the Higher system and the structure of university degrees; a syllabus of four or five Higher courses taken in the fifth year at school has for long served as the main means of preparation for, and access to, higher education in Scotland, justifying the conventional four-year Honours degree course and the three-year Ordinary degree. The relative breadth of the Higher syllabus and of the first two or three years of undergraduate study are fundamental to the conception of 'the generally educated Scot'.

This relationship, however, is now changing as the proportion of students entering university straight after their fifth year of secondary schooling declines. As many are now staying on to complete a sixth year of school before entering university, while others are seeking entry with qualifications other than Highers, the continued validity of the longer Scottish degree is being questioned. In addition, increasing numbers of students over the age of 21 are qualifying for university entrance through such schemes as the Scottish Wider Access Programme which offers study programmes provided in further education colleges and university departments of adult and continuing education. SWAP is organised by four regionally based consortia made up of further and higher education institutions in collaboration with education authorities. Entry requirements vary, although generally access courses to the humanities and social sciences only require that students should be over 21. Successful completion of the programme automatically qualifies students for entry to degree courses. Then there are other more locally based schemes, including summer schools aimed at students from schools from which few have traditionally proceeded into higher education, and the provision of part-time study programmes. Finally, all Scottish colleges and universities are involved in the Scottish Credit Accumulation and Transfer Scheme, which is designed to give students greater mobility between institutions during their academic careers.

CHANGES IN CURRICULUM AND ASSESSMENT

Far-reaching innovations affecting the curriculum and modes of assessement at all levels in local education authority schools in Scotland have taken place over the course of the 1980s and 1990s, changes which had earlier been called for in the Munn and

Dunning reports (Scottish Education Department, 1977b and 1977c). A summary of the major changes follows.

The 5-14 Development Programme

In 1987 the Secretary of State launched a major initiative with a consultation document on curriculum and assessment for all years in primary schools and the first two years in secondary schools (Scottish Education Department, 1987). The aim of the review was to achieve a clearer definition of the balance, content and objectives of the school curriculum, with a more consistent application in schools of a nationally agreed approach; and the establishment and implementation of new assessment policies in all local authority schools through the introduction of testing on a standardised basis at P4 and P7 in language and maths. The review also proposed to improve communications between schools and parents about the nature of the school curriculum and to bring about better reporting to parents of the progress of their children.

Over the next few years policy was debated and developed. Curriculum directives and guidelines reshaped the content of learning at all levels, and compulsory testing at P4 and P7 was announced in 1990. The implementation of testing was, however, to prove problematic. Local authorities, teachers' associations and parents' organisations all voiced criticisms of the scheme and, when it was introduced in 1991, parental withdrawal of children and a teachers' boycott resulted in only a third of pupils sitting the tests. The criticisms were that the tests were unnecessary, time-consuming and disruptive of the normal work of the school, and that the results would be misleading and alarmist. Since then the tests have been modified to meet some of the criticisms.

The model primary school curriculum is divided into five main areas, which are given varying degrees of emphasis: language (15 per cent), mathematics (15 per cent), environmental studies (25 per cent), expressive arts (15 per cent), and religious and moral education, including personal and social development (10 per cent), with some scope (the remaining 20 per cent) for individual schools to allocate as they see fit. The guidelines also stipulate attainment targets, which are divided into five levels, from A to E; and attainment outcomes, comprising listening and watching, talking, reading and writing. These outcomes are each made up of specific strands, for example talking to convey information, talking in groups, talking with audience awareness and so on; or reading for information, reading aloud and reading with awareness of types of text. Thus the attainment targets in each strand of each area are grouped at five levels, from the most elementary to the most advanced. Pupils entering secondary school are expected to follow the same basic syllabus, consisting of English, mathematics, sciences, geography, history, social education, a modern language, religious education, physical education, art, technical, home economics and music. The specificity of these guidelines, together with the necessity to follow them closely, represents the most far-reaching extension of national control into classroom practice in the history of primary and early secondary schooling. After two years' secondary education, pupils choose Standard Grade courses which, as is outlined below, must now include a specified range of subjects.

Replacement of Ordinary Grades by Standard Grades

One of the main stimuli to curricular reform was the large number of school leavers who gained few or no formal academic qualifications. In the mid-1970s over a third of all Scottish school pupils did not sit Scottish Certificate of Education examinations. A further 10 per cent sat such examinations but gained no passes, meaning that of all leavers, 44 per cent were classified as 'non-certificate'; and 75 per cent left with no Higher passes at all (Scottish Education Department, 1977c). Standard Grades were introduced from the mid-1980s to combat these low levels of qualification and were structured to certificate all pupils in S4, ultimately replacing the traditional Ordinary Grades in 1992.

The key features which distinguish the Standard from the old Ordinary Grade syllabuses are the incorporation of school-based work for formal assessment, including class tests, assignments, projects and the testing of practical skills in class, as well as an unseen examination component; a seven-point marking scale to replace the Ordinary five-point scale; and the division of syllabuses into Foundation, General and Credit sections, with pupils enrolled in a given section on the basis of assessed ability.

Standard Grade courses until recently were characterised by a fairly broad scope for choice in that they only had to include English and mathematics, together with religious and physical education. Courses of study in S3 and S4 are now, however, prescribed more closely: all pupils have to study subjects within each of eight modes of learning: language and communication, mathematical studies and their applications, scientific studies and their applications, social and environmental studies, technological activities, creative and aesthetic activites, physical education, and religious and moral education. Each pupil must study a range of Standard Grades including English, mathematics, a science, a social subject and a modern language. A pupil's full set of courses will cover all eight curricular modes. Within the modes, however, there is scope for choice of actual subjects. Standard Grade courses last for two years, although they may be supplemented by six-month or one-year short courses, or National Certificate modules.

Reforms in Vocational Training

It could be argued that Scottish education has traditionally had a more 'academic' character than has schooling in England and Wales. A variety of factors—the higher proportion of post-compulsory age pupils enrolling for Higher subjects (in contrast with those south of the border taking A Levels); the higher proportion of school leavers going on to higher education; the more complete introduction of comprehensive schooling in the 1960s and 1970s; and the relative lack of 'elite' schools in the private sector —might be said to have contributed to the distinctive character of Scottish education. In other ways, however, the distinction is a false one in that 'academic' qualifications have always been a crucial means of vocational advancement. Nevertheless, it is commonly argued that there has been a marked and possibly detrimental separation of 'academic' knowledge from more technically and vocationally oriented forms of learning, especially when compared with curricula in countries such as Germany. Whether or not this is the case, the assumption at least certainly underpins much educational and political analysis, as is evident in the Howie report (Scottish Office Education Department, 1992) and the then government's response (Scottish Office, 1994).

Since the 1970s and the sharp rise in youth unemployment, the demand that schools should focus on training young people more specifically for the rapidly changing workplace has become ever more prevalent. Developments over the last two decades have effectively demolished the notion of the curriculum as a 'secret garden' to be cultivated only by specialists deeply schooled in pedagogical knowledge. Prime Minister James Callaghan's speech at Ruskin College in 1976 was the start of the most recent move of government, commerce and industry to enter this garden and tell the cultivators what to plant. It was felt that only through reforms to education and training could the decline in economic competitiveness and in employment possibilities for the young be halted. The subsequent elaboration and implementation of education reforms geared explicitly to the principles of the free market and to perceived national, industrial and commercial 'needs' have had as much impact north of the border as as they have to the south.

The first major initiative in recent years affecting vocational provision in Scottish schools and colleges came with the publication of an *Action Plan* aimed at 16-18 year-olds (Scottish Education Department, 1983). According to Ainley (1990) and McPherson (1992), the Scottish Office was thereby able to maintain its control of provision for 16 to 18 year-olds, which might otherwise have been taken over by non-educationists south of the border, although by this time the Scottish Office, too, had become much more amenable to their ideas. Behind the plan and parallel measures elsewhere was concern about the fact that at the start of the 1980s barely 50 per cent of Britons aged between 16 and 18 were in education, as opposed to 86 per cent in Germany and 96 per cent in Japan.

In 1985 the plan was broadened to take account of adults going to college and (in increasing numbers) returning to school, and led to the creation of Scottish Vocational Education Council (SCOTVEC). Its remit was to design and provide a wide range of vocationally relevant qualifications to meet the requirements of the business and technical sectors of employment and to oversee student assessment. The new National Certificate courses were designed as modules requiring 40 hours of study with assessment based in schools and colleges. There are now about 3,000 of these SCOTVEC modules. Certain groupings of modules (usually four) are recognised as equivalents of a Higher at a C grade.

SCOTVEC also took responsibility for the General Scottish Vocational Qualfication, a relatively new qualification which was developed in response to the 1991 white paper, *Access and Opportunity: A Strategy for Education and Training* (Cm 1530) and was introduced in 1992: GSVQs, which cover specific but broadly defined occupational areas and also include Skillstart training in core skills (numeracy, communication, information technology, personal and interpersonal skills and problem solving), are designed for 16-19 year-olds and adults returning to formal education. The Level III GSVQ is considered to be the equivalent to three Highers. In order to attain a GSVQ a student must achieve a number of credits from a combination of mandatory core skill modules, and both mandatory and optional vocational modules. They are deemed to be relevant to a wide range of occupations and to be suitable for entry into some forms of higher education. They are principally delivered and assessed in schools and colleges.

In addition to GSVQs, SCOTVEC was also responsible for the development and accreditation of Scottish Vocational Qualifications which were first introduced in 1989, following the publication of the white paper, *Employment for the 1990s* (Cm 540, 1988). This proposed the establishment of Industry Lead Bodies, responsible for setting standards of competence relevant to employment in particular occupational areas. They were to collaborate with SCOTVEC in defining specific occupational areas, producing standards or competence statements based on key functions in these areas and in developing and testing these standards. SVQs differ from GSVQs in that they are occupationally much more specific and are designed to assess students' competence in a workplace environment, thus making them suitable for people currently in employment.

SCOTVEC also assumed responsibility for HNCs and HNDs, which are taught in further education colleges. Until the 1990s HNC and HND awards were non-modular, examination-based qualifications with graded passes at both subject and award level. They have now been transformed into modular qualifications based on units, each involving 40 hours of teaching, learning and assessment; the last of these is continuous and no longer based on examinations. Twelve credits are required for an HNC and 30 for an HND. Colleges may also submit proposals for their own HNCs and HNDs. Universities are coming to recognise HNCs and HNDs as entry qualifications alongside Highers.

The numbers of students enrolled for National Certificate courses rose steadily although this trend may now be over, at least in the short term. Figures for 1992-93 indicate that enrolments—nearly 243,000 in all—had declined slightly over the previous year. In addition the number of students registering for courses at further education colleges continued to fall, in part because of the increasing tendency for students to continue their studies at school, and in part because of the introduction of SVQs.

SCOTVEC had a major impact on Scottish further education colleges and on school provision for students not taking Highers; but it has not been alone in its provision of vocationally oriented courses. The Technical and Vocational Training Initiative was the result of a request in 1982 by prime minister, Margaret Thatcher, that new forms of technical and vocational training should be developed for school pupils. Its progress was rapid: pilot schemes were introduced in England in 1983, and in Scotland in 1984. There are now few local authority secondary schools in Scotland which are not significantly involved in TVEI schemes.

Finally, it should be noted that in 1997 SCOTVEC, and the Scottish Examinations Board which was responsible for the SCE, were incorporated in the new Scottish Qualifications Authority.

Reforms to Highers

The Higher was first introduced to Scottish schools in 1888 as a standard qualification for professions such as law, accountancy and banking. Its longevity has led to its being identified as one of the key distinctive features of the Scottish education system.

It has undergone a variety of changes over the years, most recently in the form of the Revised Higher; but its traditional role as the principal qualification for Scottish school leavers entering higher education has remained, as has its highly academic form and content, and the fundamental role accorded to the unseen examination paper. Essentially the Higher course is followed in a number of subjects each over one year in S5 and S6; ideally five subjects are taken, giving the Higher its widely acclaimed breadth, at least when compared with the fewer subjects taken in the two-year Advanced Level course across the border. Its one-year duration has to be placed in the context of the four-year Honours degree common to most Scottish universities.

Support for the Higher has at times bordered on veneration, despite mounting criticisms as to its relevance and value in the late twentieth century. McPherson (1992) notes changes to make it a group certificate as far back as 1902, although it reverted to its subject-based nature in 1951; and he goes on to describe the post-war attempts to introduce a post-Higher Scholarship Grade in order to improve the chances of prospective Oxbridge entrants from Scottish schools. (Many private schools in Scotland in fact enter their pupils for Advanced Level partly in order better to compete for places in English universities.) There was, however, much resistance to changing the Higher; arguments in its defence were mainly couched in terms of its breadth and its success in attracting students. The Higher for many epitomised the tradition of the 'generally educated Scot'. The greater staying-on rate in Scottish schools, in comparison with those in England and Wales, was held to be largely due to the one-year Higher courses; but also the universities feared that Higher courses of longer duration would lead to the abolition of the traditional four-year Honours degree (and of the three-year Ordinary degree). The eventual outcome was a compromise, with the introduction of the Certificate of Sixth Year Studies, designed as an advanced level of study.

By the 1980s pressure to reform the Higher increased, partly because of the rise in the numbers of students enrolling for Higher subjects noted above, and the rise in many universities' entrance qualifications, which reduced the proportion of qualified S5 school leavers. As we have seen, increasing numbers of students were staying on into S6 to accumulate more or improved Higher passes. This, together with the array of other courses now available in S5 and S6, resulted in a highly fragmented and piecemeal syllabus. Timetable constraints also limited the duration of effective learning to the so-called 'two-term dash'. Few pupils were taking CSYS. In addition, many students taking the Higher were either doing so in fewer subjects than the number for which it had been designed, or performing poorly. In 1990 the Secretary of State set up a committee under Professor Howie to consider the aims and purposes of post-compulsory school curricula and to propose a new structure better suited to the needs of the more heterogeneous S5 and S6 population, and to the changing demands emanating from employers and higher education.

In 1992 the Howie committee proposed a radical reform which would have had far-reaching implications for the whole of secondary schooling (Scottish Office Education Department, 1992). Its main proposals were to bring Standard Grade forward to S3 and to replace the Higher with two sorts of course beginning in S4. One, the SCOTCERT, was more vocationally oriented and designed for up to 60 per cent of students; it would be of one or two years' duration. The other, the SCOTBAC, was academically oriented and aimed at 40 per cent of students; it would last for three years. After widely publicised debate the proposals were rejected, although much of the committee's critical analysis of the current situation was accepted. Crucially, it was widely felt that Standard Grade could not feasibly be brought forward to S3 and that the dual 'pathway' model would have several negative consequences: the SCOTCERT would have much lower status; it would be difficult for students to transfer to the SCOTBAC; the choice between the two courses would come too early; and the re-source implications would restrict the number of schools able to offer both courses.

Instead, the government decided to implement an alternative set of reforms (Scottish Office, 1994c); essentially this will involve the introduction, alongside the Higher, of the Advanced Higher, which will incorporate the content of the CSYS that it will replace. The reforms still require elaboration but they would have a profound effect on the nature of secondary schooling at all levels, and lead to a major overhaul of the treatment of school leaving qualifications both by employers and higher education.

It is envisaged that the Advanced Higher will comprise two-year courses in S5 and S6, with students either sitting examinations at Higher level after one year or bypass-ing them, depending on their progress. Standard grade will encompass Foundation, General and Credit passes, and it will be necessary for pupils with a General pass to sit the Higher over two years, the first year being based on the Credit level at Standard Grade. The Higher and Advanced Higher will be modular and include courses drawn from the current academic and vocational provision. In the latter case the Higher and Advanced Higher will be developed from current National Certificate modules and Higher National units. The duration of the Higher will be 160 hours (compared with 120 hours for the current Higher) and that of the Advanced Higher 320 hours. A two-year programme of study will comprise either up to four Advanced Highers plus one Higher, or two Advanced Highers plus five Highers, in different subjects. It will still be possible to study four or five Higher subjects over one year with a view to qualify-ing for university after S5.

Students entering S5 who will not be taking a full set of Advanced Higher or Higher courses will take modules adapted from current National Certificate courses, each varying in length from 40 to 160 hours, and grouped into three levels. Students who have achieved mainly General or Foundation level passes at Standard Grade will be able to take National Certificate courses at appropriate levels. Those who do not attain Foundation level will be able to study for a Skillstart award, normally over two years.

The intention behind these reforms is to overcome many of the problems associ-ated with the current system of secondary education: the brief duration of the Higher; the greater numbers and broader ability range of students staying on after compulsory school age; the demand for both superior and more varied school-leaving qualifica-tions than are currently available, geared to the varied levels and types of ability of young people; and the division between the 'academic' and 'vocational'.

THE MANAGEMENT OF EDUCATION

In recent years there have been radical changes in the management of education insti-tutions in Scotland at all levels. There has been a drastic restructuring of the balance of power between the Secretary of State, the Scottish Office Education Department, local education authorities, schools, colleges and universities, parents, and the interests of local communities and the private sector. The Conservative government's stated policy was to devolve management by reducing the powers of the local education authorities; it was 'firmly committed to the principle that decisions affecting individual schools should wherever possible be taken at school level. It also [believed] that parents and the local community should be involved in these decisions' (Scottish Office, 1992). It could be argued, however, that the effect of many of the recent reforms has been to increase the power of the centre, in the SOED itself. The key changes began in 1980, with an increase in parents' rights to choose to which schools to send their children, but by the early 1990s they had expanded to include the whole of state education.

Placing Requests

The Education (Scotland) Act, 1981 greatly increased the opportunity for parents to send their children to schools other than those closest to where they lived. Since 1982 parents have been able to submit placing requests for the school of their choice to the relevant education authority and there has been a steady increase in the number of such requests, the vast majority of which have been granted.

Placing requests fall into three categories: those for children under the statutory age for enrolment in primary education; those for children to enrol in a primary school whose catchment does not include the parents' home; and those for children to enrol in a secondary school other than that with which their primary school is associated. Education authorities may refuse such requests on educational grounds—that the placement sought is not suited to the age, ability or aptitude of the child—or because of constraints on accommodation. Parents may appeal against the decision of an education authority and pursue the matter through to the sheriff court if they so wish. In such cases the likelihood is that the sheriff will decide in the parents' favour.

Under-age placement requests form the smallest category of such requests, and education authorities are least likely to accede to them. Over the period 1983 to 1992-93 under-age placement requests more than doubled, from over 500 to over 1,000. The number of those granted, however, increased far less dramatically, to 35 per cent of all requests.

There are many more requests by parents for their children to attend primary or secondary schools not immediately adjacent to their homes. In 1983 there were over 11,000 such requests for primary school placements, rising to over 17,500 in 1992-93. Education authorities are far more likely to grant these placements, doing so in nearly 98 per cent of such cases in 1982 and over 93 per cent in 1992-93. These figures, however, need to be considered alongside those for the school population as a whole: placement requests only affected less than 0.2 per cent of all the children enrolled in primary schools during this period in any one year.

The numbers of placement requests are somewhat smaller for secondary schools: nearly 8,800 requests in 1982, of which 93 per cent were granted, and over 10,500 in 1992-93, of which 83 per cent were granted. Placement requests constituted just over two per cent of the secondary school population in 1993, rising to nearly four per cent in 1992-93. Clearly parents of a greater proportion of pupils entering secondary education are concerned to select a school of their choice, and both the number and the proportion of pupils affected appear to be growing. It must be stressed, however, that the proportion remains small. While in some areas much higher proportions of parents exercise their right to choose a school—notably in urban areas where the figure may reach 25 per cent (Munn, 1992)—in rural areas the right is in practice much more restricted.

The Assisted Places Scheme

Parental rights were also extended by the introduction in 1981 of the Assisted Places Scheme, which was designed to give financial assistance to parents wishing to enrol their children in secondary schools in the private sector but who were deemed not to be able to afford the fees. The number of such pupils rose sharply in the early 1980s, from 1,450 in 1982-83 to 2,600 in 1985-86, and then more slowly to 3,031 in 1992-93. Assisted places are roughly equally divided between boys and girls, and about ten per cent are in Roman Catholic schools. Only about three-fifths of assisted pupils have transferred from local education authority schools.

The average level of financial assistance for each pupil in 1992-93 was £3,200, very substantially greater than the average cost of places in local authority schools (see above); just under 50 per cent of assisted pupils received full fee remission. The Labour government is phasing out assisted places, and no more children will enter the scheme after 1997.

School Boards

The School Boards (Scotland) Act, 1988 enabled the establishment in each local authority school of a board comprising elected parents and teachers together with the head teacher and other co-opted members. The actual number of board members is dependent on the size of each school's roll, but the act stipulates that the number of elected parents should form a majority and that the role of the head teacher is purely advisory.

The powers of the boards are considerably less than those of school governing bodies south of the border. Their functions are to promote communications between the school, parents and the local community; receive advice and reports from the headteacher, including an annual report containing figures on pupils' examination performance; review and approve the head teacher's plans for the use of the capitation allowance; have any matter they choose to raise considered by the head teacher and local education authority; receive information from the authority, including details of current and proposed school expenditure; participate in the appointment of senior staff; control school lets; and set the dates of some term-time holidays.

Most schools succeeded in establishing boards in 1989 and in renewing part of their parental membership two years later, although in many schools there were not enough nominations to warrant new elections. Although little research has been published on the activities of the boards, initial reports suggest that they have been overwhelmingly supportive of school policies and practices: 'boards have not acted as thorns in the schools' flesh; rather they have been harnessed to support schools and to put pressure on education authorities for more resources for schools' (Munn, 1992). In particular, the boards of many primary schools supported the demands from teachers' organisations to boycott the first national tests and few showed any interest in campaigning for their schools to 'opt out' of local education authority control and seek self-governing status.

Local Management of Schools: Management of schools may be delegated to school boards, on the initiative of either the boards themselves or local authorities. While boards generally appear to have been very reluctant to take such an initiative, some local authorities—notably Strathclyde, and Dumfries and Galloway—decided to start experimenting in devolving school management in anticipation of further government measures; Strathclyde introduced its Delegated Management of Resources scheme in 1990, two years before the publication of the government's own consultative document on devolved management of schools (Scottish Office, 1992). Schools now have considerably more control over their affairs than before, particularly with regard to staffing costs, repairs and maintenance and a variety of supplies and services, although education authorities remain directly responsible for such matters as school buildings, transport arrangements and in-service training.

Grant Maintained Schools

A prominent aspect of the Conservative government's education policy was to allow schools, following a ballot of parents, to opt out of local authority control and to be funded directly by central government. Following the model established in England and Wales, the government provided the opportunity for boards to run their schools independently of local authorities under the Self-Governing Schools, Etc (Scotland) Act, 1989. But, in contrast to the position south of the border, only a handful of Scottish schools have considered becoming grant maintained, and only one has done so. Munn interprets this as follows: 'the general trust in teachers' professional expertise, and the traditional view of education in Scotland as a collective welfare right for all, have been reflected in boards' suspicions of government policy enabling individual schools to opt out of local authority control' and by their 'concerns that opting out might lead to a two-tier education service' (Munn, 1992). But although the grant maintained schools initiative has had practically no impact on Scotland, local authorities lost control of further education colleges in 1993 when the government made them centrally funded bodies.

CONCLUSION

The changes described above, in demographic patterns, educational provision, school attendance, school leavers' qualifications and destinations, curricula and assessment, and the management of education, have all contributed to the emergence of a system of formal education in Scotland very different from that of 20 or even ten years ago, although their longer-term impact has still to be fully understood. Fluctuations in the numbers of pupils in primary and secondary schools, and students in colleges and universities, have forced government and local authorities to reappraise educational provision, as have rises in the numbers of unemployed, particularly among the young, and changing demands for formal qualifications, both from those seeking work and prospective employers. The Conservative government sought to manipulate the outcome of these changes, and at the same time impose a new model of education and training based on an ideology of the free market, by introducing an array of schemes designed to increase the influence of individuals and of dominant economic interests within the rhetoric of consumer power. The effect has been to lessen the control traditionally exercised by local education authorities and professional educators; in particular, the gates to the 'secret garden' of the curriculum, responsibility for the cultivation of which was once largely in their hands, has now been opened up for others to design and till.

Returning to the trends identified by Chitty (1989), and cited at the start of this chapter, the introduction of a model curriculum is perhaps the clearest example of the trend towards the *centralisation* of control over education; and the diffusion of occupationally oriented syllabuses in schools and elsewhere provides clear evidence of the trend towards *vocationalisation*.

Whether or not the direct consumers of education have been significantly empowered by these transfers of control is difficult to assess. More parents have more access to information about the nature of their children's schooling, and some have more choice in deciding where and how they should be educated. Prospective students, including adult returners, now have a much wider choice of courses to follow in different institutions, although the effect this will have on their employment opportunities remains crucially conditioned by the state of the labour market. The sustained increase in both the proportion of individuals with formal qualifications and in the standards they have attained, particularly marked among girls and women, will not of itself create jobs; indeed, continuing in education and training may be not so much a means to, as a substitute for, work (Fiddy, 1983; Bates *et al*, 1984; Finn, 1987; Gleeson, 1989).

The overall impact of the changes also has to be seen in relation to the widespread manifestations of opposition to much of what has been proposed, particularly by teachers' associations and parent groups and, to a certain extent, local education authorities. The result has been a dilution in the implementation and effectiveness of some of the changes, as those opposed to the Conservative government sought to lessen, for example, the extent of testing and the impact of the publication of crude data by individual schools. Parents in Scotland—unlike a significant number south of the border—have, so far at least, been unwilling to question the power and expertise of local authorities, schools and their staff by seeking grant maintained status for their children's schools. In this sense, in Scotland there has not been a marked trend towards what Chitty labelled *privatisation;* furthermore, a smaller proportion of pupils attend fee-paying schools, although the assisted places scheme did not suffer from a lack of demand. Increasing numbers of parents, particularly those with higher levels of education and socio-economic status who tend strongly to prefer schools reputed to have a superior academic standing, are exercising their new rights to choose their children's school within the state sector (Echols, McPherson and Willms, 1990). Such a trend is likely to lead to further *differentiation*, in the sense of a polarisation between schools along an axis of examination performance differentials of their pupils.

As for the 'Englishing' of the Scottish education system, one could certainly argue that many of the changes outlined in this chapter run parallel to the reforms in England and Wales, and that the changes being implemented in post-compulsory schooling, with the proposed introduction of the two-year Advanced Higher, mark the end of one of the most distinctive features of Scottish schooling. One can also note the increasing numbers of students educated south of the border who compete successfully for places in Scottish higher education. But arguments about how far all this amounts to an anglicisation of Scottish education continue what is an old and probably a never-ending debate.

NOTE ON SOURCES: In addition to references in the text, statistics are from HM Inspectors of Schools Audit Unit (various reports); and Scottish Office, *Statistical Bulletin: Education Series.*

BIBLIOGRAPHY

Adler, R (1985) *Taking Juvenile Rights Seriously,* Scottish Academic Press

Ainley, P (1990) *Training Turns to Enterprise: Vocational Education in the Market Place,* Tufnell Press

Baggott, R (1992) *Health Care and the National Health Service,* Macmillan

Bannister, J, Dell, M, Donnison, D, Fitzpatrick, S and Taylor, R (1993) *Homeless Young People in Scotland: The Role of Social Work Services*, HMSO

Barbour, R, Palmer, J, Liberman, S & MacLeod, L (1990) *Extending Community Care,* Scottish Council of Voluntary Organisations

Bartlett, W & LeGrand, J (1994) 'The Performance of Trusts' in Robinson, R & LeGrand, J (eds), *Evaluating the NHS Reforms,* Policy Journals (for King's Fund Institute)

Bates, I, Clarke, J, Cohen, P, Finn, D, Moore, R & Willis, P (1984) *Schooling for the Dole? The New Vocationalism,* Macmillan

Berridge, D & Brodie, L (1996) 'Residential Child Care in England and Wales: The Inquiries and After' in Hill, M & Aldgate, J (eds), *Child Welfare Services: Developments in Law, Policy, Practice and Research,* Jessica Kingsley

Birchall, E & Hallett, C (1995) *Working Together in Child Protection,* HMSO

Bochel, D & McLaren, M (1979) 'The Establishment and Development of Local Health Councils', *Scottish Health Service Studies,* 41

Booth, C (1903) *Life and Labour of the People in London,* Macmillan

Borland, M (1991) 'Permanency Planning in Lothian Region: the Placements', *Adoption and Fostering,* 15: 4

Bradshaw, J & Lynes, T (1995) *Benefit Uprating Policy and Living Standards,* Social Policy Research Unit, University of York

Buglass, D (1993) *Assessment and Care Management,* Social Work Research Centre, University of Stirling

Carlen, P, Gleeson, D & Wardhough, J (1992) *Truancy: The Politics of Compulsory Schooling,* Open University Press

Carstairs, V & Morris, R (1991) *Deprivation and Health in Scotland,* Aberdeen University Press

Cashmore, J & De Haas, N (1992) *The Use of Closed-Circuit Television for Child Witnesses in the ACT,* (Report for the Australian Law Reform Commission and the Australian Capital Territory Magistrates' Court)

Central Advisory Committee on Education (1967) *Children and Their Primary Schools,* HMSO

Central Regional Council (1993) *Pre-Fives and Out of School Care: Policy Report,* Stirling: Central Regional Council.

Central Statistical Office (1995) *Regional Trends,* HMSO

Challis, D & Davies, B (1986) *Care Management and Community Care*, Gower

Chitty, C (1989) *Towards a New Education System: The Victory of the New Right?*, Falmer Press

Cohen, B (1995) *Childcare Services for Rural Families*, European Commission

Cd 4499 (1909) *Report of the Royal Commission on the Poor Laws and Relief of Distress*, HMSO

Cd 8731 (1917) *Report of the Royal Commission on the Housing of the Industrial Population of Scotland, Rural and Urban*, HMSO

Cmd 5563 (1938) *Report of the Committee on Scottish Administration*, HMSO

Cmd 6404 (1942) *Social Insurance and Allied Services*, HMSO

Cmd 6550 (1944) Social Insurance, *HMSO*

Cmnd 2306 (1964) *Children and Young Persons, Scotland*, HMSO

Cmnd 3605 (1966) *Social Work and the Community: Proposals for Reorganising Local Authority Services in Scotland*, HMSO

Cmnd 4510 (1969) *Report of the Royal Commission on Local Government in Scotland*, HMSO

Cmnd 4728 (1971) *Fair Deal for Housing*, HMSO

Cmnd 4734 (1971) *Reorganisation of the Scottish Health Service*, HMSO

Cmnd 5174 (1972) *Education: A Framework for Expansion*, HMSO

Cmnd 5175 (1972) *Education in Scotland: A Statement of Policy*, HMSO

Cmnd 6852 (1977) *Scottish Housing: A Consultative Document*, HMSO

Cmnd 7212 (1978) *Special Educational Needs*, HMSO

Cmnd 7615 (1979) *Report of the Royal Commission on the National Health Service*, HMSO

Cmnd 9517 (1985) *Reform of Social Security*, HMSO

Cmnd 9691 (1985) *Reform of Social Security: Programme for Action*, HMSO

Cm 412 (1988) *Report on Inquiry into Child Abuse in Cleveland 1987*, HMSO

Cm 540 (1988) *Employment for the 1990s*, HMSO

Cm 555 (1989) *Working for Patients*, HMSO

Cm 849 (1989) *Caring for People: Community Care in the Next Decade and Beyond*, HMSO

Cm 1530 (1991) *Access and Opportunity: A Strategy for Education and Training*, HMSO

Cm 2144 (1993) *Children Act Report 1992*, HMSO

Cm 2286 (1993) *Scotland's Children*, HMSO

Cm 2584 (1994) *Children Act Report 1993*, HMSO

Cm 2813 (1995) *Social Security Departmental Report*, HMSO

Cm 3201 (1996) *Public Expenditure: Statistical Analyses 1996-97*, HMSO

Cm 3212 (1996) *Social Security Departmental Report*, HMSO

Cm 3214 (1996) *Serving Scotland's Needs: The Government's Expenditure Plans 1997-2000*, Stationery Office

Cm 3551 (1997) *The Scottish Health Service: Ready for the Future*, Stationery Office

Cm 3614 (1997) *Serving Scotland's Needs: The Government's Expenditure Plans 1997-2000*, Stationery Office

Cm 3658 (1997) *Scotland's Parliament,* Stationery Office

Cm 3807 (1997) *The New NHS: Modern, Dependable,* Stationery Office

Cm 3811 (1997) *Designed to Care,* Stationery Office

Constitution Unit (1996) *Scotland's Parliament: Fundamentals for a New Scotland Act,* The Constitution Unit

Cooper, J (1983) 'Scotland: The Management of Change' in Coooper, J (ed), *The Creation of the British Social Services 1962-1974,* Heinemann Educational Books

Corby, B (1993) *Child Abuse: Towards a Knowledge Base,* Open University Press

CoSLA, NALGO, NUPE, TGWU & GMB (1992) *Caring for the Future: Report of the Inquiry into Staff Employed in Residential Care,* Convention of Scottish Local Authorities

Croxford, L (1994) 'Equal Opportunities in the Secondary School Curriculum in Scotland 1977-91', *British Journal of Educational Research,* XX: 4

Currie, H & Murie, A (1996) *Housing in Scotland,* Chartered Institute of Housing

Davidson, R (1993) 'Financial Assistance from Social Work', in Davidson, R & Erskine, A (eds), *Social Work Response to Poverty and Deprivation,* Jessica Kingsley

Davies, G, Wilson, C, Mitchell, R & Milsom, J (1995), *Videotaping Children's Evidence: An Evaluation,* Home Office

Deacon, A (1982) 'An End to the Means Test? Social Security and the Attlee Government', *Journal of Social Policy,* 11:3

Department of Health (1995) *Child Protection: Messages from Research,* HMSO

Department of Social Security (1993) *The Growth of Social Security,* HMSO

Directors of Social Work in Scotland (1992) *Child Protection Policy, Practice and Procedure,* HMSO

Duguid, G (1996) *Deprived Areas in Scotland,* Scottish Office Central Research Unit

Durndell, A & Lightbody, P (1993) 'The Persistence of the Gender Gap in Computing', *Computers and Education,* XXI

Echols, F, McPherson, A & Willms, J (1990) 'Parental Choice in Scotland', *Journal of Educational Policy,* 3

English, J (1987) 'Access to Public Sector Housing' in Pacione, M (ed), *Social Geography: Progress and Prospect,* Croom Helm

English, J (1988) 'Building for the Masses' in Grant, C (ed), *Built to Last?,* ROOF magazine

Enthoven, A (1985) *Reflections on the Management of the National Health Service,* Nuffield Provincial Hospitals Trust

Erickson, P (1982) 'The Client's Perspective' in Martin, F & Murray, K (eds), *The Scottish Juvenile Justice System,* Scottish Academic Press

Fiddy, R (ed) (1983) *In Place of Work: Policy and Provision for the Young Unemployed,* Falmer Press

Finn, D (1987), *Training Without Jobs: New Deals and Broken Promises,* Macmillan

Fitzpatrick, B (1995) *Services for Elderly Patients Following Discharge from Acute Hospital Care,* Department of Social Policy and social Work, University of Glasgow

Ford, R & Taylor, R (1995) *Implementing Community Care in an Area Team* (privately circulated)

Fowles, R (1988) 'Monitoring an Initiative Using Section 12 Funds' in Freeman, I & Montgomery, S (eds), *Child Care*, Jessica Kingsley

Fox, S (1991) *Children's Hearings and the International Community*, HMSO

Francis, J (1995) 'Culture Club', *Community Care*, 30 June-5 July

Freeman, I & Montgomery, S [eds] (1988) *Child Care*, Jessice Kingsley

Freeman, I, Morrison, A, Lockhart, F & Swanson, M (1996) 'Consulting Service Users: The Views of Young People" in Hill, M & Aldgate, J (eds),*Child Welfare Services: Developments in Law, Policy, Practice and Research*, Jessica Kingsley

Galbraith, L (1994) *Child Protection Referrals in Tayside*, Tayside Regional Council

Gibson, J (1985) *The Thistle and the Crown*, HMSO

Gilbert, B (1966) *The Evolution of National Insurance in Great Britain*, Michael Joseph

Gilbert, B (1970) *British Social Policy 1914-39*, Batsford

Gillham, B (1991) *The Facts About Child Sexual Abuse*, Cassell

Gleeson, D (1989) *The Paradox of Training: Making Progress Out of Crisis*, Open University Press

Glennerster, H, Matsaganis, M, Owens, P & Hancock, S (1994) 'GP Fundholding: Wild Card or Winning Hand?' in Robinson, R & LeGrand, J (eds) *Evaluating the NHS Reforms*, Policy Journals (for King's Fund Institute)

Green, D (1988) *Everyone a Private Patient*, Institute of Economic Affairs

Green, D, Neuberger, J, Young, M & Birstall, M (1990) *The NHS Reforms: What Happened to Consumer Choice?*, Institute of Economic Affairs

Griffiths, R (1988) *Community Care: Agenda for Action*, HMSO

Griffiths, R (1983) *NHS Management Inquiry: Report to the Secretary of State for Social Services*, DHSS

Hallett, C and Birchall, E (1992) *Coordination and Child Protection: A Review of the Literature*, HMSO

Ham, C (1991) 'Revisiting the Internal Market', *British Medical Journal*, 302:2 February

Ham, C (1994) 'Public v Public is Not the Issue', *Independent*, 24 August

Ham, C, Costain, D & Benzeval, M (1988) *New Horizons in Acute Care*, National Association of Health Authorities

Hamilton, D (1981) *The Healers: A History of Medicine in Scotland*, Canongate Press

Harding, L (1991) *Perspectives in Child Care Policy*, Longman

Harrison, A (1989) 'The NHS: Under-Resourced for Ever?' in Harrison, A & Gretton, J (eds), *Health Care in the UK 1989*, Policy Journals

Harrison, S, Hunter, D, Marnoch, G & Pollitt, C (1992) *Just Managing: Power and Culture in the NHS*, Macmillan

Heald, D (1992) *Formula-Based Territorial Public Expenditure in the United Kingdom*, Department of Accountancy, University of Aberdeen

Hendrick, H (1992) *Child Welfare*, Routledge

Heywood, J (1978) *Children in Care*, Routledge and Kegan Paul

Hill, M (1987) *Sharing Child Care in Early Parenthood*, Routledge and Kegan Paul

Hill, M, Murray, K, & J. Rankin (1991) 'The Early History of Scottish Child Welfare',

Children and Society, 5:2

Holman, B (1988) *Putting Families First,* Macmillan

House of Commons (1992) *Report of the Inquiry in Child Care Policies in Fife* (HC191/92-93), HMSO

House of Commons (1993) *Report of the Inquiry into the Removal of Children from Orkney in February 1991* (HC195/92-93), HMSO

Hubbard, M (1992) *School Leavers with Multiple Disabilities,* unpublished Ph.D. thesis, University of Stirling

Humes, W & Paterson, H (eds) (1983) *Scottish Culture and Scottish Education 1800-1980*

Hunter, D & Wistow, G (1987) *Community Care in Britain: Variations on a Theme,* King Edward's Hospital Fund for London

Hunter, R & Richards, M (1990) *Towards a Joint Framework for Planning in Scotland,* Scottish Office Central Research Unit

Information & Statistics Division, NHS in Scotland (1995) *Scottish Health Statistics 1995,* NHS in Scotland

Kendrick, A. (1995a) *Residential Care in the Integration of Child Care Services,* Scottish Office Central Research Unit

Kendrick, A. (1995b) 'Supporting Families Through Inter-Agency Work: Youth Strategies in Scotland' in Hill, M, Kirk, R & Part, D, *Supporting Families,* HMSO

Klein, R (1995) *The New Politics of the NHS* (3rd ed), Longman

Kohls, M (1989) *Stop, Start, Stutter: A Report on Joint Planning,* Care in the Community Scottish Working Group

Labour Party (1995) *Renewing the NHS: Labour's Agenda for a Healthier Britain*

Lambert, L, Buist, M, Triseliotis, J & Hill, M. (1990) *Freeing Children for Adoption,* British Agency for Adoption and Fostering

Levitt, I (1992) *The Scottish Office: Depression and Reconstruction 1919-1959,* Scottish History Society

Lilley, R (1995) 'Let Privatised Hospitals Take the NHS off the Critical List', *Sunday Times,* 31 November

Lockyer, A (1992) *Citizen's Service and Children's Panel Membership,* Macdonald Lindsay

Lockyer, A (1994) 'The Scottish Children's Hearings System: Internal Developments and the UN Convention' in Asquith, S & Hill, M (eds), *Justice for Children,* Martinus Nijhoff

Long, G (1995a) 'Family Poverty and the Role of Family Support Work' in Hill, M, Kirk, R & Part, D (eds), *Supporting Families,* HMSO

Long, G (1995b) *A Voucher System for Scotland,* Scottish Network, Family Policy Resources Unit

MacDermid, A (1996) 'City Hospital Fuels Fear of Two-Tier Care', *[Glasgow] Herald,* 31 January

Macdonald, C & Myers, C (1995) *Assessment and Care: The Practitioner Speaks,* Social Work Centre, University of Stirling

MacLeod, S & Giltinan, D. (1992) *Child Care Law: A Summary of the Law in Scotland,* British Agency for Adoption and Fostering

Martin, C (ed) (1994) *The Children Act Review: A Scottish Experience,* HMSO

Martin, F, Fox, S & Murray, K (1981) *Children Out of Court,* Scottish Academic Press

McCrone, D (1990) 'Anglicising Scotland: University Admissions' in Brown, A & Parry, R (eds), *Scottish Government Yearbook 1990,* Unit for the Study of Government in Scotland

McCrone, D (1992) *Understanding Scotland: The Sociology of a Stateless Nation,* Routledge

McGhee, J (1995) 'Consumers' Views of a Post-Placement Support Project', *Adoption & Fostering,* 19:1

McPherson, A & Rabb, C (1988) *Governing Education: A Sociology of Policy Since 1945,* Edinburgh University Press

McPherson, A & Willms, D (1987) 'Education and Improvement: Some Effects of Comprehensive Reorganisation in Scotland', *Sociology,* XXI: 4

McPherson, A (1990) 'How Good is Scottish Education and How Good is the Case for Change?' in Brown A & Parry, R (eds), *Scottish Government Yearbook 1990,* Unit for the Study of Government in Scotland

McPherson, A (1992) 'The Howie Committee on Post-Compulsory Schooling' in Paterson, L & McCrone, D (eds), *Scottish Government Yearbook 1992,* Unit for the Study of Government in Scotland

McPherson, A, Munn, P & Raffe, D (1990) *Highers and Higher Education,* Association of University Teachers

McPherson, A, Munn, P & Raffe, D (1991) *Aiming for a College Education: A Strategy for Scotland,* BP Educational Services

Means, R & Smith, R (1994) *Community Care; Policy and Practice,* Macmillan

Munn, P (1992) 'Devolved Management of Schools and FE Colleges: A Victory for the Producer over the Consumer?' in Paterson, L and McCrone, D (eds), *Scottish Government Yearbook 1992,* Unit for the Study of Government in Scotland

Murray, K (1995) *Live Television Link: An Evaluation of its Use by Child Witnesses in Scottish Criminal Trials,* HMSO

NAHSPO (National Association of Health Service Personnel: Scotland) (1991) *The Role and Preparedness of the Personnel Function,* NAHSPO

NCH Action for Children (1994) *The Hidden Victims: Children and Domestic Violence*

Newman, R & Beardow, R (1990) 'What's Up Doc?', *Health Services Journal,* August

O'Hara, G (1991) 'Placing Children with Special Needs: Outcomes and Implications for Practice', *Adoption and Fostering,* 17:1

OPCS (1993) *1991 Census: Report for Great Britain,* HMSO

Orton, P & Fry, J (1995) *UK Health Care: The Facts,* Kluwer Academic Publishers

Paterson, L with Hill, M (1994) *Opening and Reopening Adoption: Views from Adoptive Families,* Scottish Office Central Research Unit

Pitcairn, T & Waterhouse, L (1993) 'Evaluating Parenting in Child Physical Abuse' in Waterhouse, L (ed), *Child Abuse and Child Abusers: Protection and Prevention,* Jessica Kingsley

Ranade, W (1994) *A Future for the NHS? Health Care in the 1990s,* Longman

Registrar General for Scotland (1996) *Annual Report 1995,* HMSO

Riddell, S (1992) 'Gender in Education: Progressive and Conservative Forces in the Balance' in Brown, S & Riddell, S (eds), *Class, Race and Gender in Schools*, Scottish Council for Research in Education

Roberts, R, Taylor, C, Dempster, H, Bonnar, S & Smith, S (1993) *Sexually Abused Children and Their Families*, Report to the Child and Family Trust

Rowntree, S (1901) *Poverty: A Study of Town Life*, Macmillan

Ryburn, M (1992) 'Contested Adoption Proceedings', *Adoption and Fostering*, 16:4

Saraga, E (1993) 'The Abuse of Children' in Dallos, R & McLaughlin, E (eds), *Social Problems and the Family*, Sage

Saunders, A, Epstein, C, Keep, G & Debbonaire, T (1995) *It Hurts Me Too: Children's Experiences of Domestic Violence and Refuge Life*, National Institute for Social Work, ChildLine & Women's Aid Federation

Scotland, J (1969) *The History of Scottish Education*, University of London Press

Scottish Education Department (1977a) *Truancy and Indiscipline in Schools*, HMSO

Scottish Education Department (1977b) *The Structure of the Curriculum in the Third and Fourth Years of the Scottish Secondary School*, HMSO

Scottish Education Department (1977c) *Assessment for All: Report of the Committee to Review Assessment in the Third and Fourth Years of Secondary Education in Scotland*, HMSO

Scottish Education Department (1983) *16-18s in Scotland: An Action Plan*, HMSO

Scottish Education Department (1987) *Curriculum and Assessment in Scotland*, HMSO

Scottish Home & Health Department (1968) *Administrative Reorganisation of the Scottish Health Services*, HMSO

Scottish Home & Health Department (1977) *Scottish Health Authorities: Revenue Equalisation [SHARE]*, HMSO

Scottish Home & Health Department (1979) *Reorganisation of the NHS in Scotland*, HMSO

Scottish Home & Health Department (1989a) *Self Governing Hospitals* (Scottish Working Paper 3), HMSO

Scottish Home & Health Department (1989b) *NHS Consultants: Appointments, Contracts and Distinction Awards* (Scottish Working Paper 6), HMSO

Scottish Homes (1993) *House Condition Survey 1991*, Scottish Homes

Scottish Homes (1996) *Third Survey of Consumer Preference in Housing*, Scottish Homes

Scottish Homes (1997) *House Condition Survey 1995*, Scottish Homes

Scottish Office (1988) *New Life for Urban Scotland*, HMSO

Scottish Office (1991) *Review of Child Care Law in Scotland*, HMSO

Scottish Office (1992) *School Management: The Way Ahead*, HMSO

Scottish Office (1992) *The Structure of Local Government in Scotland*, Scottish Office

Scottish Office (1994a) *Health in Scotland 1993*, HMSO

Scottish Office (1994b) *Community Care: The Housing Dimension* [Circular SWSG7/94/Env27/94/NHS MEL(1994)79]

Scottish Office (1994c) *Higher Still: Opportunity for All*, HMSO

Scottish Office (1995a) *Government Expenditure and Revenue in Scotland 1993-1994,* Scottish Office

Scottish Office (1995b) *The New Councils,* HMSO

Scottish Office (1996) *Health in Scotland 1995,* HMSO

Scottish Office CRU (1996) *Partnership in the Regeneration of Urban Scotland,* HMSO

Scottish Office Education Department (1992) *Upper Secondary Education in Scotland,* HMSO

Scottish Office Education Department (1995) *The Future of Scottish Pre-School Education,* SOED

Secombe, I & Buchan, J (1994) 'The Changing Role of the NHS Personnel Function' in Robinson, R & LeGrand, J (eds), *Evaluating the NHS Reforms,* Policy Journals (for King's Fund Institute)

Smith, R, Gaster, L, Harrison, L, Means, R & Thistlewaite, P (1993) *Working Together for Better Community Care,* School for Advanced Urban Studies, University of Bristol

Social Services Inspectorate (1995) 'Implementing Caring for People: Impressions of the First Year', *Communicate,* 4

Social Services Inspectorate & Social Work Services Group (1991) *Case Management and Assessment: Managers' and Practitioners' Guide,* HMSO

Social Work Inpectorate (1992) *Another Kind of Home,* HMSO

Social Work Services Group (1990) *Inspection of Establishments* [Circular SWSH 9/90]

Social Work Services Group (1993) *The Future of Adoption Law in Scotland,* Scottish Office

Social Work Services Group & Social Work Services Inspectorate (1996) *Guidance Package,* Scottish Office

Stalker, K, Taylor, R & Petch, A (1994) *Implementing Community Care in Scotland: Early Snapshots,* Social Work Research Centre, University of Stirling

Stone, S. (1994) 'Contact between Adopters and Birth Parents: The Strathclyde Experience', *Adoption and Fostering,* 18:2

Strathclyde Regional Council, Greater Glasgow Health Board, Glasgow City Council, Scottish Homes and Bearsden and Milngavie District Council (1995) *Greater Glasgow Community Health Plan 1995-98*

Strathclyde Social Work Department (1993) *1993 Overview Report: Child Care,* Strathclyde Regional Council

Strathclyde Social Work Department (1995) *Child Care Plan,* Strathclyde Regional Council

Strong, P & Robinson, J (1990) *The NHS Under New Management,* Open University Press

Swanson, M (1988) 'Preventing Reception into Care: Monitoring a Short-Stay Refuge for Older Children' in Freeman, I & Montgomery, S (eds) *Child Care,* Jessica Kingsley

Taylor, R & Ford, G (1995) *Caring in the Community: A Study of Carers in the East End of Glasgow,* Princes Royal Trust, Glasgow

Taylor, R, Ford, G & Dunbar, M (1995) 'The Effects of Caring on Health: A Community-Based Longitudinal Study', *Social Science and Medicine,* 40:10

Teague, A (1989) *Social Change, Social Work and the Adoption of Children,* Avebury

Timmins, N (1988) *Cash, Crisis and Care: The Independent Guide to the NHS Debate,* Newspaper Publishing

Timmins, N (1996) 'NHS Now Top Private Sector Operator', *Financial Times,* 30 September

Tisdall, K with Donaghie, E (1995) *Scotland's Families Today,* HMSO

Titterton, M (1990) *Caring for People in Scotland,* Evidence to the House of Commons Social Services Committee (unpublished)

Treasury (1979) *Needs Assessment Study: Report,* HM Treasury

Triseliotis, J (1988) *Groupwork in Adoption and Foster Care,* Batsford

Triseliotis, J (1991) *Adoption Services in Scotland,* Scottish Office

Triseliotis, J, Borland, M, Hill, M & Lambert, L (1995) *Teenagers and the Social Work Services,* HMSO

Waterhouse, L and Carnie, J (1989) *Child Sexual Abuse: The Professional Challenge,* Social Work Services Group

Watson, J & Taylor, R (1996) 'Assessing Carers' Needs: Current Practice and Recommendations for Change', *Community Care,* 8-14 February

Whitehead, M (1994) 'Is it Fair?: Evaluating the Equity Implications of the NHS Reforms' in Robinson, R & LeGrand, J (eds), *Evaluating the NHS Reforms,* Policy Journals (for King's Fund Institute)

Wilcox, S (1995) *Housing Finance Review 1995/96,* Joseph Rowntree Foundation

Wilkinson, E & Stephen, C (1994) *The Functioning of Family Centres in Tayside Region,* Department of Education, University of Glasgow

Wistow, G, Knapp, M, Hardy, B, & Allen, C (1994) *Social Care in a Mixed Economy,* Open University Press

Younghusband, E (1978) 'Developments in Scotland Leading up to and Following the Social Work (Scotland) Act, 1968' in Younghusband, E (ed), *Social Work in Britain 1950-1975,* Allen & Unwin

INDEX

Acts of Parliament:
  Act of Union (1707) 1
  Carers (Recognition of Services) Act
    (1995) 78-9
  Children (Scotland) Act (1995) 94, 97, 99,
    100, 104, 108, 109, 110, 115, 116, 117
  Children Act (1908) 95, 115
  Children Act (1948) 94
  Children Act (1963) 94-5
  Children Act (1989) 96, 109-10
  Children and Young Persons (Scotland) Act
    (1932) 94, 95
  Education (Scotland) Act (1981) 158
  Housing (Homeless Persons) Act (1977) 137
  Local Government (Scotland) Act (1994) 15
  National Health Service Act (1946) 42
  National Health Service (Scotland) Act
    (1947) 40
  National Health Service (Scotland) Act
    (1972) 42
    National Health Service and Community
    Care Act (1990) 49, 75-6, 77, 79,
    83, 85, 89, 138
  National Insurance Act (1946) 41
  Poor Law Amendment (Scotland) Act
    (1845) 2, 36
  School Boards (Scotland) Act (1988) 159
  Secretary for Scotland Act (1885) 2
  Self Governing Schools, etc (Scotland) Act
    (1989) 160
  Social Work (Scotland) Act (1968) 93, 95-6,
  105
*Access and Opportunity: A Strategy for
  Education and Training* (Cm 1530) 154
Acute Hospital Trusts 69, 70
*Administrative Reorganisation of the
  Scottish Health Services* 42
Adoption 91, 113-14, 115
Allocation/access to social housing 134-5, 137
Assisted Places Scheme 159

Barnett formula 6-8

Benefits Agency 26
Benefits:
  and incentives 33-7
  adequacy/uprating 31-3
  cost 29-31
  system 27-9
Beveridge report (Cmd 6404) 20, 21-4, 28, 31,
  32, 35, 39

Care and Repair 139
Care management 86-7
Carers 88-9, 108, 115
Caring for People (Cm 848) 75, 76, 88
Child benefit 21, 22-3, 24, 28, 35
Child protection 102-5
Child witnesses 101-2
Children's panels 98
Children's hearings 93, 96, 97-101, 115
Children:
  away from home 110-14
  in need 109-10
  older 108-9
  with special needs 107-8
Community care plans 75, 83
Contingency benefits—*see non-contributory
  benefits*
Contributory benefits 19, 21, 27, 28
Council housing 118, 122, 124, 128-34
  deprived estates 119, 135-6
  large scale voluntary transfers 118, 129-31
  residualisation 131-2

Department of Social Security 3, 18, 25, 26,
  36, 37
Designed to Care (Cm 3811) 40, 62, 68-70
Devolution 1, 5
Domiciliary care 75, 76-80, 82
Dunning report 151-2

Early years services 106-7
Education, management of 157-60
Educational curricula and assessment 151-7

Educational Priority Areas 143
Elderly 72, 73, 76-8, 82, 84, 86, 139
Employment for the 1990s (Cm 540) 155
Enthoven, Alain 47-8, 53, 59

Family allowances—*see child benefit*
Family credit 24, 25, 28, 31, 33, 37
Family income supplement—*see family credit*
Family support 105-10
Fostering 91, 111-13, 115
Fowler reviews 24-6, 33, 36
Fundholding GPs 40, 49, 50-1, 52, 53, 65, 66, 68, 69, 71, 75, 84, 87
Further education—*see post-school provision*

Gilmour Committee 3
Glasgow Eastern Area Renewal (GEAR) 135
Goschen formula 5, 6
Grant maintained schools 160
Griffiths report (community care) 74
Griffiths report (NHS) 44, 54, 60, 61-3

Health boards 42-4, 49, 50-1, 52, 53, 64, 69, 75, 80, 82-5, 88
Health Improvement Programmes 69, 71
Health needs 54-6
Health Service Commissioner 42, 45-6
Higher education—*see post-school provision*
Highlands and Islands Medical Service 41
Homelessness 119, 136-8
House condition survey 121-2
Household size 120
Housing:
    associations 123-4, 133-4, 139
    completions 123-4
    departments 74, 75, 97, 139
    improvement 119-20, 121, 127
    overcrowding 119, 121
    plans 119
    rents and subsidies 125, 132-3, 140
    sheltered 77, 139-40
    slum clearance 118, 119, 121, 123, 125, 129
    special needs 138-40
    stock 119-22
    tenure 119, 122-36
Housing Association Grant 134
Housing benefit 25-6, 28, 33, 35, 123, 132
Housing Support Grant 132-3

Incapacity benefit 26

Income related benefits—*see means testing*
Income support 25, 26, 28 37, 75, 83, 91
Intermediate Treatment 108-9

Job seeker's allowance 26, 27, 28, 35, 37

Kilbrandon report (Cmnd 2306) 95-6

Learning difficulties, people with 72, 73, 79, 80
Leaving care 113
Local government 11-17
    reorganisation 11-15, 76, 96, 97, 117
Local Health Councils 42, 45
Local Health Care Co-operatives 69, 70, 71
Lone parents 91-2

Means testing 23, 27, 33-4, 36, 37, 38
Mentally ill 72, 73, 78-79, 82
Minimum wage 34-5, 36
Mortgage Interest Tax Relief 127
Munn report 151-2

National assistance 20, 21-2, 24, 27
National Health Service:
    Common Services Agency 42, 45-6
    expenditure 46-8, 57-8, 68
    history 40-6
    internal market 40, 44, 46-54, 58-9, 75, 80
    long-term service agreements 70, 71
    management 60-1
    privatisation 65-7
    professional advisory committees 42, 45
    purchasing contracts 51-2
    trusts 49, 52-4, 61, 64, 65, 69
    waiting lists 63-4
National insurance—*see contributory benefits*
Needs Assessment Study 5-6, 9, 57
New Life for Urban Scotland 135
New towns 130
Non-contributory benefits 28-9
Nursery schools—*see pre-school education*
Nursery vouchers 107, 144

Orkney affair 93, 96, 105
Owner occupation 118, 119, 122, 124, 125-7, 129, 133

Patient's charter 40, 63-5
Physical disabilities, people with 79-80, 140

Plowden report 143
Poor law/relief 18, 19, 20, 21, 36, 41, 94
Post-school provision 146-7, 153-5, 156
Poverty trap 33-5, 36, 38
Pre-school education 142, 143-4
Primary Care Groups 70, 71
Primary Care Trusts 69, 70
Private renting 122, 124, 127-8, 131
Public authority renting—*see council housing*
Public expenditure 4-11

Regional hospital boards 41, 42
Rent to mortgage scheme 126
Reorganisation of the Scottish Health Services (Cmnd 4734) 42
Residential care 75, 76-80, 82, 85, 91, 96-7, 110-11
Revenue support grant 8, 15, 17
Right to buy 118, 124, 125-7, 128, 129, 130, 131, 132, 139, 140
Royal Commission on the Housing of the Industrial Population of Scotland 119
Royal Commission on the National Health Service 44
Royal Commission on the Poor Laws 18

Savings trap 37-8
Schools:
  boards 159-60
  leavers' destinations 150-1
  leaving qualifications 148-50, 155-7
  local management 160
  placing requests 158-9
  rolls 142-3
  secondary 142, 145
  special 145-6
Scotland's Children (Cm 2286) 97
Scotland's Parliament (Cm 5658) 1
Scottish block 6-9, 57
Scottish Health Services Planning Council 42, 44
Scottish Health Services Revenue Equalisation (SHARE) 44, 49, 69
Scottish Homes 4, 118, 121, 122, 129, 130, 140
Scottish Qualifications Authority 155
Scottish Special Housing Association 118, 129, 130
Scottish Vocational Education Council 154-5
Sheriff court 99-100, 158
Social fund 25, 28

Social housing—*see council housing*
Social insurance—*see contributory benefits*
Social services departments—*see social work departments*
Social Work and the Community (Cmnd 3065) 95
Social work departments 72, 73, 74, 75-6, 80-1, 82-5, 87, 91, 95-6, 97
State Earnings Related Pension Scheme (SERPS) 24, 26, 27, 28, 39
Supplementary benefit 24, 27, 75

Take-up of benefits—*see means testing*
The New NHS: Modern, Dependable (Cm 3807) 68
Tolerable standard 121-2
Trust Implementation Plans 69

UN Convention on Rights of Child 92, 115, 117
Unemployment benefit 26, 27
Unemployment trap 35-7
Universities—*see post-school provision*

Vocational training 154-5
Voluntary hospitals 41
Voluntary sector 73, 75, 76, 81-2, 85, 93-4, 105, 106, 108

Warnock report 145
Welfare pluralism 93-4, 116
Wheatley report (Cmnd 4510) 11, 14
Working families tax credit 39
Working for Patients (Cm 555) 40, 46, 48, 50, 53, 59, 61, 62, 65, 67, 69-70, 71